Gateway Second Edition
to
Canada

Virginia Sauvé

OXFORD
UNIVERSITY PRESS

Oxford University Press is a department of the University of Oxford.
It furthers the University's objective of excellence in research, scholarship,
and education by publishing worldwide. Oxford is a registered trade mark
of Oxford University Press in the UK and in certain other countries.

Published in Canada by
Oxford University Press
8 Sampson Mews, Suite 204,
Don Mills, Ontario M3C 0H5

www.oupcanada.com

Copyright © Oxford University Press Canada 2012

The moral rights of the author have been asserted

Database right Oxford University Press (maker)

First Edition published in 2012

Library and Archives Canada Cataloguing in Publication

Sauve, Virginia L. (Virginia Louise), 1946–
Gateway to Canada / Virginia L. Sauvé. — 2nd ed.

Includes index.
ISBN 978-0-19-544335-6

1. English language—Textbooks for second language learners. 2. Readers—Canada.
3. Readers (Adult). I. Title.

PE1128.S368 2012   428.6'4   C2011-901414-9

This book is printed on permanent (acid-free) ∞ paper.

Printed and bound in China.

1 2 3 4 — 15 14 13 12

Contents

This book is dedicated to Tetsuo (Ted) Aoki,
my teacher, mentor, and friend for many long years.
For your excellence as an educator and your
generosity in sharing that, I thank you.

To the Reader

To those of you familiar with the first edition of this book, I offer this second edition in the hopes you will continue to find it of value. It has been updated, not only in terms of statistics but also in terms of the many changes that Canada has been experienced in the 13 years between editions. At your suggestion, I have kept the same format and the content that is still relevant and of interest to our readers is still there. However, one chapter has been added ("Canadians Enjoying Life: Sports and Recreation") and two others have been thoroughly rewritten. In addition, you will find on the Oxford website (www.oupcanada.com/gateway) some teacher notes for the use of the book in differing contexts and many more exercises which students or teachers can use to supplement what is in the book.

For those of you not familiar with the book, allow me to introduce it to you. *Gateway to Canada* has been written primarily for intermediate and advanced learners of EAL/ESL, although a few teachers have told me they use it with beginners who like the pictures and the friendly tone the book is written in. When I asked how they can use it with beginners, they said they introduce key vocabulary before they begin. With that thought in mind, there will be a section in the web supplement to give them a hand with that task.

It is my hope that the book gives the reader a good helping of cultural capital that will support them in quickly feeling like they belong in Canada and can easily converse with Canadians about things that matter to both the learner and to the average Canadian. Many employers have told me that it is not so much a new Canadian's English that gets in the way of success in the workplace, as it is the person's lack of cultural understandings. EAL/ESL is beginning to put more emphasis on this area and that is good. Meanwhile, we need materials that support teacher and learner alike in understanding what Canada is about, what our issues and challenges are, and what values define us as Canadians. I think you will find much in this book to assist you with that learning or teaching.

Chapters 1 and 2 present some basic history and information about our government systems and how they work. Chapters 3 and 4 cover the arts, education, sports, and recreation. Chapter 5, "The Mosaic of Canada", is like a patchwork quilt of cultural and religious expressions across the country. Chapters 6 through 11 look at the geography, economy, and uniqueness of each of our regions: Pacific, Prairie, Central, Atlantic, and the North. Chapter 12 attempts to acknowledge a sampling of those Canadians of whom we are proud: inventors, scientists, doctors, literary figures, musicians, entertainers, and others. Chapter 13 leaves us with more questions than answers as it endeavours to present some of the larger challenges facing Canadians today as we learn to take our place at the global table.

I draw your attention also to the glossary at the back of the book. It may be helpful in finding a word that is introduced elsewhere in the book.

Lastly, I trust that you will use this book in the ways that work best for you. That may mean starting with what you are most interested in rather than going in the order that is given. I hope that you have as much fun reading the book as I have had writing it. I have been privileged to see all our provinces and spend time with people in each one. I have tried to capture the joy of that experience and my pride at being a Canadian, in the hopes that both will be contagious. I hope you will be motivated to go and see new parts of Canada for yourselves. There is no part of this great country where I do not feel welcome, where I do not feel a sense of belonging. That is my wish for you.

Acknowledgements

Thirteen years ago, my oldest daughter, Monique Sauvé, and I wrote the first edition of *Gateway to Canada*, and we have been delighted that so many people in Canada and abroad have found the text valuable in their studies of English and Canadian culture. Needless to say, some updates were long overdue but I didn't realize how many until I began to research this second edition. Much has changed. I am thankful to those educators who sent in their ideas to Oxford about the types of changes they wanted. Mostly, they liked the format as it was, especially the lovely coloured photos and maps which the publisher so generously included in the first edition. I am grateful once again to Oxford for their support in putting this edition out in its new and updated format. It was Jason Tomassini who initiated this second edition and Cindy Angelini who has done a splendid job of working with me on editing it. I am deeply grateful for her thoroughness, her support, and her patience in answering all my questions. In addition, thanks to Nadine Coderre who assisted her with the editing.

My daughter has relocated and was not involved in this edition but we owe most of the content in the early history chapter and the Quebec chapter to Monique Sauvé and I am most grateful for all her assistance in the first edition.

Lastly, I am deeply grateful to all the learners and teachers who have told me through the years of their joy in using the book. It is my hope that this second edition will support its readers in years to come in falling in love with this country we call Canada and being active participants in her ongoing transformation.

About the Author

Virginia Sauvé is now semi-retired after a long and interesting career in many different contexts and roles involving adult EAL learners. She has worked in public institutions and private colleges teaching all levels from Literacy to ELT (Enhanced Language Training for immigrant professionals). For 12 years, she administered and wrote curriculum for a private school she initiated. Since the closure of that school, she has worked as a consultant doing project work for funders and providers and creating workplace training for a variety of jobs filled by EAL and literacy learners in hospitals, garment factories, and a large variety of other venues. She also taught TESL in two universities and coordinated the Korean Teacher Education Project (K-TEP) at the University of Alberta for five summers. She was a frequent plenary speaker at TESL conferences across Canada during the eighties and nineties and an active member of both her ATESL association and of TESL Canada. She has written two other books, both for teachers, and several articles, some for journals and some as chapters in edited works. She now enjoys being a grandmother to five lovely children.

Introduction to Canada

Quick Facts

» Canada's land mass makes it the second-largest country in the world.

» Almost half of the country's land area is covered by the rocky Canadian Shield.

» Canada has a population of approximately 35 million, which is small for such a large country.

The People

Canada's population density

There are about 35 million people living in Canada today, a relatively small population for such a large country. (If you want a good estimate of Canada's population now, go to Statistics Canada's website and read the Population Clock.) Canada is also a young country (about 150 years old), and most of the population comes from immigration over the last 400 years. Only Aboriginal peoples inhabited the land before that time.

The Land

If you had to use two words to describe Canada, they might be *large* and *diverse*. Canada is the second-largest country in the world. It has a total area of 9 970 610 square kilometres and is bordered by three oceans: the Pacific to the west, the Arctic to the north, and the Atlantic to the east. Across the country, Canadians experience many different landscapes, from rolling plains and mountains to the cold tundra of the North.

Geographically, Canada can be divided into five major regions: the Pacific Region, the Prairie Provinces, Central Canada, the Atlantic Provinces, and the North.

The Pacific Region

The Pacific Region includes Canada's western-most province, British Columbia. The region is known for its mild coastal climate, forests, and spectacular mountains, the famous Rockies. The Rocky Mountains are the youngest and highest mountains in Canada. British Columbia is in the

landform region called the Western Cordillera. (*Cordillera* means a system of mountain ranges.) Between the mountain ranges are areas of high plateaus and deep trenches. Since the landscape is very rugged, most people live in the south and near the coast. Vancouver and Victoria are the largest cities in British Columbia.

The Prairie Provinces

Alberta, Saskatchewan, and Manitoba are Canada's Prairie Provinces. They are known for their rolling plains and extreme climate with long, cold winters and hot, dry summers. Much of the area is covered with farms producing large quantities of canola, as well as wheat and other grains. The region is also rich in oil and natural gas.

The Prairie Provinces are not only characterized by their rolling plains, however. Northern Saskatchewan and Manitoba are covered by the great Canadian Shield—a rocky landscape with lakes, rivers, and forests that stretches over almost half of Canada. Southwestern Alberta has the Rocky Mountains and some of the most spectacular scenery in the country.

Central Canada

This region, which includes Ontario and Quebec, is not the geographic centre of Canada. The region gets its name because, historically, it has been the centre of political and economic power in the country. Canada's capital city is Ottawa, Ontario. Central Canada is the most heavily populated and industrialized area of Canada, particularly in the south around the Great Lakes and St. Lawrence River.

The Great Lakes are the largest body of fresh water in the world. In order of size (from largest to smallest area), they include Lake Superior, Lake Huron, Lake Michigan, Lake Erie, and Lake Ontario. Some of the first settlements in Canada were built along the St. Lawrence River and the Great Lakes. Today, these waterways are still an important transportation route from the Atlantic Ocean to Canada's interior.

Though heavily populated, the Great Lakes–St. Lawrence Lowlands in the south is only a small geographic region in Central Canada. The largest part of Central Canada is covered by the rocky Canadian Shield. In the far north we find the Hudson Bay Lowlands, which are cold, flat, and swampy, with very few towns or cities. This area is home mainly to Inuit and other Aboriginal peoples who have lived there for centuries.

The Atlantic Provinces

The easternmost region of the country includes the Maritime provinces of New Brunswick, Prince Edward Island, and Nova Scotia, as well as Newfoundland and Labrador. Fishing, shipping, and farming are important activities for the people of this area. The region has many small coastal communities, although there are also major industrial centres such as Halifax and Sydney in Nova Scotia.

There are mountains in this region, the Appalachian Mountains, but they are not at all like the grand, rugged mountains of the Pacific Region. The Appalachians are old, rounded mountains. Valleys in the region, such as the Annapolis Valley in Nova Scotia, are important farming areas producing fruit, vegetables, and dairy products.

The North

Canada's North includes the Yukon Territory, the Northwest Territories, and Nunavut, along with all of Canada's Arctic islands. To most Canadians this region is quite remote since 90 percent of Canada's population lives in the south, within 160 kilometres of the Canada–United States border. However, the North is home to about 110 000 people, many of them indigenous peoples, and to a great variety of wildlife including caribou and polar bears.

The North covers a large area and has a varied landscape which includes mountains of the Western Cordillera, the Innuitian Mountains, the Arctic Lowlands, and parts of the Interior Plains and Canadian Shield. This varied landscape has one feature in common: extremely long, cold winters. It is so cold that the earth is frozen for most of the year and never thaws more than half a metre from the surface. This permanently frozen layer of earth is called permafrost. It has made construction in the North a real challenge for architects and builders.

Much of the North is treeless tundra, but in the spring and summer the tundra plays host to a variety of beautiful wildflowers and shrubs. In the summer months, there is no darkness; the sun never sets. The summer season may be short, but it is all the more appreciated for its contrast with the long darkness of the winter.

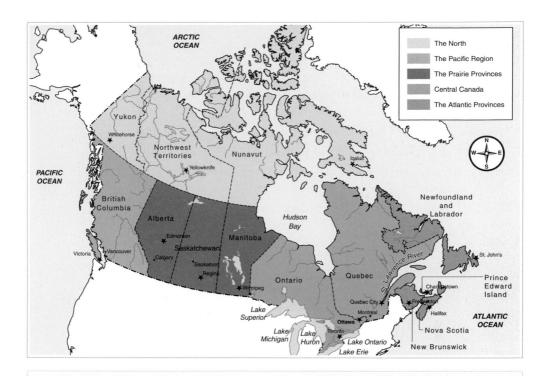

Regions of Canada

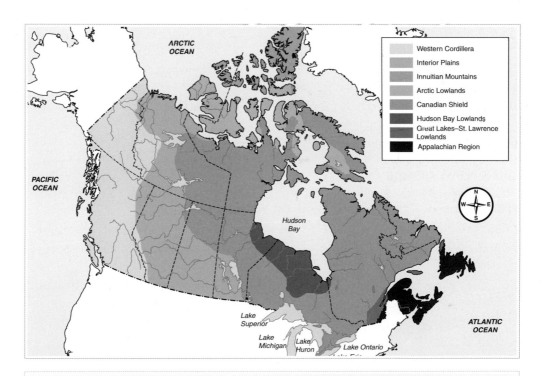

Landforms of Canada

COMPREHENSION CHECK

1 In land area, is Canada the largest, second-largest, or fourth-largest country in the world?

2 What is the name of Canada's newest and highest mountain range?

3 What rocky landform region covers almost half of Canada?

4 How many lakes are there in the largest body of fresh water in the world? What is this group of lakes called?

5 In which part of Canada do you find tundra?

VOCABULARY

indigenous	born in or native to an area
inhabited	lived in
colonize	establish a settlement in an area, often a conquered area
conquer	overcome by force
diverse	varied
tundra	a vast, nearly level and treeless Arctic area with a marshy surface and underlying permafrost (permanently frozen layer of earth)
spectacular	amazing, striking
plateaus	high, flat areas of land
trenches	long, narrow cuts through some surface of the earth
rugged	rough, broken, uneven
prairie	a large area of nearly treeless grasslands
swampy	consisting of wetland areas with trees, shrubs, and grasses partly covered with water
remote	distant, far away

USING NEW WORDS

Fill in each blank with a word from the list above.

1 Soldiers dug _____ during the war to protect themselves from enemy fire.

2 Buffalo and indigenous peoples _____ the prairies long before the Europeans arrived.

3 Houses in the far north do not have basements because it is impossible to dig deep holes in the _____.

4 The English _____ed the French in the famous battle on the Plains of Abraham in 1759.

⑤ When one country _____s another, there is sometimes conflict between the two peoples.

⑥ Pine and spruce trees are both _____ to the Rocky Mountains.

⑦ Canada can seem like a _____ location to people who have always lived in the tropics.

⑧ The fireworks display delighted adults and children alike with its _____ colours and patterns.

⑨ The farmers harvested a bumper crop of wheat on the _____s this year.

⑩ The _____ land was not good for growing anything.

⑪ Canadians celebrate the _____ cultures within their borders.

⑫ The coastline was too _____ for boats to land.

⑬ _____ are often chosen for building sites because there is no fear of flooding.

FOR DISCUSSION

» Why do you think the majority of people in Canada live within 160 kilometres of the American border?

» What are some problems Canadians face because of the country's geography? What are some advantages of Canada's geography?

Chapter One

Canada: Early Beginnings

Quick Facts

» Before European settlement, indigenous peoples inhabited the land.

» France and England were the first nations to colonize the area in large numbers.

» Fur traders and fishermen explored the land before colonists arrived.

» The British conquered the French in 1759 on the Plains of Abraham in what is now Quebec City.

» Canada became a country in 1867.

» In 1885, the national railroad was completed, linking the eastern and western regions of the country.

The People

Origins—Canada's First People

We do not know for certain where Canada's first people came from. Different theories attempt to explain their origins. Many of Canada's first people have their own creation myths. Aboriginal elders have handed down these stories of their origins from generation to generation. An example of a creation myth is the one told by the Blackfoot about Napi, the creator of the world. *Napi* is the Blackfoot word for *old man*.

The Blackfoot tell of how water originally covered the whole world, and Napi became curious to find out what was underneath the water. He therefore sent various animals to dive into the water, but the animals failed to find anything except a muskrat. The muskrat came back to the surface of the water with a ball of mud. Napi took this mud and blew on it until it became the earth. He then piled rocks to make mountains and covered the plains with grass. Napi dug large holes and filled them with water to produce rivers and lakes. He made birds and animals and then people. He taught people how to work and to live. When the world was complete, Napi climbed a mountain and disappeared. Other Aboriginal groups have their own creation myths.

Archaeologists have a different theory about where the first inhabitants of this land came from. They believe that early humans came here from Siberia by crossing a land bridge during the last Ice Age. This land bridge connected Siberia and Alaska across what is now the Bering Strait. Archaeologists base their argument on the fact that all physical evidence of early humans has been found in Africa, Asia, and Europe, not in the Americas. All agree, though, that the original people of this land were here at least 10 000 years before Europeans arrived.

How Canada's First People Lived

By 1500, historians believe that the population of present-day Canada was about half a million. There were many groups of indigenous people, with different cultures and languages. Half of

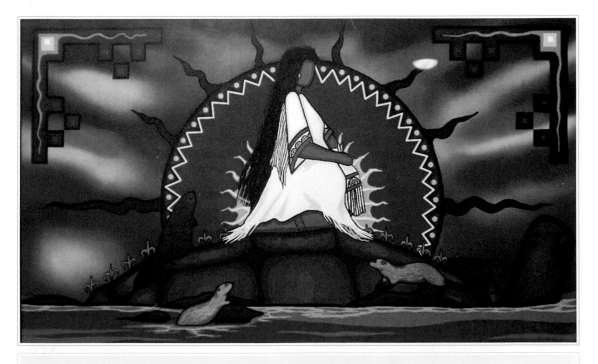

An Iroquois creation myth tells of the birth of the earth on the back of a turtle

the total population lived along the Pacific Coast and in what is now southern Ontario. Many First Nations lived along the Pacific Coast because the climate was mild and there was an abundant source of food for them in the sea. These coastal inhabitants tended to remain in the same place. They did not need to migrate, as did Aboriginals in northern areas and on the prairies.

Aboriginals in northern areas had to be migratory to follow the animals they needed for food and to find sheltered areas in the harsh winters. Prairie Nations migrated with the buffalo. They relied on the buffalo for their food and used its hide and bones to make their clothing, shelter, and tools.

First Nations who lived in what is now Ontario and Quebec tended to move around less because they grew crops such as corn and beans for food. They also hunted large and small animals for food, clothing, shelter, and tools.

Aboriginals lived in harmony with nature. They respected nature as a provider of life and took only what they needed to survive. Before the

A Cree family on the prairie

Europeans arrived, each Nation's way of life was determined by the kind of natural resources it had, and by how scarce or plentiful these resources were. Each Aboriginal community controlled its affairs in its own way. This changed drastically with the arrival of the Europeans.

COMPREHENSION CHECK

❶ Where do archaeologists think that Aboriginals came from originally? Why?

❷ About how long did Aboriginals live in North America before the Europeans arrived?

❸ Which Aboriginal groups were migrants who moved from place to place throughout the year? Why did they migrate?

❹ What was the relationship between Aboriginals, animals, and the land?

VOCABULARY

relatively	as compared to, or in relation to others
theories	possible explanations based on available facts
myths	stories used to explain or teach values and truths within a culture
muskrat	a large, semi-aquatic member of the rat family (semi-aquatic means living partly on land and partly in water)
archaeologists	scientists who study history primarily by excavating (digging) for remains
migrate	move from place to place with the seasons
hide (n)	the skin of an animal
harmony	a combination which forms an orderly and peaceful whole; agreement

Note: In everyday speech, Canada's indigenous peoples are referred to as Aboriginals, First Nations, or native people.

USING NEW WORDS

Fill in each blank with a word from the Vocabulary section.

➊ Ducks _____. They fly south for the winter and north for the summer.

➋ _____ pelts were sold by Aboriginals to fur traders, who then sold them to be made into fur coats and hats.

➌ The _____ of the buffalo was used by Aboriginals for clothing and for making teepees, their mobile houses on the prairies.

➍ Every culture has its _____. They are not lies; rather, they are creative ways of telling a truth.

➎ Mary Leakey was one of the _____ who found the bones of our very early ancestors.

➏ There are different _____ about who the first Europeans were to settle in North America; some think it was the Vikings.

➐ You speak English _____ well for a newcomer.

➑ The couple decided to end their marriage because there was no longer any _____ between them.

Match each word with its meaning.

plentiful	try
attempt	depended on
origins	in short supply; few in number
scarce	in great supply; many in number
drastically	beginnings
relied on	having a strong and far-reaching effect

FOR DISCUSSION

» How, in your view, does the Aboriginals' relationship with nature compare to most modern North Americans' relationship to nature?

RESEARCH

» Find out which First Nations or Inuit originally inhabited your area. Are there reserves or cultural centres for Aboriginals in your area today?

» One Nation, called the Beothuk, who lived in Newfoundland a long time ago, is now extinct. There are none of these people left alive. Find out how they became extinct and when.

Exploration and Settlement

Early Contact—The Vikings

The Vikings, from Norway, Sweden, and Denmark, may have been the first Europeans to arrive in North America. Viking explorers had reached the east coast of North America by the year 986. People first learned of their voyages through the Vikings' stories, called sagas, which they passed down from generation to generation. One of these famous Viking explorers was Leif Ericsson. Historians believe Ericsson built the first European settlement in North America. The remains of a Viking settlement have been found at L'Anse aux Meadows in Newfoundland. Historians are not sure why the Vikings abandoned this colony, but the Vikings never did establish a permanent settlement in North America.

Viking explorers reached North America by the year 986

Searching the World for Wealth

It was not until approximately 500 years after the Vikings arrived that Europeans again sailed to the Americas. Traders were bringing treasures of silk and spices to Europe from Asia, but the overland route was slow and dangerous. Europeans were anxious to find a faster sea passage to the riches of the East.

In 1492, Christopher Columbus set sail from Spain across the Atlantic Ocean to find the passage to Asia, but landed instead in Central America. He thought he had discovered a western route to India and called the indigenous people Indians. Up to that time, Europeans were totally unaware that North America or its people existed, and in fact believed that the world was flat.

Columbus brought back silver and gold to Spain from the Americas. With the promise of such riches, other European countries rushed to send their own explorers across the Atlantic. John Cabot sailed from England in 1497 and landed on what is now Newfoundland. He claimed the area for England. Off the coast of Newfoundland, the English discovered the wealth of an abundant fish supply.

France sent Jacques Cartier in 1534. Cartier made three voyages to the New World. On the first, he reached the Gulf of St. Lawrence and thought it was the passage to Asia. Many explorers would make similar mistakes: when they discovered a body of water, they believed it was the route to Asia. To prove that he had reached the new lands, Cartier kidnapped two sons of an Iroquois chief and took them back to France.

Cartier returned to North America in 1535. This time he sailed farther up the St. Lawrence River to the Iroquoian settlements of Stadacona, present-day Quebec City, and Hochelaga, now Montreal. Cartier returned to France in the spring of 1536. On the way, he found the strait separating Newfoundland from Cape Breton Island and proved that Newfoundland was an island.

In 1541, the king of France was ready to establish a settlement in the New World. He put a French nobleman named Roberval in charge of this expedition. Cartier was Roberval's guide. This first attempt at settlement failed due to the harsh winter and sickness. Cartier found what he thought were gold and diamonds, but they turned out to be fake; they were combinations of

French explorer Jacques Cartier

Fish and Furs

Long before the Europeans began extensive explorations in North America, European fishermen visited the east coast frequently. Initially, they would catch the fish, preserve them with salt on their ships, and then bring them back to Europe to sell. Because salt was expensive, fishermen began taking their fish to shore to let them dry. These fishermen were the first Europeans to establish summer settlements along the east coast of present-day Canada.

Aboriginals began to trade with the fishermen. The Aboriginals gave the Europeans furs in exchange for their fish. Furs were worth a lot of money in Europe. Fur hats and coats were very fashionable and people were willing to pay a high price for them. The European fishermen also began to trade common items such as knives and copper kettles for the Aboriginals' furs.

Soon, the European traders settled in what is now Quebec and Ontario for the whole year—not just the spring and summer—to be closer to the Aboriginals and their fur supply. Thus, both the abundant fish stocks in the Atlantic and the fur trade contributed to the first successful European settlements in Canada.

quartz and iron. These bad experiences discouraged France from sending any more explorers to Canada for the next 60 years.

These voyageurs helped transport furs

COMPREHENSION CHECK

Check your understanding by completing the following puzzle.

Across

3. perhaps the first Europeans to reach North America

4. what Europeans were looking for by sea : _____ to Asia

5. the "riches" found off the coast of Newfoundland

6. the French explorer who made three voyages to the New World

8. the major river Cartier travelled on

Down

1. what Columbus called the indigenous people

2. the area with silks and spices

5. what Aboriginals traded with the Europeans

6. the explorer who claimed Newfoundland for England

7. where the Vikings built a settlement, now part of a province of Canada

(You can find the answers to the puzzle on page 250 at the back of the book.)

VOCABULARY

permanent	lasting; not temporary
passage	a way to pass through
kidnapped	stolen away without permission (a person is taken illegally)
strait	a narrow passage connecting two seas or bodies of water
harsh	unpleasant and difficult
extensive	covering a broad area, far-reaching
preserve	maintain without change
fashionable	popular for a time, especially clothing
kettles	metal pots used for cooking

USING NEW WORDS

Fill in each blank with a word from the Vocabulary section.

1. The _____ connecting the two lakes was too shallow for ships to pass through.

2. The child got stuck trying to squeeze through the narrow _____ between the shed and the house.

3. When the babysitter woke up, she noticed that the baby had been _____ and she frantically called the police.

4. Clothing which is _____ one year may be considered out-of-date the following year.

5. Knives, guns, and _____ were often given by the traders in exchange for furs.

6. Many immigrant groups work hard to _____ their original languages and cultural traditions in Canada.

7. Large cities have _____ libraries, whereas smaller communities cannot afford to buy a large number of new books each year.

8. The woman was much too _____ to be a teacher of young children.

9. Very few things in life are _____.

FOR DISCUSSION

» How might history have been different if Cartier had taken real diamonds and gold back to France with him?

» How do you think Cartier justified the kidnapping of two Aboriginal youths to take back to France with him? Can you think of other examples of one group of people dehumanizing another?

» Cabot claimed Newfoundland for England and Cartier claimed the St. Lawrence region for France. How do you think Aboriginals felt about these claims to the land on which they had lived for thousands of years?

The Colony of New France

French Interest Renewed

By 1600, the wealth from the fur trade and the fishing industry renewed French interest in North America. The king of France decided to settle what is now eastern Canada. The colony would be named New France. Jacques Cartier's voyages had established a French claim to the Gulf of St. Lawrence area, but for that claim to be internationally recognized, the region had to be successfully colonized by the French. To avoid the high costs of building the settlements, the king of France made an agreement with a private fur-trading company. If the company brought settlers to New France, it would have a monopoly on the fur trade. Only this company would be allowed to trade for furs in New France and it would receive all the profits.

Acadia

Early attempts at colonization, from 1598 to 1601, failed. In 1604, however, a French nobleman and a mapmaker named Samuel de Champlain together established the first permanent French settlement in the New World. Their first small community was on an island just off the south coast of present-day New Brunswick. At that time, this area was called *Acadie* (Acadia in English). The settlers spent a terrible first winter on the unprotected island. In the summer of 1605, they moved to a more sheltered harbour in what is now Nova Scotia. This new settlement was called Port Royal.

Champlain's arrival in Acadie

The French colonists successfully made it through the winter of 1605–06, but by 1607, France had decided that *Acadie* was too far from the centre of the fur trade and chose to establish a new French settlement along the St. Lawrence River. The French settlers left Port Royal and went back to France, but in 1610, some returned and stayed to farm. These people are the ancestors of the French-speaking Acadian people in Nova Scotia and New Brunswick today.

Settlement along the St. Lawrence

In 1608, Champlain was chosen to found the first French settlement along the St. Lawrence River. For his role in settling this area and Port Royal, he is known as the Father of New France.

Champlain chose the old Iroquois village of Stadacona for the settlement. It was at a narrow part of the St. Lawrence River and had a good harbour. The settlement was called Quebec, from the Algonquian word *Kebec*, meaning *narrows*. Twenty-eight settlers died the first winter, leaving only Champlain and seven others. Champlain realized that the colony of New France needed many more settlers if it was going to survive, but his efforts failed. By 1627, there were only 65 settlers in Quebec.

A Royal Colony

By 1663, the population of New France was still very small. The fur traders were more concerned with their trading than with farming and settlement. War between the French and the Iroquois also made settlers feel unsafe. Louis XIV, then king of France, decided to end the rule of the fur traders and make New France a royal colony governed by the king. On behalf of the king, a governor, a bishop, and an intendant ruled in New France. They ensured that more settlers came to the colony and they encouraged farming and industry.

By 1700, New France was not the great farming colony that Louis XIV had wanted. Furthermore, since 1688, France had been almost constantly at war. It did not have the time or the money to spend on the colony.

COMPREHENSION CHECK

❶ Why did the French government give a monopoly to the fur-trading company in New France?

❷ Who was called the Father of New France?

❸ Where does the name Quebec come from originally and what did it mean?

❹ Why did Louis XIV make New France a royal colony?

VOCABULARY

monopoly	complete possession or control over some aspect of trade or business by one person or company
ancestor	person from whom we are descended
bishop	a leader within the Roman Catholic Church appointed by the Pope
intendant	an agent appointed by the king to supervise justice, finance, and other affairs of government
found	establish or begin a new community or organization

USING NEW WORDS

Fill in each blank with a word from the list above.

❶ The _____ decided whether a man accused of a crime was guilty or innocent and, if guilty, what his punishment was to be.

❷ Nowadays, many people believe it is not good business to give any company a _____ over any aspect of trade.

❸ Queen Victoria was an _____ of Britain's Queen Elizabeth II.

❹ All the priests in the Roman Catholic Church report to their _____.

❺ The department store that we now call The Bay was originally called the Hudson's Bay Company and was _____ed by fur traders.

ROLE PLAY

» In small groups, imagine you are part of the first group of settlers in Quebec. How would you survive that first winter on the shores of the St. Lawrence River? Discuss your experiences and what you would do for food, shelter, drinking water, clothing, warmth, and entertainment. Present your solutions.

The Struggle for Power

France versus Britain

France and Britain did not have good relations. They fought over colonies in North America and also over the fur trade. France was largely Roman Catholic and Britain was mainly Protestant. This difference also caused tension.

In 1756, the Seven Years War broke out between France and Britain. They fought in each other's colonies all over the world. In North America, they fought over three areas: the present-day Atlantic provinces, the interior (due to the wealth-producing fur trade), and the Ohio Valley in what is now the United States. The British colonists on the east coast wanted new farmland for their growing population, and the French fur traders had forts in the Ohio area which they refused to move.

The British Conquest

By 1758, the British had captured the French fortress of Louisbourg, which guarded the entrance to the St. Lawrence River. This was the beginning of the end for French rule in North America. New France now lay unprotected. The British arrived on the St. Lawrence River before the French could transport reinforcements to New France.

In September of 1759, the British attacked the French in the famous battle on the Plains of Abraham just outside Quebec City. The British were victorious and the following spring, they conquered the last French stronghold, Montreal. French rule in North America ended, but the French influence continues to be felt in Canada. Today, more than five million French-speaking descendants of these early settlers live in the province of Quebec.

You can see that the bitterness between French and English in Canada goes back a long way. These events help to explain why English–French relations in this country continue to threaten Canadian unity.

Changes under British Rule

The British changed the name of New France to Quebec. In the Quebec Act of 1774, the British allowed the French to keep their Roman Catholic religion, civil law system, and language so that they would not try to break away from Britain. Many French, however, still felt that their culture was threatened by British rule and by the large number of British settlers moving into the region.

From 1775 to 1784, many British came to Quebec from the American colonies to the south. During the American Revolution (1775–83), the American colonies were fighting for their independence from Britain. The people who fled north to the British colonies such as Quebec and Nova Scotia wanted to remain loyal to Britain. They were known as United Empire Loyalists.

With so many new settlers, Britain had to create two new colonies: New Brunswick and Upper Canada. New Brunswick was created in 1784. In 1791, the British passed an act that divided Quebec into Upper and Lower Canada. Upper Canada was the English-speaking colony and Lower Canada was the French-speaking colony.

Due to unrest in both Upper and Lower Canada, the British government reunited the two in 1841. Upper Canada became Canada West and Lower Canada became Canada East. The capital of the two was Montreal. They would eventually become the provinces of Ontario and Quebec with Confederation in 1867.

COMPREHENSION CHECK

1. What were two reasons that the English and French fought each other in many parts of the world?
2. Where was the last stronghold for the French?
3. Why did the British agree to many demands of the French people in Quebec?
4. Why did the United Empire Loyalists leave the American colonies?
5. What provinces today used to be called Upper Canada and Lower Canada?
6. Has the old bitterness between the French and the English been resolved today?

VOCABULARY

Protestant	Christian but not Roman Catholic; so named when Luther made protests against the Roman Catholic Church in Germany in the early 1500s
reinforcements	fresh troops (soldiers) sent to renew the strength of one's force in battle
victorious	winning, conquering
stronghold	a place of strength and power
descendants	those who are descended from a person, family, or group; we are the descendants of our ancestors
bitterness	the feeling of anger and resentment towards someone you believe has wronged you
threaten	present a danger to
get along	have a good relationship
formerly	before, in the past
unrest	disturbance; a lack of peace and harmony

USING NEW WORDS

Fill in each blank with a word from the list above.

1. There can be no real harmony between two people as long as there are strong feelings of _____.

2. To _____ someone usually creates anger or fear in that person.

3. Presbyterians, Anglicans, and Lutherans are sometimes called _____s.

4. The English language is spoken in many countries today partly because the English were _____ in many battles throughout history.

5. The United States of America has been a _____ of much power in the world since the end of World War II.

6. Canadians are the _____ of people from many different countries and races.

7. Eritrea was _____ part of Ethiopia.

8. The staff could not handle the riot at the prison and asked the army to send _____.

9. There has been longstanding _____ between the Roman Catholics and Protestants in Northern Ireland.

WORD FORMS

Fill in the blanks with the correct form of the words given.

VERB	NOUN	ADJECTIVE	ADVERB
reinforce			- - - - - - - - -
	threat		
embitter			

(You can find the answers on page 250 at the back of the book.)

WRITE

» Imagine that you are a French or English soldier who must fight in the famous battle on the Plains of Abraham in 1759. Describe the night before the battle. What are your hopes and your fears? What do you do on this night and with whom?

The Birth of a Nation

Reasons for a Union

In the 1860s, people were talking about a possible union of all the British North American colonies. There were five major reasons for this drive for union. The first was the civil war between the northern and southern United States from 1861 to 1865. When the North (the northern states) won, the British North American colonies worried that the Northern armies might attack them to get revenge against Britain for its support of the South during the war. Some Americans also believed that it was the United States' destiny to control all of North America. If they were united, the British North American colonies felt they could better defend themselves against any American aggression.

A second reason for union was the need for a strong defence against the Fenians. The Fenians were Irish Americans who believed that if they invaded British North America, they could get back at Britain and possibly force the British to free Ireland. At this time, all of Ireland was under British rule. In 1866, 1500 Fenians captured Fort Erie in present-day Ontario.

The third reason for a union was trade. The British North American colonies had a special advantage in trade with Britain, but in 1846 the British started a free-trade policy which eliminated this advantage. The colonies then made a special trade agreement with the United States, but this ended in 1865 because it was no longer profitable for the Americans. Some British North American colonies argued that the only solution was free trade amongst themselves. This would be easier if the provinces were united.

A railway to link the colonies also seemed essential. A railway line to join western Canada with the Atlantic Ocean had been started in 1860, but had gone bankrupt. Many believed that the only way it could be finished was if the colonies united. They could then share the cost of building the railroad. They also argued that this railroad was necessary to defend Canada in case of war. It was needed to get British troops from Halifax to Canada during the winter when the St. Lawrence River was frozen solid.

Finally, British attitudes toward the colonies were also changing. Some British citizens wanted to get rid of the colonies because they thought they were too expensive to defend. They believed it was time for the British North American colonists to pay their own way.

The Charlottetown and Quebec Conferences

In August of 1864, political leaders of Canada West and Canada East, Nova Scotia, Prince Edward Island (PEI), and New Brunswick met in Charlottetown, the capital of PEI, to discuss a union of all the British North American colonies. The idea of a union seemed a favourable one. Confederation, a union of the colonies under a central government, became a real possibility after this conference. The leaders met again at Quebec later that year and were joined by delegates from Newfoundland. This time, they organized a plan for the union.

The Fight for Confederation

The leaders had to convince the people of their colonies to accept the plan. From 1864 to 1867, the issue was debated in the colonies. Prince Edward Island and Newfoundland rejected the plan. The people of Prince Edward Island felt the concerns of their small island would be lost in the united government. Newfoundland decided to keep its independence and its strong ties with Britain. The colonies of Canada West, Canada East, Nova Scotia, and New Brunswick agreed to Confederation. In the spring of 1867, the union was approved by the British Parliament when the British North America Act was passed.

On July 1, 1867, the four colonies (now called Ontario, Quebec, New Brunswick, and Nova Scotia) were officially united into the Dominion of Canada. Celebrations were held across the new country to celebrate the event. John A. Macdonald became Canada's first prime minister.

Canada's first prime minister, John A. Macdonald

In the following years, the country grew quickly. The North-West Territories became part of Canada in 1870. This massive region included most of the North (except the Arctic Islands), as well as present-day Alberta and Saskatchewan, and much of Manitoba, northern Ontario and northern Quebec. Manitoba became a province of Canada in 1870, although at that point it was just a small portion of land around Winnipeg. British Columbia joined in 1871, and Prince Edward Island joined in 1873.

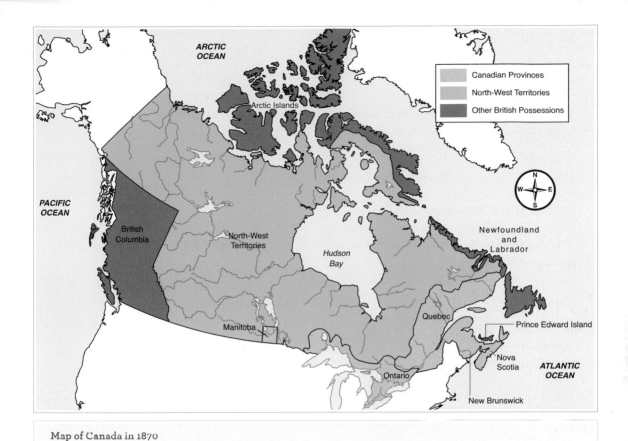

Map of Canada in 1870

In 1898, the Yukon became a separate territory from the North-West Territories. Alberta and Saskatchewan both became provinces of Canada in 1905. Newfoundland remained independent from the rest of Canada until 1949. Finally, in 1999, Nunavut became Canada's third territory.

COMPREHENSION CHECK

Are the following statements true or false?

1. The British North American colonies feared that the United States might attack them.
2. The colonies believed they needed a railroad for defence and to encourage trade.
3. Some people in Britain no longer wanted to pay to defend the colonies.
4. Ontario, Quebec, Nova Scotia, and Newfoundland were the four provinces that formed Canada in 1867.
5. British Columbia was the last province to join Canada.
6. John A. Macdonald was Canada's first prime minister.

VOCABULARY

civil war	a war between two groups of people within a country
destiny	one's future as it is intended to be
invaded	entered with force; taken over by another people
bankrupt	totally without financial resources; broke
delegates	representatives to a meeting or conference
rejected	refused; pushed aside

USING NEW WORDS

Match each word on the left with the word or group of words on the right which is closest in meaning.

destiny	getting even
delegates	taken over by an enemy
rejected	hostility
revenge	refused
bankrupt	fate
aggression	broke
invaded	representatives

FOR DISCUSSION

» Canadians and Americans are often seen as friendly neighbours, but there is also some real tension between them. What historical reasons can you see for this tension?

» People in some colonies protested strongly against Confederation in 1867. Why do you think some people did not want to become part of a large country with a central government? Why are some large countries today breaking up?

Building the National Railroad

The Promise of a Railway

In May 1870, the people of British Columbia told John A. Macdonald, Canada's prime minister, that they wanted to join Confederation. They asked that a wagon road be built across the prairies and through the mountains to connect British Columbia with Canada. Macdonald agreed to do even more. He promised a railway would be started within two years and finished within ten. Without the railway, Macdonald worried that British Columbia might leave Confederation and join the United States. He also wanted to bring farmers to settle the prairies and to produce farm products for Canada's eastern markets.

Construction Begins

Macdonald and his government's first attempt at getting Canada's railway underway failed because of a political scandal. People accused Macdonald and his government of taking bribes from the company that was hired to build the railway. Macdonald and his party were forced out of power in 1873. The new government was less interested in building the railway. Not much work was done on the project over the next five years.

In 1878, Macdonald returned to power and the railway project was once again underway. George Stephen and Donald A. Smith formed a new Canadian Pacific Railway Company to complete the project. Workers had built 1100 kilometres of railway lines, but another 3040 kilometres of track still had to be laid. William Van Horne was hired to supervise railroad construction. Under his direction, workers laid 1500 kilometres of railway on the prairies in 15 months. It was a remarkable accomplishment.

A Dangerous and Difficult Project

Building other sections of the railway, however, proved to be very complicated and dangerous for the workers, especially the section through the mountains of British Columbia. The workers had to build bridges over steep mountain canyons and use explosives to blast through rock. Some claim that along the British Columbia section of the railway, every kilometre of tunnel and track was stained with blood. Workers were killed by explosions, flying rocks, or falls from narrow passages. To keep costs down, many Chinese workers were brought in to work on the British Columbia section of the railway. The Chinese workers were willing to work for lower wages than other labourers. Many Chinese men died working on the railway. They played an extremely important role in this part of Canada's history.

Will They Finish?

By 1885, the Canadian Pacific Railway faced serious financial problems. The company was out of money and sections of track still had to be built. The opposition Members of Parliament did not want the Canadian government to loan any more money to the railway. John A. Macdonald argued that the railway had already proved its usefulness. Troops had been sent out to Manitoba from Ottawa in only nine days to put down a rebellion earlier

Chinese workers building the railroad

that year. Macdonald convinced the Canadian government to loan the Canadian Pacific Railway Company enough money to finish the project; and on November 7, 1885, at 9:22 a.m., workers hammered in the last spike of the railway. The section of railway from Ontario to British Columbia had been completed in five years.

Settling the West

The completion of the railway was a very important event in Canadian history. It eventually brought almost a million settlers to western Canada. It also encouraged trade within Canada, instead of with the United States, because it made transportation from east to west across Canada easier and faster.

Settlers from Britain, the United States, and Europe moved into western Canada. Many were looking for political or religious freedom, land, and the opportunity for a better life. By 1912, almost one-fifth of the people in Canada were not of British or French origin. Though people of Asian, African, Jewish, and southern European origins were not welcomed into Canada until later, the make-up of the country's population had changed. As Canada entered the twentieth century, it was experiencing the greatest immigration boom in its history.

COMPREHENSION CHECK

1. Who promised British Columbia that Canada would build a railroad there within ten years?
2. Why did he make that promise knowing how difficult and expensive it would be?
3. Which group performed a lot of the labour on the mountain sections of the railway?
4. What problems did the government and the Canadian Pacific Railway Company have in completing the project?
5. Why was the completion of the railway important for Canada?

VOCABULARY

wagon	a wooden vehicle on four wheels pulled by a team of horses
scandal	an event which causes extreme embarrassment to individuals because of some immoral, illegal, or unethical activities
bribes	money or services offered to a person to act dishonestly or illegally
track	the long, straight metal pieces laid parallel to one another along a course for the train to follow
canyons	narrow valleys with high, steep sides usually with a stream or river at the bottom
spike	a large, pointed metal peg or nail used to hold the railway tracks in place

USING NEW WORDS

Match each word on the left to the most appropriate expression on the right.

spike	You don't want to fall into one of these!
track	If you are involved in one of these, shame on you!
wagon	Look out if you get caught taking these!
canyons	You wouldn't want one in your eye!
bribes	Not much good if it loses a wheel!
scandal	Being on this is better than being off it!

FOR DISCUSSION

» What do you think would have happened if the railway had not been built across the country when it was?

» What effects can a large number of new immigrants have on the people already living in the area?

CHAPTER REVIEW

Match these key events in Canadian history with the correct dates listed below.

» Canada becomes a country _____

» Champlain starts the first French settlement in North America _____

» Britain defeats France on the Plains of Abraham _____

» The national railroad is completed _____

» Jacques Cartier makes his first voyage to the New World _____

   1534   1604   1759   1867   1885

Chapter Two

Contemporary Canada: Recent History, Government, and Economy

Quick Facts

» Canada has a federal system of government, with ten provinces and three territories.

» Canada is a member of the British Commonwealth, whose head of state is the Queen of England.

» The leader of Canada is the prime minister; the leaders of the provinces are the premiers.

» The capital city of Canada is Ottawa.

» The Canadian Parliament has two houses: the House of Commons, whose members are elected, and the Senate, whose members are appointed.

» Economically, Canada is rich in natural resources such as forests, minerals, fish, oil, and gas.

» Most Canadians work in service jobs, such as in businesses, education, and health care.

Introduction

This chapter and the next provide you with a brief introduction to Canada today: its government, economy, educational and training systems, arts, and entertainment. First, here is a look at some important historical events of the past century that have affected life in Canada today.

Canada in the Past Century—A Timeline

1914–18	World War I Canadians join other members of the British Commonwealth in the war against Germany and Austria-Hungary. Canada gains international recognition for its role in the war.
1918	Women win the right to vote in federal elections and have the right to vote in six of the provinces.
1920	Women gain the right to run for office in the Canadian government.
1929–39	The Great Depression A time of serious economic difficulties in Canada and throughout the world. The stock market collapses in 1929. The world market for wheat also collapses, hurting farmers in western Canada badly. Many people are unemployed.
1939–45	World War II Canada joins Britain against Germany and its allies. In 1941, following the bombing of Pearl Harbor in Hawaii by the Japanese, Japanese Canadians are interned and their property is confiscated. Many of these same people had fought for Canada in World War I. Women join the workforce in large numbers.
1945–68	Postwar Canada Canada's economy and population grow significantly. There is a Baby Boom (those born in this period are called "Baby Boomers"). Many new immigrants also come to Canada. In the 1960s, Canada introduces social programs such as medicare and the Canada Pension Plan.
1948	People of Asian origin receive the right to vote.
1949	Newfoundland (later named Newfoundland and Labrador) joins Canada as the tenth province.
1950	Inuit Canadians gain the right to vote in federal elections.
1959	The St. Lawrence Seaway is completed, allowing ships to pass from the Atlantic Ocean into the Great Lakes. Canada also increases trade and economic ties with the United States.
1960	First Nations and Métis people gain the right to vote in federal elections.
1965	Canada gets its own flag with the red maple leaf. (Up to this time, the Union Jack of Britain had been our flag.)
1967	Canada celebrates its hundredth birthday.
1969	Prime Minister Pierre Trudeau and his Liberal government pass the Official Languages Act. The Act states that all federal government services must be provided in both French and English. Funds are given to the provinces to support bilingualism.

1970	Quebec nationalism and the separatist movement gained strength throughout the 1960s. In October of 1970, members of an extremist separatist organization called the FLQ murder a Quebec government official and kidnap a British official. The Canadian army moves into Quebec to settle the crisis.
1976	A separatist party, the Parti Québécois, is elected to head the Quebec government. The government takes action to protect the French language in Quebec, but loses a referendum for Quebec sovereignty (political independence from Canada) in 1980.
1982	Prime Minister Trudeau and his government bring Canada's constitution (the British North America Act of 1867) home from Britain. Canada now has the power to make changes to its own constitution. The British North America Act is renamed the Constitution Act, 1982 and the Charter of Rights and Freedoms is added. Quebec, however, is the only province that does not sign the constitution.
1984–89	Brian Mulroney and the Progressive Conservative Party win the federal election in 1984. The government promotes closer economic and political ties with the United States. The Free Trade Agreement is passed in 1989 between the two countries. The government also attempts to change the constitution to include Quebec, but these attempts fail.
1990	The issue of Aboriginal rights and land claims receives increased attention when Mohawks at Oka, Quebec, hold an armed standoff to protect their land.
1993	Brian Mulroney steps down as prime minister and is replaced by Canada's first female prime minister, Kim Campbell. She loses her first election six months later, however, and the Liberals under Prime Minister Jean Chrétien take power.
1994	Canada signs the North American Free Trade Agreement (NAFTA) with the United States and Mexico.
1995	Another sovereignty referendum is held in Quebec. The vote is very close, but Quebec remains part of Canada.
1999	Nunavut is born. This is the third territory in Canada's North and gives the Inuit more control over their own affairs.
2002	Canada hosts the G8 Summit in Kananaskis, Alberta. Canada promises more than 10 billion dollars over 10 years to eliminate the spread of weapons and materials of mass destruction in the world. (The G8 Summit is a meeting of the governments of the world's largest economies.)
2005	Parliament passes Bill C-38, The Civil Marriage Act, giving marriage rights to same-sex couples. This makes Canada the fourth nation in the world to do so.
2007	Prime Minister Stephen Harper commits to providing 1.5 billion dollars in incentives over nine years to producers of renewable alternatives to gasoline and diesel fuel.
2007	Prime Minister Harper pledges 7 billion dollars for the protection of Canadian sovereignty in the Arctic.
2010	Canada hosts the Winter Olympic Games in Vancouver to a rousing display of patriotism and the winning of 26 medals, our best showing so far at these games.

COMPREHENSION CHECK

True or false?

1. Women have always had the right to vote in Canada.
2. Alberta and Saskatchewan were the last provinces to join Canada.
3. The Great Depression was especially difficult for farmers in western Canada because they could not sell their wheat.
4. The Second World War lasted about six years.
5. Japanese Canadians all decided to move inland from the west coast during World War II because they were nervous about the war.
6. Canada got its own flag in 1867.
7. Canada is a bilingual country.
8. In the sovereignty referendum of 1995, the people of Quebec voted in favour of political independence from Canada.

VOCABULARY

run for office	stand for election
collapses	falls apart; fails suddenly
interned	forced to live in a confined area
confiscated	taken away
Baby Boom	the period after World War II when many people had children and the economy consequently grew steadily
social programs	government-funded programs (such as old-age pensions or social assistance) which help to protect people from hardship
medicare	a program in which every person has equal access to basic health care whether they are rich or poor
pension	a regular payment to people who have reached a certain age (65 in Canada), when they are no longer working
bilingualism	the ability to speak two languages (in the case of Canada, English and French), a policy which is officially encouraged in Canada
nationalism	strong emotion for one's nation (usually a country, but in the case of Quebec, many of the people consider Quebec their nation)
referendum	a vote in which the people can make an important decision about some issue
constitution	an official act which sets out rules and principles for the government of a nation or other organization; a set of relatively permanent laws about the exercise of power in a country
charter	an official agreement which grants privileges or recognizes rights (for example, human rights)

USING NEW WORDS

Nationalism is a strong feeling of loyalty to one's people or nation. A nationalist is a person who supports or demonstrates this feeling. Below are some other terms you may come across which describe a person's behaviours or beliefs. Match each word on the left with its definition on the right.

separatist	a person who supports the protection of our natural environment
federalist	a person who wants Quebec to separate from the rest of Canada and become an independent nation
activist	a person who supports a strong central government
environmentalist	a person who discriminates against people of other races
racist	a person who is very active in supporting his or her beliefs

FOR DISCUSSION

» Based on the events in the timeline, what do you think are two of the most important issues in Canada today? Why?

» Are there recent important events you think should be added?

» Does your country of origin have social programs such as employment insurance and medicare? Are you willing to pay higher taxes to have these programs?

Government in Canada

The Three Levels of Government

Canada is a democratic country in which our political representatives are elected by citizens 18 years of age and over. Canada has three levels of government: federal (national), provincial, and municipal (city, town, or rural area). Our federal representatives are called Members of Parliament or MPs. Our provincial representatives are called Members of the Legislative Assembly (MLAs) in most provinces. In Ontario, they are called Members of the Provincial Parliament (MPPs), in Newfoundland and Labrador, they are called Members of the House of Assembly, and in Quebec, they are called Members of the National Assembly (MNAs). Municipalities have their own systems of local government. Municipal representatives are usually called councillors.

• What are elected representatives in your province and municipality called?

• At what age can a person vote in your community?

The responsibilities of the different levels of government are defined in Canada's constitution. The federal government is responsible for matters that affect the whole country such as immigration, employment, international trade, criminal law, taxation, citizenship, health care, defence, communications (including the postal system), and transportation. The provincial governments are responsible for such matters as education, social services, labour laws, land titles, corporate registrations, tourism, workers' health and safety, highways, the sale of alcoholic beverages, and motor vehicle licences. Municipalities deal with local affairs such as schools, property, care of roadways, urban transportation, business licences, libraries, police, and fire services. Municipal councillors also pass laws (called bylaws) governing such matters as speed limits, noise levels, animal licensing, and local planning and development.

Canada's House of Commons

All levels of government can tax the public. The federal government collects income tax and GST (goods and services tax) of five percent on most goods and services sold in Canada. All provinces except Alberta have also a provincial sales tax which varies in size. Many provinces have combined their federal and provincial taxes into an HST (harmonized sales tax) which is sometimes quite controversial. The combined system of taxation means that more monies are collected than in previous totals of federal and provincial tax. Municipalities collect property taxes and business taxes.

There is some overlap in the responsibilities of the federal and provincial governments. In these cases, the federal government often gives money to the provinces to run the programs, but asks the provinces to follow federal policies on these services. A good example is medicare. The Canadian government believes that all citizens should have basic health care whether they are rich or poor. Since the program requires a great amount of money, both levels of government pay for part of health care. Many of the provinces, for example, collect a monthly fee called healthcare premiums. Do you pay a monthly fee in your province for basic health care?

Political Parties

In Canada, most people who want to represent us in government belong to a political party. There are many different political parties in Canada. The three main parties at the federal level are the Conservative Party of Canada, the New Democratic Party of Canada (NDP), and the Liberal Party of Canada. In 2011, the Green Party of Canada won its first seat in Parliament, while the Bloc Québécois—which used to be an important party within Quebec—lost all but four of its seats. Each party has its own set of beliefs and policies. Sometimes an individual who does not belong to a political party runs for office. These individuals can sit in the government as Independents.

Some people would show the relationship between the parties like this:

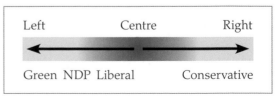

The Bloc Québécois is not on the diagram because it is not a national party. It was formed to give Quebec a stronger voice in the federal government and to work for Quebec independence. It has representatives only from Quebec.

The largest federal parties have representatives at the provincial level as well. The provincial parties, however, do not necessarily follow the same policies as the federal parties. It is important to find out what a party's policies are before voting in any election.

COMPREHENSION CHECK

1. Which level of government makes the decisions about how Canada as a whole is governed?
2. If you are having problems with sponsoring a family member who wants to immigrate to Canada, who would you ask for help: an MP or an MLA/MPP?
3. If you and members of your ethnic community want to start a bilingual school for your children, which level of government could you talk to?
4. Would you contact the federal or provincial government to find out where you could get a driver's licence?
5. Which level of government decides how much postage stamps cost?
6. If you want to become a citizen of Canada, which level of government would you contact for information?
7. Which level of government decides how fast you can drive your car in the city?
8. Bonus question: What do you think will happen if you drive your car too fast and the police stop you?

VOCABULARY

democratic	governed by the people or elected representatives of the people
representatives	people who speak or work for others at their request
councillors	members of a council; a council is a group of people elected to work on behalf of a larger group (such as a city council)
taxation	the requirement by governments that people pay money for services (for example, income tax based on a person's income, property tax based on the value of land and buildings owned, and sales tax based on the value of what you buy)
corporate	having to do with a corporation (company, business)
registration	the act of officially recording information (registration of children at school, registration of a marriage)
tourism	the business of serving visitors to a country or community
licence (n)	a paper which gives permission to do, own, or use something (such as a driver's licence)
urban	of the city (rural: of the country)
assess	determine the value of something
overlap (n)	something shared in common
policies	guidelines for decision-making in governments and other organizations

USING NEW WORDS

Fill in each blank with a word from the Vocabulary section.

1. José did not come from a _____ country. A general in the army controlled the government.
2. _____ is an important industry in the beautiful Rocky Mountains region of Alberta. Many people like to visit the area from other countries.
3. If you drive your car without a _____, the police can fine you.
4. When you apply for a job in a country where English is your second language, the employer will often _____ your English language skills before he or she decides to give you a job.
5. _____ life is often more stressful than life in the country. Would you rather live in a city or on a farm?
6. Many people believe there is too much _____ in Canada.
7. It is important to know a party's _____ before voting.

Unscramble the following words. Use the clues on the right to help you.

palover — There should not be an _____ between a man's date with one woman and his date with another, or he will have no dates at all!

rocporate — _____ taxes are at a lower rate than personal taxes to encourage people to go into business and to create jobs.

nillcocours — It is important for every community to have both male and female _____ in municipal government.

tinoratregis — When a police officer stops a driver, he asks to see the driver's licence and _____.

peersentratives — Each member of the United Nations has _____ in New York to speak on behalf of that nation.

FOR DISCUSSION

» Are there parties on the left and right in your country of origin?

» What does it mean to be a leftist? To be a right-winger?

» Which groups of people traditionally support the left? The right?

MAKING CONTACT

» Find out who your elected provincial representative (MPP or MLA) is. Search online for "Who is my MPP (or MLA)" and the name of your province to find a list of representatives from your province. You will need to enter your address or postal code to find your local representative.

» Find out who your elected federal representative (MP) is.

» Telephone your city hall or municipal office and find out if your municipal representatives are elected on the ward system (each part of a community elects its own representatives) or for the whole community.

Bonus assignment: Ask three Canadians for the names of their federal and provincial representatives. How many said that they did not know or were wrong in their answers? Do you find that people in Canada are more or less interested in politics than people in your country of origin?

Elections in Canada

Since Canada is a democratic country, we elect our representatives. The candidates with the most votes win the election.

To vote in an election, your name must be on a voters' list. You will receive a card in the mail telling you where to vote. If you do not receive a card and think you were missed, you can contact the returning officer (search online or call 411 to find your returning officer) who will help you to get on the voters' list.

When you go to the polling station to vote (it is usually in a school, church, or community centre), you are given a ballot. The people who work at the polling station will show you how to vote. Be sure to follow their directions because if you do not, your vote may not be counted. Your vote is secret.

You do not have to tell anyone how you voted. You are free to vote for the person or people you think will serve you and your family best.

COMPREHENSION CHECK

1. What should you do if you think you are not on the voters' list for an upcoming election?
2. If you are asked to mark an X beside the name of the person you want to vote for and instead you circle the name, will your vote be counted?

VOCABULARY

voters' list	a list of the people who are registered to vote, who have permission to vote
returning officer	the person in charge of running the election in an electoral district
polling station	a place where one or more polls are located; a poll is an official area in an election and is designated by a number. You need to vote at the poll in which you are registered.
ballot	the piece of paper on which are listed the names of people running for office or the questions being asked in the election

USING NEW WORDS

Fill in each blank with one of the words or terms from the Vocabulary section.

Mai-Ling and her husband, John, were excited to vote in Canada for the first time. However, when they checked the _____, their names were not on it and they did not receive a card in the mail. They did not know that they were supposed to contact the _____ to correct the mistake. When they arrived at the _____ on election day, they were worried that they would not be allowed to vote. Then they learned that they just needed to show proof of their identity and address to be added to the voters' list. Happily, they each marked a _____ and put it in the box.

FOR DISCUSSION

» Some people think that their vote does not matter, and so they do not bother to find out what the election issues are and they do not vote. What do you think of this opinion?

» Some people who are still learning English think they should not vote because they do not yet understand the issues well enough. If you want to learn more about an election and what each of the candidates represent, what can you do?

The Elements of Government

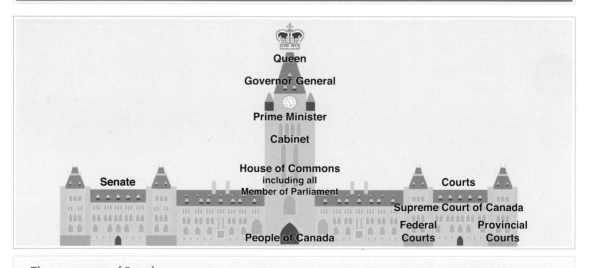

The government of Canada

In the above chart, you can see that the Queen of England is the head of state in Canada's government. Does this surprise you? (Many Canadians are very supportive of the monarchy, while others believe that it is no longer relevant to today's reality and would like to end this connection with Britain.) The Queen appoints a representative in Canada called the Governor General. This system of appointing a representative for the Queen is used throughout the British Commonwealth.

In fact, the Governor General is more of a figure-head than an actual policy-maker, although most Canadians have a lot of respect for the men and women who have served Canada as Governor General. The Governor General appoints a Lieutenant-Governor in each province. The premier of each province suggests people for this position, just as the prime minister suggests people for the Governor General's position to the Queen.

The actual leader of the country is the prime minister. He or she is the leader of the party that has the most seats in the House of Commons. The House of Commons is made up of Members of Parliament (MPs) elected by the people. The prime minister appoints a cabinet from members of his or her party elected to the House of Commons. Each cabinet minister is the leader of a government department such as Health Canada, Service Canada, Department of National Defence, or Citizenship and Immigration Canada. The cabinet has a lot of power to influence decisions made by the government. Any Member of Parliament can present a bill for a vote by the House of Commons, but most bills come from the prime minister and cabinet. Bills passed by the House of Commons become laws when they are approved by the Senate and signed by the Governor General.

The Senate is an appointed, not elected, body of men and women. People who are appointed senators can serve to age 75. They are appointed by the prime minister. The function of the Senate is to see that no laws are passed without very careful thought. Senators examine legislation passed by the House of Commons, and if they think it is not good legislation or needs changes, they send it back for further consideration.

While Parliament (the House of Commons and Senate) makes the laws for us to follow, the courts have the power to interpret and apply those laws. In Canada, a person is presumed innocent until proven guilty. It is up to the courts to prove that a person is guilty. In other words, the benefit of the doubt goes to the accused. Every effort is made to ensure that innocent people are not convicted of crimes they did not commit.

Some laws in Canada are very controversial. When people are not in agreement with laws, they may write letters to their MPs or to the editors of newspapers, or join in demonstrations to express their views. Two examples of very controversial laws in Canada today are the laws on abortion and possession of marijuana.

Current abortion laws say that doctors may perform an abortion in a hospital or approved clinic as long as the pregnancy is not beyond four months. People who disagree with abortion call their view pro-life. Others who feel women should be able to have abortions call their view pro-choice.

Marijuana is commonly used by many people as a recreational drug and for pain control, even though it is usually illegal to sell marijuana.

COMPREHENSION CHECK

Are the following statements true or false?

1. The prime minister of Canada is the head of state.
2. Canada is the only country in the British Commonwealth with a Governor General representing the Queen.
3. Senators are appointed, not elected.
4. In Canada, someone accused of a crime must prove his or her innocence or be presumed guilty.
5. Abortion and the use of marijuana are two controversial subjects in Canada.
6. Pro-choicers believe that all women who get pregnant by accident should get an abortion.

VOCABULARY

monarchy	a government headed by a king or queen; a government wherein royalty still has wealth and influence
British Commonwealth	a group of nations formerly colonized by Britain which are now independent, but have chosen to keep economic and political ties with one another
figurehead	a person who appears to have power, but who really does not
cabinet	the group of men and women who supervise the departments of government and who make, with the prime minister or premier, the executive decisions of government
presumed	thought to be true, even though you are not sure
benefit of the doubt	an expression which means that when we are uncertain as to which decision is best, we give a person the decision which is in their best interest. The principle of "innocent until proven guilty" favours the accused in court. (In some countries, it is up to the accused to prove his or her innocence.)
convicted	judged guilty of a crime
controversial	arguable; not clearly one thing or another
abortion	the act of ending the life of a fetus in the mother's womb

USING NEW WORDS

Fill in each blank with one of the words or terms from the list above.

1. The man was _____ by a jury of his peers.
2. The federal _____ is chosen very carefully so that it includes representatives from all provinces.
3. India, Australia, New Zealand, and Nigeria are some other members of the _____.
4. Canada's immigration policy is a _____ subject.
5. Henry Morgentaler is a well-known Canadian doctor who challenged Canada's _____ laws across the country and won. He believed that Canadian women should have the right to be responsible for their own bodies and that includes the right to end an unwanted pregnancy.
6. The _____ is controversial in most democratic countries today.
7. A person who has little or no real power in spite of his or her position is called a _____.
8. The little girl told her rural school teacher that a cow ate her homework. Although the teacher found this hard to believe, she gave the little girl the _____.

FOR DISCUSSION

» Some people do not like to be asked controversial questions because they do not want to get into an argument with others. Do you feel this way? Why or why not? With whom do you feel comfortable talking about controversial topics such as politics or religion? With whom would you feel unsafe or uncomfortable discussing such topics?

» The use of marijuana is very controversial in Canada. Some people think it should be decriminalized (made legal) while others think it is important to maintain the laws against it. What do you think, and why?

» If you were an elected Member of Parliament in Canada today, can you think of some laws you would like to see changed? Explain why.

The Canadian Economy

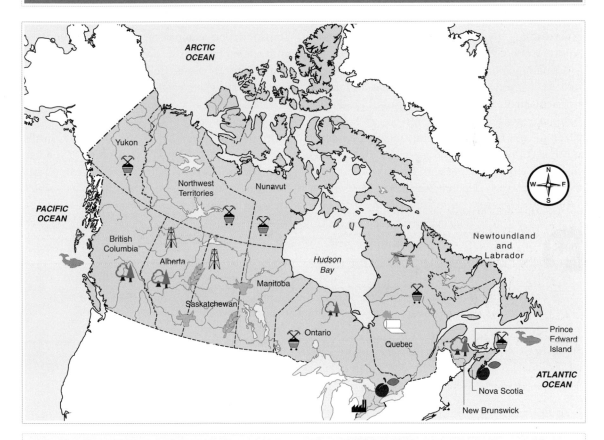

Economic activities across Canada

Canada is a very large country blessed with many natural resources. From trees in the forests across the country, we make pulp and paper. From mines, we extract coal, gold, silver, iron, uranium, and many other minerals. On the prairies, we grow grain, raise cattle, and extract oil and gas from beneath the ground. From the oceans on our east and west coasts, we take fish and other seafood.

Can you think of any Canadian goods which were imported by your original country?

In Japanese restaurants, customers may buy Alberta beef and British Columbia salmon. In Russia, people sometimes eat bread made from Canadian wheat. In the United States, many of the newspapers are made from Canadian pulp, and people use Canadian oil and gas in their cars.

Because Canada has a relatively small population and abundant natural resources, much of our international trade is in exporting those resources and buying manufactured goods. The United States is by far Canada's largest trading partner at this time. In 2009, 51 percent of our imports came from the US and 75 percent of our exports went there. We imported 11 percent of our goods from China that year and exported 3 percent of our goods to China. The European Union is also a significant trading partner with 10 percent of our imports coming from the EU and 5 percent of our exports going there. Additionally, 3 percent of our exports went to the United Kingdom in 2009.

Canada exports a lot of food products: wheat and other grains, beef and other meat, oil, dairy products, sugar beets, and maple sugar products, to name a few. Copper, gold, iron ore, nickel, potash, and zinc are the minerals most often sent to other countries. Natural gas and oil are other important exports, along with forestry products.

Though largely dependent on natural resources, Canada also has a strong manufacturing industry.

Extracting oil on the prairies

Transportation equipment, such as automobiles and automobile parts, are our most important manufactured goods, followed by food, paper products, and chemicals.

Canada is also a world leader in the telecommunications industry. The Canadarm, a remote-controlled arm used by NASA astronauts in the American space program, is a major Canadian achievement. Canadians have also developed and built powerful communications satellites, which are used by countries around the world.

COMPREHENSION CHECK

1. What differences do you notice between the Canadian economy and the economies of countries such as Japan or Korea, which export a lot of manufactured goods?
2. Name two of Canada's most important exports.
3. For what industry is Canada well-known by other nations?

VOCABULARY

pulp	a semi-liquid mixture made from the wood of trees; used to make paper
extract	take out
uranium	a mineral element used in producing nuclear power
seafood	sea fish or shellfish which can be eaten; shellfish include shrimp, lobster, clams, and scallops
imported	bought from other countries
exporting	selling to other countries
customer	a person who buys goods or services from someone
sugar beets	large root vegetables used for the production of sugar
maple sugar	a Canadian treat made from the sap of the sugar maple tree
dependent	unable to do without; needing something in order to survive
equipment	machines or articles needed for a specific purpose

satellites	human-made structures sent into space to travel around the earth or another planet for research or communications
remote-controlled	moveable from a distance by radiowaves

USING NEW WORDS

Here is a small puzzle to review the vocabulary words. Note that not all words are from the vocabulary list. You may want to do the puzzle with a partner and see who finishes first.

Across

2. what we call wheat, oats, and barley

3. wonderful!

4. to be fortunate; to be gifted by God

6. fuel for cars

7. what keeps moving parts moving

8. milk, butter, and cheese

Down

1. many cows

3. a very precious metal

5. a word for fish, shrimp, scallops, and lobster

(Find the answer to the puzzle on page 250.)

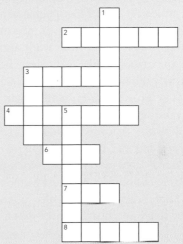

OUR CURRENCY

» Currency is the money system of a country. Canadians use the dollar as their basic unit of currency. Two dollars will buy you a loaf of bread or a bottle of pop from a vending machine. Our dollar coin is called a "loonie" because it has a picture of a bird called a loon on the front. We make a lot of jokes about the loonie. Do you know why? Other coins are called the toonie (2 dollars), quarter (25 cents), the dime (10 cents), the nickel (5 cents), and the penny (1 cent).

» All Canadian coins have a picture of Queen Elizabeth II of England on the back. Can you explain why?

» What could you buy with the following amounts of money? Match the amount on the left with the item you think best fits on the right. (Prices are approximate and all prices are before tax.)

❶ $2.75	_____	a) a one-way bus ticket within a city
❷ $350 000	_____	b) a pair of good running shoes, not on sale
❸ $0.59	_____	c) a stamp to mail a letter within Canada
❹ $12.50	_____	d) a ticket to see a movie in the theatre
❺ $150	_____	e) a new three-bedroom house
❻ $35 000	_____	f) a new mid-size car
❼ $1.80	_____	g) a cup of coffee

Canadians at Work

Employment is of great concern across the country as young people look for jobs when they finish school and as new immigrants seek to become independent as soon as possible. The employment picture in Canada is changing. It used to be that a person could expect to learn one set of skills for a job and work in that job all of his or her life. That is no longer true. Most people can expect to have several different kinds of jobs in their lifetimes. There is less full-time work and more part-time or casual work available. The number of jobs in high-tech industries and in communications is growing and, with them, the amount of training workers need. Most jobs require some computer knowledge today. The size of the workforce has also increased. Whereas in our grandparents' generation, most women did not work outside the home, now most women have paid jobs. High school students also often look for part-time work and take an extra year to complete high school.

Another change is in the number of people who are starting their own small businesses. In part, this is because many services which used to be provided by the government are now provided by contracted businesses. Perhaps, when you are looking for a job, you might think about starting your own business instead of applying for work with an employer. Some small business owners even work from their own homes. If you want to do this, you will have to ask about the zoning restrictions in your community. Some kinds of business can be run from anyone's home, while others have to be located in areas which are intended for that business purpose.

If you look at the chart to the right, you will see that most jobs today are in the service sector. Do you know what each of the categories in the chart means? Can you give examples of jobs in each of these categories?

One thing that is important to know if you are going to work in Canada is that all provinces have laws which tell us the rights and responsibilities of employees. They may be called labour standards or employment standards in your province. Each province has a minimum wage and there are laws about how many hours an employer can ask you to work before he or she must pay overtime. You must be paid vacation pay and you must have deductions taken off your paycheque for employment insurance, Canada Pension Plan, and Canada Revenue Agency taxation, unless you are a self-employed contract worker and not an employee. There are also laws about discrimination. It is against the law to discriminate against someone based on such differences as race, gender, age, or religion, for example. If you think that you have been denied a job because you are a woman, because you are Black, or because you belong to a particular religion, there may be laws to help you fight that decision. For starters, you have to know what laws are there to protect you—they vary from province to province.

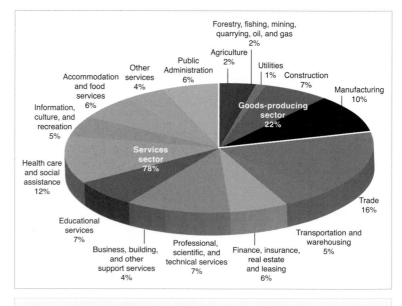

Employment in Canadian industries

COMPREHENSION CHECK

❶ How is women's role in the workforce in Canada different from women's role in the workforce in other countries you know?

❷ How has privatization (the shift from government services to private businesses) affected the kind of work available to some people who are ambitious and creative?

VOCABULARY

casual   not regular or permanent; work which varies from week to week as the employer needs you (for example, one week, you might work full-time and another week, not at all)

deductions   money taken off an employee's paycheque before he or she receives it (including money for Canada Pension Plan, Employment Insurance, and taxes)

self-employed   working for oneself; a worker who is not an employee of a company or other business and therefore does not have employee benefits, but who can deduct self-employment expenses from his or her income tax

USING NEW WORDS

Match each word on the left to its opposite on the right.

self-employed   regular

casual   additions

deductions   employed by a company or business

MAKING CONTACT

» Find out the minimum wage for workers in your province. Are there different rates for different jobs? Are there any jobs which are not covered by the minimum wage guidelines? Are there different rules for youths and adults? What are they?

» What is the legal vacation pay in your province for an employee of less than one year? More than ten years?

» Talk to a Canadian worker about the differences between the Canada Pension Plan and company pension plans. Ask that worker if he or she expects to see any changes to the Canada Pension Plan in the near future and why.

» Talk to a self-employed person and ask what benefits there are in being self-employed rather than being an employee.

CHAPTER REVIEW

Name the following.

❶ Canada's head of state

❷ the current prime minister

❸ the Governor General

❹ the mayor of your community

❺ two major manufactured goods in Canada

❻ Canada's most important customer for exports

Chapter Three

Arts and Education

Quick Facts

» Canadians enjoy a wide variety of arts and entertainment from ballets and symphonies to winter carnivals, fiddling contests, and street performers.

» The Canadian Broadcasting Corporation (CBC) is Canada's government-owned national television and radio network that provides programs created and produced by Canadians.

» From a group of 20 street performers at its beginnings in 1984, *Cirque du Soleil®* is a major Quebec-based organization presenting different shows simultaneously around the world.

» Education in Canada is a provincial responsibility and programs vary from province to province.

» In addition to elementary, secondary, and post-secondary education, programs are available to teach heritage languages, English as a second language, and job skills.

» Education from kindergarten to Grade 12 is free to everyone. Further education requires the payment of tuition but is still heavily subsidized by governments.

Arts and Entertainment

Rick Mercer and Jian Ghomeshi both host shows on the CBC

National Arts Companies

Canada has produced many gifted artists and entertainers. While many of these people choose to stay in Canada, others have moved to the United States. Some of these artists felt that to advance their careers, they had to expand their horizons beyond Canada. Canada is a large country with a small population, and this can create problems. One problem is the difficulty we have in keeping our cultural identity beside a very large and powerful neighbour, the United States.

One national institution that works to maintain a distinctive Canadian culture is the Canadian Broadcasting Corporation (CBC). The CBC is our government-owned national television and radio system, which offers programs in English and French across the country. The Canadian Radio and Telecommunications Commission (CRTC) is the government organization which decides how much programming must be Canadian. The CRTC has complex rules about how much Canadian content is required in order to be licensed as a TV or radio station in Canada. These rules are intended to support and protect Canadian culture.

The CBC helps Canadians on one side of the country stay informed about the lives of Canadians in other parts of the country, even in the most remote northern communities. Many Canadians set their morning alarm clocks to CBC radio and eat their breakfast listening to the most recent news. Travellers adjust their car radios so they can listen to a variety of documentaries and musical programs as they drive from one area to another. CBC television documentaries have revealed aspects of the Canadian experience many people knew nothing about.

The National Film Board of Canada (NFB) is another organization which has supported Canadian talent. NFB films continue to win international recognition for their excellence. The films are also used in schools from coast to coast to teach students about issues facing Canadians today.

Nonetheless, Canadians are heavily influenced by American popular culture. There are many more American TV and radio stations than Canadian ones, and American programs are very popular in Canada. Some people purchase satellite dishes to get as much American programming as possible. Others believe it is very important to maintain a distinctive Canadian identity by controlling the amount of entertainment we get from the United States. Many parents are also concerned about the amount of violence on some American TV programs.

But the arts are alive and well in Canada. More and more entertainers, musicians, actors, writers, and artists are gaining recognition internationally for their work and still calling Canada home. In Chapter 12, you will learn more about a number of individuals who have distinguished themselves as singers, musicians, and artists in Canada.

Cirque du Soleil

In 1984, Quebec City was celebrating the 450th anniversary of Canada's discovery by Jacques Cartier, and they needed a show that would carry the festivities out across the province. Guy Laliberté presented a proposal for a show called *Cirque du Soleil,* and succeeded in convincing the celebration's organizers to put on the show. The artistic company soon attracted other talented artists and creators to work with them and their imaginative, grand productions have become well-known all over the world. The company now makes its home in many countries outside Canada as well as within it. There are no animals in this circus and yet the audience instantly recognizes that they are in an imaginative circus-style production. More than 100 million spectators in more than 300 cities on six continents have seen a *Cirque du Soleil* show. Their creations have earned them many awards including multiple Geminis and Emmy Awards. Canadians are very proud of this talented group who have always been proud ambassadors of Quebec and Canada in each city and country they have visited.

Canadian Voices

Rita MacNeil is a popular singer from Cape Breton, Nova Scotia. She sings a variety of songs that can be described as folk and country music. Although she spends a lot of time travelling and giving concerts outside the country, Canada is still home for her. She is well-known for her Christmas concerts across the country with the miners' choir called Men of the Deeps. This is what it means to her to be a Canadian:

The place where we are born or where we establish our roots affects us all our lives. I have a deep appreciation for Canada because I've been able to travel from coast to coast getting to know the landscape and the people. I feel safe here and proud when I hear the national anthem, "O Canada." It can't be summed up in a word—it's a feeling inside when you can say I am from Canada.

Local Arts and Entertainment

Every major city in Canada has its symphony orchestra and theatre companies. There are also many fine ballet companies across the country including the National Ballet based in Toronto, the Royal Winnipeg Ballet, and Les Grands Ballets Canadiens from Quebec, to name a few. These companies have sent dancers to many countries of the world and brought many famous international dancers to Canada. There are also many smaller music, dance, and theatre groups, which offer a wide variety of performances from modern to traditional in communities across the country.

Canadians enjoy a number of popular festivals, especially in the summer months when people flock outdoors to enjoy the warm weather.

Stratford Festival: Seana McKenna as King Richard III.

In late August in Halifax, for example, crowds of people go to the docks to watch the International Busker Festival. In Winnipeg, Toronto, and many other communities, people go to the park to enjoy outdoor theatre such as Shakespeare in the Park and outdoor concerts. The waterfronts in Vancouver, Toronto, and Halifax are home to a number of performances of various kinds. In mid-August, over 200 000 people flock to English Bay in Vancouver to watch the final night of the Celebration of Light, an international fireworks competition. We love our fireworks! Some small communities also offer high quality theatre and music productions by visiting performers or local groups.

During the winter months, many communities organize winter carnivals with ice sculpting contests, skating, cross-country skiing, skidooing, and even dogsled races. There are also concerts in the cities' concert halls, plays in theatres and dinner theatres, and various performers such as bands and singers in small clubs and lounges throughout the country. In rural areas, parties and other social gatherings are held in community centres and church halls. Some traditional events include square dances, fiddling contests, and First Nation powwows.

COMPREHENSION CHECK

1. What do some people think threatens Canada's cultural identity?
2. What is the name of Canada's national radio and TV broadcasting company?
3. If you wanted to see an outdoor concert or play, where could you go?
4. What are some events at winter carnivals?

VOCABULARY

gifted	talented, able to do something well which most others cannot do
expand their horizons	increase their opportunities
maintain	keep in good condition

documentaries	films or other programs made to communicate factual information about a particular topic
flock	go in great numbers to see or do something
buskers	street entertainers such as jugglers, unicycle riders, and comedians, who perform for donations (small amounts of money) from people who watch
square dances	group folk dances performed to the music of a fiddle with rapid spoken instructions given by a caller
powwows	celebrations of First Nations peoples usually including Aboriginal dancing, feasting, and other ceremonies
volunteer	a person who does work without expectation of pay

USING NEW WORDS

Fill in each of the blanks below with one of the words or expressions above.

1 Those who cannot read and write sometimes learn well with the help of a _____ tutor.

2 When people see fire engines, they often _____ to watch the fire.

3 People who take courses in the evening are usually trying to _____ _____ _____.

4 A car or an appliance will last you for a long time if you _____ it in good condition.

5 When some Koreans visited the Stoney _____ near Banff, they felt a kinship with their Aboriginal "cousins" who share common ancestral roots.

6 Several people from visible minorities are working with a film crew to prepare a number of _____ on racism.

FOR DISCUSSION

» Volunteering is very popular in Canada. Men and women who have time often volunteer their talents because they enjoy it. Some people who are unemployed volunteer to learn new skills, get Canadian work experience, and make contact with employers. Volunteers do a lot of very important work in Canada. However, from time to time, they are exploited. Have you ever volunteered? What did you gain from that experience? Do you know anyone who has been exploited as a volunteer?

» Name some popular Canadian artists, actors, or musicians you know. Are they also popular outside Canada?

» Do you think that Canadians should try to protect their culture from American culture? Why or why not?

» Is the culture from which you come in danger in any way? Has it been in the past?

Education and Training

Elementary and Secondary Schooling

Schooling in Canada is free and universal. That means that it does not cost money to go to a public school and everyone can go if they are between the ages of 6 and 18. Schooling is a provincial responsibility. In most provinces, the government provides kindergarten through Grade 12. Schooling is compulsory from the ages of 6 or 7 to 14 or 18 (depending on your province). After that, children can legally drop out of school if they are considered to be adults in their province of residence. In many communities, home schooling is also an option with a teacher assigned to supervise and provide resources.

Most provinces have public schools, separate schools, and private schools. Separate schools are usually, but not always, Roman Catholic and are funded with public (tax) dollars. In communities where Roman Catholics are in the majority, the public school board may be Roman Catholic and the separate school board Protestant. Property owners are asked if they wish to support the public or separate school board, and their tax money then goes to the school board of their choice. The provincial government makes decisions about teacher qualifications and curriculum, while local school boards make decisions about the building of schools and how money is to be spent.

Private schools are generally not supported by public money. Usually, parents have to pay to send their children to private schools. In some provinces, public money is available to support private schooling, but parents usually still pay at least part of the costs. Many, but not all, private schools are religious. Increasingly, school boards in some parts of the country are offering alternative kinds of schooling. (They may be called charter schools or special programs.) This gives parents more options in communities where there are open boundaries and children can go to any school in the community as long as it is not full.

Teachers in all schools must be licensed. Most often, they have a university degree called a B.Ed. (Bachelor of Education) and a teacher's certificate which they get from the province after two years of successful experience in an approved school.

Schools are described as elementary (or primary) and high (or secondary) schools. Elementary schools are usually from Grade 1 to Grade 6 or 8, while high schools may be from Grade 7 or 9 to Grade 12. Some provinces have junior high or middle schools for Grades 7 to 9 and senior high schools for Grades 10 to 12. The system, however, varies across the country. For example, in Quebec, students take six years of elementary education followed by five years of secondary studies. Then students have the option of taking two years of pre-university studies or three years of technical studies at a CEGEP (college). Public education from kindergarten to college is free for Quebec residents. How are schools organized in your community?

The hours for schooling also vary greatly. Most schools are closed for two months in the summer (July and August) and have short breaks at Christmas and in the spring, usually in March. Older children generally have longer hours at school than very young children. An average school day for a high school student might be 8:30 a.m. to 3:30 p.m., with a one-hour lunch break and a one-hour spare. Kindergarten children often go for only half a day.

All of the older children and some of the younger children are expected to do homework in most schools. This might be reading, mathematics (often called arithmetic in the younger grades), or worksheets of some kind. Teachers expect parents to make sure that their children do their homework. Parents are generally invited to the school for parent-teacher interviews, home and school nights, or other special events. Parents can also make appointments to see teachers if they wish. As for discipline in the schools, it is against the law for teachers to hit students. Disobedient children are normally punished by being given extra assignments, detentions, or time outs. Children who are disruptive on a regular basis can be suspended or expelled from the school.

In some areas, schools or programs are available for children who want part of their education in their heritage language. In Edmonton, for example, children can attend bilingual programs in French, Ukrainian, German, Cree, Mandarin, Spanish, and Arabic, in addition to English. In Winnipeg, immigrant families can send their children to after-school language programs located in their schools. In Vancouver, bilingual French programs are so popular that there is a lottery to decide who can get in. Other parents who want

Students working in an elementary classroom

specialized education for their children might choose from the available alternative schools. There are schools with special programs in art, theatre, ballet, business, and community involvement, for example. Correspondence schools are also available for children who live too far away to attend a regular school. Each province has its own curriculum and materials for these students, who return their lessons by mail.

Extra-curricular programs are an important part of schools, especially high schools. These programs may include sports, drama, yearbook, school newspaper, debating, band or orchestra, or any number of interesting and educational opportunities of a voluntary nature.

COMPREHENSION CHECK

1. Who must go to school in Canada?
2. What choices do parents have about their children's schooling?
3. If a child is five or six years old, is it necessary for the parents to send that child to school?
4. Who can send their children to school for free?
5. What qualifications do public school teachers need to have?
6. What opportunities do parents have to talk to teachers?

VOCABULARY

universal	available to all
compulsory	required; without choice
qualifications	the necessary training and experience for a job
curriculum	the program of studies in a school
spare (n)	a supervised or unsupervised period of time when a student can choose what work to do at school
discipline	a means of correcting unacceptable behaviour
disobedient	not following the rules
detentions	extra time a student is required to stay after normal school hours; a form of punishment
disruptive	creating disorder; preventing others from working
suspended	not allowed to attend school for a specified period of time (e.g., one week)
expelled	not allowed to attend a particular school in future
alternative	a different choice
correspondence	having to do with mail or email, with writing back and forth
yearbook	a book of individual photos of all students, pictures of school events, and other memorabilia for any given year in high school

USING NEW WORDS

Fill in the blanks with one of the words from above.

❶ The boy's parents were very happy that their son had been _____ rather than _____; at least, he had a second chance to improve his behaviour.

❷ A child who often starts fights may be described as _____ at school.

❸ What _____ are necessary to do your job in Canada?

❹ A good ESL _____ must include opportunities for listening, speaking, reading, and writing.

❺ A driver's licence is _____ for anyone who wants to drive a car in Canada.

❻ Basic health care is a _____ right in Canada. No one should go without proper treatment due to a lack of money.

❼ When you move to a new address, be sure to ask the post office to forward your _____ to the new location.

❽ _____ are sometimes used by the schools to ensure that children follow the rules of the school.

FOR DISCUSSION

» What kind of problems do immigrant children sometimes have at school?

» When racism is one of these problems, what can you do?

» What kinds of problems can develop between immigrant children and their parents when the children are in school? What can be done about these problems?

» What are the advantages and disadvantages of bilingual schools for immigrant children?

Post-Secondary Education and Training

When a student completes Grade 12—or Secondary 5 in Quebec—he or she receives a diploma. This gives the graduate the right to apply for a program at a university, college, or technical school. These schools offer what is called post-secondary education. The high school graduate may also decide to look for a job. Acceptance at a post-secondary institution depends on good grades being achieved in the final year of high school. The following are the five main types of post-secondary institutions in Canada.

University: an institution which offers general programs in arts and sciences, as well as study for the professions (such as medicine, law, education, commerce, and engineering). Graduates may receive a bachelor's degree (for example, B.A., B.Ed., or B.Sc.), master's degree, or doctorate depending on the length of study and the program.

College: an institution which offers only the bachelor's level of study or the first two years of a bachelor's degree with the right to transfer to a university to complete the program.

CEGEP: an institution (unique to Quebec—translated into English, CEGEP stands for College of General and Vocational Education) which allows students to complete either a two-year pre-university program or a three-year technical program.

Community college: an institution which offers a variety of programs to the community including two-year diploma programs that lead to employment in a particular field (such as nursing or computer technology), shorter programs leading to certification in a particular area

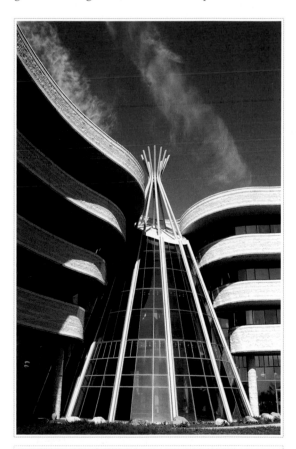

First Nations University of Canada in Regina, Saskatchewan

(such as early childhood education or mixology), and general interest courses.

Technical school: an institution which offers programs in the trades and technical areas (for those pursuing careers as electricians, plumbers, denturists, draftspersons, computer technicians, and so on). Technical schools also have apprenticeship programs.

What does it cost to go to one of these post-secondary schools? Tuition varies across Canada, but in all cases is highly subsidized by the government. For example, the program of study for a university student might actually cost between $12 000 and $20 000 per year. Students may pay tuition of about $3500 per year; the rest is paid for by the government. Students, however, pay for their own books, supplies, and living expenses. Sometimes parents pay for some of their children's higher education, but often, the students work during school vacations to pay their expenses or take out a student loan. The loans must be paid back after the students have graduated.

The post-secondary school year is generally eight months long, from September to the end of April, and the year is usually divided into two semesters of four months each. Between April and September, most students try to get summer jobs to save money for their winter courses. Students can also choose to take courses in the spring session (May–June) or summer session (July–August).

For the many international students who come to Canada from other countries to study, most institutions require a score of at least 80 on the TOEFL examination (Test of English as a Foreign Language). This test is held monthly in all urban centres, and there are courses and books available to help students prepare for the TOEFL. International students usually pay a higher tuition than Canadian students. It is generally about three times the regular tuition.

The primary function of all of these institutions is to prepare people for the workplace. However, they also have a continuing education function. Many Canadians are believers in lifelong learning. They continue to take courses to learn and adapt to a quickly changing world. Many people, for example, return to school to update their skills to meet the changing demands of their jobs.

Federally Funded Training

Two areas where the federal government has taken some responsibility for training are in employment and in English as an additional language (EAL). School boards, universities, community colleges, and various non-governmental organizations offer EAL (often called English as a Second Language, or ESL). Most of these charge a fee. Citizenship and Immigration Canada has a program called LINC (Language Instruction for Newcomers to Canada), which is for new immigrants to Canada. Citizens, visitors to Canada, and refugee claimants are not eligible. LINC is free and is offered by many different schools. To apply, you must go to an assessment centre and take a test. LINC programs teach only the beginning levels of English. Some provinces prefer to design their own immigrant language programs and do not offer LINC. Immigrants can go to their local settlement agencies to get information about the type of programs they are eligible to take.

Service Canada pays for many different job training programs. These programs are available for people on Employment Insurance (EI). You can check with your local Canada Employment Centre (CEC) to find out what is available in your community.

COMPREHENSION CHECK

1. If you wanted to become an apprentice carpenter, where would you take courses?
2. What can a student do if he or she wants to go to university, but has no money?
3. If you were born in another country and learned English as a second language, what test must you pass before you can go to university in Canada? What score do you need?
4. How long is the usual school year at a university?

VOCABULARY

apprenticeship	a teaching-learning relationship between a master tradesperson and someone wanting to learn that trade
tuition	the money paid to take a course of studies
subsidized	partially funded or paid for
loan (n)	money lent which must be repaid at some time in the future
semesters	the periods of time over which a course or set of courses is completed
primary	most important
charge	1. expect money in return for something 2. formally accuse someone of a crime
fee	money paid for a service
refugee claimants	people seeking refugee status
eligible	having the right qualifications or attributes to participate; acceptable to participate in a program
settlement agency	an organization that exists to help immigrants, often in their first languages, get the kinds of support they need, especially in the early months of their settlement in Canada

USING NEW WORDS

Fill in the blanks below with the best possible word from above.

1. Gillian really wanted to take swimming lessons, but even after saving her babysitting money she was still short $10, so her parents _____ the fee for her lessons.
2. Most people have to get a _____ when they buy their first new car.
3. Juan was very frustrated because he could not get his papers as an electrician in Canada until he could find an employer who would give him an _____.
4. When young people in Canada decide to get married, their _____ consideration in choosing a partner is usually love.

⑤   High schools usually have two _____, fall and winter.

⑥   The _____ to take one English course was $325.

⑦   They paid $120 for the hotel room, but the hotel did not _____ for parking.

⑧   _____ are in a very difficult situation because they are not eligible for many government services.

⑨   The girl was not _____ for the training program because she was not a citizen or landed immigrant of Canada.

⑩   A volunteer from the _____ _____ came to the airport to meet the new refugee family and take them to an apartment where they could stay for a couple of weeks until they found their own apartment.

⑪   Immigrants are often surprised to learn of the many licences they need to buy, each of which requires a _____: fishing licence, driving licence, permit to do renovations in your house, and so on.

An acronym is a word formed from the first letters of other words and used to stand for those words. What do the following acronyms stand for?

ESL   _____

LINC   _____

CEC   _____

EAL   _____

EI   _____

(You can find the answers on page 250 at the back of the book.)

FOR DISCUSSION

» Many students who borrowed a lot of money to go to university have not been able to find a good job when they finished. Some think they made a big mistake to borrow so much money. What do you think?

» Compare our system of higher education to that of another country. What are some of the differences?

» Do you know anyone who has taken a federal job training program? Did that person get a job?

» What other services are available in your community to help people who are unemployed?

MAKING CONTACT

» Find the names of some settlement agencies in your community and some of the programs they offer to immigrant adults or children.

» Go online to look at the programs for one of the post-secondary institutions in your province. If you have questions that are not answered online, phone someone in the appropriate department and ask your questions.

CHAPTER REVIEW

» By searching online or asking Canadians, find out who these famous Canadians are and what they are known for.

| Karen Kain | Bryan Adams | Oscar Peterson |
| Graham Greene | Nikki Yanofsky | Tom Thomson |

At which kind of post-secondary institution would you most likely study the following:

» to become a doctor?

» to become a welder?

» to become a massage therapist or professional dancer?

» to do the first two years of a B.A. program?

Chapter Four

Canadians Enjoying Life: Sports and Recreation

Quick Facts

» Hockey is Canada's favourite sport with many children learning to play at a young age. It originated in Canada.

» Skiing, skating, and curling are favourite winter pastimes for many Canadians.

» The Stanley Cup is awarded to the best hockey team in North America annually, after a playoff series in the spring.

» The Grey Cup is awarded to the best Canadian football team after a playoff series in November.

» Lacrosse is Canada's official summer sport; it was first developed by the Algonquians, an Aboriginal people.

» The inventor of basketball, James Naismith, was a Canadian.

» The 2010 Winter Olympics in Vancouver and Whistler, BC, not only showed Canadian winter athletes at their finest but showed Canadians at their patriotic best. We came away with 26 medals in total, 14 of which were gold medals, Canada's best yet in the Winter Olympics.

» There are only four statutory holidays that are common to all Canadians: New Year's Day, Canada Day, Labour Day, and Christmas.

Introduction

In English, we have an expression, *All work and no play makes Jack a dull boy*. Canadians take that to heart and enjoy their recreation time either participating in a variety of sports and other interesting activities, or observing them with great enthusiasm. This chapter looks at popular sports, entertainment, festivals, and typical activities enjoyed during summer and winter. Because different provinces have different statutory (legal) holidays, a chart is provided that shows which holidays people get off from work in the different provinces. The chapter closes with the highlights of the 2010 Winter Olympics, hosted in British Columbia (BC).

Participant Sports

The kinds of sports enjoyed depend somewhat on where one lives and what season of the year it is. In most parts of Canada, children learn to play hockey or to figure skate. Cities have indoor and outdoor skating areas for both hockey and figure skating and they are well-used. Most towns of any size have an arena which is used as an ice rink in the winter and a place for agricultural displays and 4-H events in the summer. Some parents in rural areas either make a backyard ice rink for their children to skate on or use nearby lakes and ponds as skating rinks during our long winters. In the cities, children line up to get onto the various leagues for their age groups and ice time is at a premium, with some teams having to play late in the evening or on Sunday mornings.

Another popular winter sport is skiing, both downhill and cross-country. Canada boasts some

Downhill skiing

world-class ski resorts such as those at Whistler in BC; in Banff, Alberta; and Mont Tremblant in Quebec. Canadian downhill skiers have become well-known internationally for their skill in competition. A popular event for cross-country skiers is the Canadian Birkebeiner Ski Festival which takes place in the countryside east of Edmonton on the second Saturday of February. It is a family event with varying distances, or, for the serious cross-country skier, a 55-kilometre competition with full pack in often very cold weather.

Curling has been *the* adult winter sport for rural Canadian adults and many urban Canadians too, and the popularity of this sport increased after our success in the 2010 Winter Olympics held in Vancouver, BC, where the Canadian men's curling team took the gold medal and Canadian women's curling team took the silver medal. The

Cross-country skiing

rest of us were glued to our TV screens watching a game which many of us had previously known little or nothing about.

Basketball and volleyball are often played in schools and occasionally for fun in gyms across the land. The original rules of basketball were typed out on two sheets of paper by inventor James Naismith in 1891. A doctor and educator from Ontario, Naismith had moved to Springfield, Massachusetts, for a job and it was there that he invented the game of basketball. His original documents were sold in 2010 at an auction in New York for almost $4.5 million.

Summer participant sports include swimming, soccer, golf, baseball, beach volleyball, tennis, and badminton, among others. Cities and towns across Canada have indoor and outdoor swimming pools where large numbers of children take lessons in summer. Organizations such as the YMCA and YWCA, and many large urban high schools also have swimming pools available for recreation and classes, as do universities and colleges.

While few Canadians played soccer 50 years ago, most children now learn to play soccer at school and it has become a popular team sport, due in no small part to the growing number of immigrants to Canada from countries where soccer is *the* sport of choice.

Golf is a very popular sport, especially among business people. Canadian golf courses are often

Golf is a very popular sport

very beautiful and much less expensive to play on than courses in smaller countries where land is at a premium. It is not unusual for tourists to come to Canada primarily to play golf on their vacation.

Spectator Sports

Professional Hockey

Canadians love cheering for their professional sports teams, especially those in the NHL (National Hockey League) and CFL (Canadian Football League). Canada is home to only seven of the NHL's 30 teams but the Stanley Cup playoffs are one of the most-watched TV series in Canada each year. The NHL has both Canadian and American teams. For those unfamiliar with hockey, it is a game played by two teams of six members each on the ice at any given time: the

goalie, two other defensive players, and three offensive players. The offensive players' job is to get the puck into the opposing net while the defensive players' job is to keep the other team's puck out of the net. It is a fast, aggressive game and crowds fill the arenas shouting for their favourite teams. Canadian teams include the Montreal Canadiens, Ottawa Senators, Toronto Maple Leafs, Edmonton Oilers, Calgary Flames, and Vancouver Canucks. In addition, Winnipeg has been granted the return of a home team to their city after losing the Jets to the Americans. They are rejoicing! Players such as Wayne Gretzky, Sidney Crosby, Alexander Ovechkin, Daniel and Henrik Sedin, and Jonathan Toews are role models for a lot of young players who aspire, one day, to be good enough to play in the NHL. Scouts are always on the lookout for Canadian talent, and many Canadians play on American teams as well. Each player is assigned a number which is on his jersey. The really good players' numbers are "retired" and not reassigned after the player retires. Virtually every Canadian-born person knows that number 99 belongs to "The Great One," as Wayne Gretzky is still called.

Hockey is also an Olympic sport and Canada selects its best players from the NHL teams to play for Team Canada. While the Soviets were the team to beat in previous years of men's hockey, in recent years the competition has been fiercest between the US and Canada. Canada also has a champion women's hockey team that has won the gold or silver medal at every Winter Olympics in which they have competed. We are proud of our talented hockey players, both men and women.

Number 99 belongs to The Great One

Professional Football

Another popular spectator sport is professional football, played by teams in the CFL (Canadian Football League). Canadian football is played a little differently than American football so Canadian teams play with one another and not with the American teams. One difference is the size of the playing field. The Canadian field is longer and wider than the American field. In a Canadian game, there are 12 players from each team on the field at any given time, while an American team has 11 players on the field. There are also many differences in the complex rules of play.

There are eight teams in the CFL. They are the BC Lions in Vancouver, the Edmonton Eskimos, the Calgary Stampeders, the Saskatchewan Roughriders in Regina, the Winnipeg Blue Bombers, the Hamilton Tiger-Cats, the Toronto Argonauts, and the Montreal Alouettes. The playing season culminates in the fall with the ever-popular Grey Cup following a series of playoffs. The final Grey Cup game is held in a different Canadian city each year and is a big tourist attraction, with people travelling from across the country to see the best of the best vying for the cup. The final game is normally played in late November on a Sunday afternoon but the festivities begin as early as Wednesday and it is seen as one big party by the host city and all of its guests.

COMPREHENSION CHECK

1. What is the highest award professional hockey teams can win in Canada?
2. What is the highest award professional football teams can win in Canada?
3. How many gold medals did Canadian athletes win in the 2010 Winter Olympics?

④ What already-popular winter sport became even more popular as Canadians watched their own teams play their way to one gold and one silver medal in the 2010 Winter Olympics?

⑤ Why do some foreign travellers come to Canada to play golf in the summer?

⑥ Wayne Gretzky and Sidney Crosby are well-known for their skills as _____ players.

⑦ How many professional football teams are there in the Canadian Football League (CFL)?

⑧ What nickname was given to Wayne Gretzky in recognition of his excellent skills as a hockey player?

VOCABULARY

take (something) to heart	take (something) very seriously, to recognize the importance (of something)
highlights	main points or events
playoff series	a series of games that comes at the end of a season of play and determines the winner or winners
at a premium	hard to find because it is (or they are) popular
boast	speak of with pride
glued to our TV sets	feel compelled to keep watching something of great interest; to watch with few interruptions
role models	people who others can learn from and want to imitate
on the lookout (for)	searching (for something)
culminate	finish or be at the end of something
vying	competing

USING NEW WORDS

Fill in the blanks with one of the words or expressions from above. (Note, in one of the phrases, you have to change the possessive pronoun.)

❶ Parents need to be good _____ for their children.

❷ A university degree program _____s with a graduation ceremony and a celebration of some kind.

❸ The NHL _____ happens in the spring, after a winter of hockey games across Canada and the US.

❹ I am always _____ for a comfortable, wide pair of winter boots because I have trouble finding the right size.

❺ The Canadian Broadcasting Corporation (CBC) sponsored a TV series in which well-known Canadian figure skaters were matched together with hockey players in a pairs skating competition. This program became very popular and many people were _____ to watch these big strong men learn the complexities of figure skating.

6. The _____ of a grandmother's year are the special times she enjoys with her grandchildren.

7. It is not good to _____ too much or people will think you are arrogant.

8. When the playoffs are on, tickets are _____ and scalpers sometimes sell their tickets at much higher prices than they paid for them.

9. The parents told their children it was very important to _____ their education _____.

10. When the Flames and the Leafs were both _____ for the Stanley Cup in the final playoffs, Calgarians and Torontonians alike watched the game with anxious excitement.

FOR DISCUSSION

» In Canada, hockey is the most popular team sport for spectators, so newcomers often find that they are lost in social discussions when they do not understand such terms as "a shutout" or "a hat trick." What are some ways you can learn about the basic rules of hockey and some of the terminology used to describe the game?

» The Birkie or Canadian Birkebeiner Ski Festival can be very dangerous when the temperatures are well below zero degrees Celsius. Why do you think some men and women would compete in a competition that is both difficult and dangerous? Can you think of other sports that people do in conditions that are dangerous? Do they do them for similar reasons?

» Hockey is an aggressive sport, and at times a violent one. Professional hockey players are often admired as role models by young children. Do you think this is a good thing or a bad thing? Why?

Entertainment

Canadians feel very lucky to enjoy many forms of cultural expression in our cities, and in the country as well. We enjoy world-class symphonies, ballet companies, and opera companies across the country. In addition, there are both professional theatre troupes and amateur theatre groups across Canada. In a country whose winter is regarded as far too long by many of us, we enjoy the opportunity to attend performances indoors during the long winter months. In the summer, people in some cities enjoy special outdoor theatre or symphony presentations at local parks.

Younger Canadians enjoy large concerts with performers from all over the world. In the summer, folk festivals, jazz festivals, fringe festivals, and other special events keep us very busy during the long, hot days of summer. The Big Valley Jamboree, in central rural Alberta, is a huge gathering of country music fans who camp by night and cheer to big-name performers onstage by day, for several days.

Different regions of the country have favourite forms of entertainment that are not widely available to everyone. People in rural areas are often partial to country and western music and entertainers in local bars provide this music to the public. Singers such as Gordon Lightfoot, Anne Murray, and Shania Twain are well-known in the United States as well as Canada. The Atlantic provinces are well-known for the excellent folk music which has developed there and for musicians such as fiddler Ashleigh MacIsaac, singer Rita MacNeil, and folk group the Barra MacNeils, all from Cape Breton Island. The Barra MacNeils' lively music is rooted in Celtic origins, but is also mindful of northern Atlantic history. And while comedy clubs may be found in all the major cities, Winnipeg is probably the best known for producing people skilled at the art of making people laugh.

Holidays

There are a number of statutory holidays in Canada but these differ from one province to another. As we can see below, only New Year's Day, Canada Day, Labour Day, and Christmas Day are federal statutory holidays in the whole country.

Other special days are not official days off. Mother's Day and Father's Day, in May and June, respectively, are days when we honour our fathers and mothers with cards, gifts, or a night out. Valentine's Day is a day when we celebrate love and people give a gift, candy, or flowers to their loved one or take them out for dinner. Halloween is a time when many costumed children go door-to-door to get gifts of candy from the homeowners, while others enjoy dressing up in costumes and going to a party at their school, local shopping centre, or friend's house.

Holiday	Date	BC	AB	SK	MB	ON	QC	NB	NS	PE	NL	YT	NT	NU
New Year's Day	January 1	✓	✓	✓	✓	✓	✓	✓	✓	✓	✓	✓	✓	✓
Islander Day	February 14									✓				
Family Day	Third Monday in February		✓	✓		✓								
Valentine's Day	February 14	Not an official holiday												
Good Friday	Three days before Easter Monday	✓	✓	✓	✓	✓		✓	✓	✓	✓	✓	✓	✓
Easter Monday	Varies (March/April)						✓							
Mother's Day	Second Sunday in May	Not an official holiday												
Victoria Day	Monday before May 25	✓	✓	✓	✓	✓	✓					✓	✓	✓
Father's Day	Third Sunday in June	Not an official holiday												
Saint-Jean-Baptiste Day	June 24						✓							
Canada Day	July 1	✓	✓	✓	✓	✓	✓	✓	✓	✓	✓	✓	✓	✓
Civic Holiday	First Monday in August	✓			✓	✓		✓						✓
Labour Day	First Monday in September	✓	✓	✓	✓	✓	✓	✓	✓	✓	✓	✓	✓	✓
Thanksgiving	Second Monday in October	✓	✓	✓	✓	✓	✓					✓	✓	✓
Halloween	October 31	Not an official holiday												
Remembrance Day	November 11	✓	✓	✓				✓		✓	✓	✓	✓	✓
Christmas Day	December 25	✓	✓	✓	✓	✓	✓	✓	✓	✓	✓	✓	✓	✓
Boxing Day	December 26					✓								

Not all special days are on the chart. Many people celebrate St. Patrick's Day, especially if they have Irish origins, while others celebrate Robbie Burns Day, particularly if they are from Scotland. Many of Canada's first immigrants came from Scotland, England, and Ireland. The Lunar New Year in early February is a popular celebration for the Chinese, Korean, and Vietnamese people living in Canada. Ukrainians and Coptic Christians celebrate their Christmas about two weeks after the rest of the country. And the growing Muslim population celebrates Eid at the end of their 30-day fast period, which is called Ramadan. As more and more people from other cultures come to make Canada their home, we are coming to see more celebrations that were previously unknown to us.

Summer Recreation

In a country with long winters, as you can imagine, Canadians want to spend as much time as possible outdoors when the weather is good! And many of us like to leave the cities and spend time in the great outdoors. Camping is a favourite summer pastime for many. Some go in their trailers or motorhomes, but most like to pack a tent, some sleeping bags, and a camp stove and go to their favourite park. Canada has wonderful national parks and there are also many provincial parks.

Camping in Banff, Alberta

Usually, there is a fee charged to use these parks for camping purposes or even to visit them during the day. You can buy a yearly pass that includes unlimited use for all national parks, although the cost for using the campgrounds within those parks is extra. Camping is a wonderful way to see the country at a low cost and a wonderful way to meet a lot of nice people. But whatever you do, do not feed the bears or other wild animals. They may look cute but they are very dangerous! And never, ever get between a mother bear and her cub.

If you do go camping, be sure to give yourself time to do some stargazing. In the cities, we seldom see many stars but out in the countryside or mountains, the stars are bright and beautiful because there is no competition from city lights.

For those who prefer to travel in luxury, there are usually some nice hotels and motels in, or close to, many of our parks. You can also stay in one of the many youth hostels throughout the country, in both urban and rural areas. This is an inexpensive way to travel all over the world and many travellers also find it a good way to meet people from many different countries.

Another popular activity in the summer is to spend time on Canada's many lakes and rivers in a canoe or kayak. Sometimes these boats are available for rent at popular lakes, but many people prefer to buy their own and travel wherever they want. Many people like to go for fishing weekends in the mountains or at one of the many lakes across the country. Summer is also a good time to ride a bicycle. City dwellers often enjoy an evening bike ride after dinner while others go for a long walk. We all enjoy our long summer evenings where the sun doesn't set until as late as 10 p.m.

Summer is the best time to enjoy our many large city parks. Because many of our cities have been built along river valleys, there are some beautiful urban parks at which one can hike, picnic, or paddleboat. Many of the lakes in these parks become big skating rinks in the winter and are available for good cross-country skiing, tobogganing, or snowshoeing.

Possibly the most popular summer activity for the majority of Canadians is barbecuing! Whether you have a barbecue at home in your backyard or prefer to barbecue in a park over a wood fire,

Kayakers can get a great view of killer whales

nothing makes meat taste better than grilling it in the fresh air. Many people cook most of their meat and vegetables on home barbecues in summer and, if the mosquitoes are under control, also eat with friends outside in the warm evening air.

If you happen to live along one of our coastlines, you have special treats in-store for you in the summer. From Vancouver, for example, you can take a ferry over to the Gulf Islands to spend time exploring the area, and there are also many islands on the Atlantic coast. On either coast, you can go whale-watching on a large boat for the day or rent a kayak and possibly visit with the whales or dolphins up-close and personal. But be careful of the waves from other boats!

Hiking and mountain climbing are popular sports for many people. Just remember to sign in and sign out before and after you go on any hike overnight in the national parks. That way, if you run into problems, someone knows where to look for you. And be sure to read the fire-hazard signs. If a sign says "No fires," this is because in dry weather, it only takes one spark to start a huge forest fire.

For many Canadians, flower and vegetable gardening is a favourite summer activity. Apartment dwellers can often rent small plots in neighbourhood gardens, both public and private, or they can grow some things in pots on their balconies or sundecks. Serious gardeners sometimes rent a large gardening space on a nearby farm so that they have produce to freeze or store for winter and give their friends any surplus. People in cities who don't garden themselves love to go to farmers' markets. These are places where you can buy fresh vegetables, local meats, organic eggs, honey, homemade bread, and a multitude of other things including arts and crafts. They are also friendly, fun places to be!

If it's a rainy day in summer, you can always go bowling, roller-skating, or to a museum or art gallery. There is no shortage of things to do in the city. And don't forget the small-town rodeos and annual exhibitions with rides for the children and agricultural contests for mom and dad.

Last, but not least, people in many cities enjoy some sort of multicultural festival in the summer. Edmonton hosts the three-day Heritage Festival at Hawrelak Park and typically has as many as 250 000 visitors at more than 60 pavilions where one can see ethnic dancing, enjoy ethnic foods, and buy small cultural artifacts from all over the world. Winnipeg's Folklorama festival is spread out over the city and you can visit each community's pavilion in its own location. Toronto boasts a large annual Caribbean festival and everyone enjoys a colourful parade and several days of wonderful steel-drum music and dancing. First Nations communities across Canada host pow-wows where people from various Nations perform Aboriginal dances and celebrate their history and culture together, and visitors are always welcome. Be sure to try some bannock baked over a campfire—it's delicious!

Dancers at the Edmonton Heritage Festival

COMPREHENSION CHECK

1. What is the difference between an amateur theatre group and a professional theatre troupe?
2. What kind of music do people listen to at the Big Valley Jamboree in rural Alberta during the summer?
3. What are the four statutory holidays that are common to all Canadian provinces?
4. When do children wear costumes and knock at the doors of neighbours, asking for candy?
5. What is the name of the celebration that ends the period of Ramadan for Muslims?
6. What summer activity gives people the opportunity to experience fresh air and exercise, stargaze, sleep in a tent, and eat their food cooked over a campfire?
7. If you wanted to rent a kayak and go whale-watching, where would you go in Canada?
8. During the summer, where could you go to buy fresh produce, eggs, and locally produced meats from the farmers who produced them?

VOCABULARY

fringe festival	a festival of new, unpublished, and often experimental plays
powwow	a First Nations celebration of dancing, drumming, and singing usually held on reserves during the summer
heritage	our history as a people, nation, or race
up-close and personal	the opposite of *from a distance*
Labour Day	the first Monday in September, which is a day off for most workers in celebration of the work they do for the country
Thanksgiving	a celebration started in the late 16th century to celebrate an explorer's homecoming, and later to celebrate the harvest season. It is a time now when families gather and usually eat turkey and other special foods.
Good Friday	a special day for Christians to remember the crucifixion of Jesus

USING NEW WORDS

Fill in the blanks with the words from above:

1. _____ weekend is usually a time for families to gather and enjoy good food and one another.
2. When the Korean students came to Canada in the summer, their teacher took them to a big _____ at the Morley Reserve and the Aboriginal dancers invited them to come up on stage and dance with them.
3. We all want to be proud of our _____ and share it with others.

④ The first _____ festival happened in Edinburgh, Scotland, and actors from all over the world still love to go there and try out their new plays.

⑤ _____ marks the death of Jesus, while Easter marks his resurrection.

⑥ While we love to read about our heroes and heroines, it is always more fun to meet them _____.

⑦ _____ is on the first Monday in September.

FOR DISCUSSION

» You will notice that Quebec is the only province that has a statutory holiday for Saint-Jean-Baptiste Day. While they call it a national holiday, no other province celebrates this day. Why do they call it a "national" holiday?

» In the winter, Canadians enjoy the outdoors when they toboggan, ski, skate, or snowshoe. Do you think you would enjoy any of these activities? Why or why not?

» There is a strong influence of Celtic music in Nova Scotia and Newfoundland in particular. Why do you think that is? (If you are not sure, look up information on early immigration to those provinces and see where the early settlers came from.)

» In Canada, weather has a big influence on the activities people choose to do at different times of the year. What other factors influence the kinds of activities people enjoy in their free time?

The 2010 Winter Olympics in Vancouver and Whistler, BC

When the people of Vancouver heard that the Olympics were going to be held in their city, there was as much grumbling as there was joy, because they knew that taxpayers pay higher taxes for many years after such an expensive undertaking. However, when the big day arrived, that grumbling was nowhere to be heard. Both Vancouver and the whole country were caught up in the excitement of hosting the world in a beautiful city, the only area in Canada that is unlikely to be covered in snow in February.

Canadians watched the Olympic Torch relay before the games began, as torchbearers ran across the country, cheered on every step of the way by crowds lining the roadways. They also listened to Nikki Yanofsky, the young singer from Quebec who enchanted the country with the words of "I Believe."

Canadians who could not attend the Olympics in person were glued to their TV sets for 17 wonderful days. In their homes and in local bars and stores, people watched the world's best athletes compete for medals, and they watched the joy and enthusiasm of everyone who was in attendance at the Olympics.

We were enormously proud of our athletes for their skill, courage, and positive attitude. We watched the opening and closing ceremonies

The Olympic torch burns in Vancouver

Top Three Countries in Medal Wins

	Medals	Gold	Silver	Bronze
US	37	9	15	13
Germany	30	10	13	7
Canada	26	14	7	5

Sad and Courageous Moments

- The death of Georgian luge athlete Nodar Kumaritashvili on a training run at Whistler before the games began
- The fall and consequent injuries of Slovenian cross-country skier Petra Majdic and her determination to do her race in spite of serious injuries during the training run (She was hospitalized for some time afterwards.)
- Joannie Rochette's bronze-medal–winning short program performance, two days after the death of her mother

Proud Moments for Canada

- The first gold-medal win of the 2010 Olympics, by Quebecois skier Alex Bilodeau
- The first gold-medal win ever by Canada in ice dancing, by Tessa Virtue and Scott Moir

with tears of pride. We held our breath when the weather at Cypress Mountain threatened the downhill skiing events planned there. We gritted our teeth as British journalists complained about nearly everything at the beginning of the games, and we silently cheered all the hard-working volunteers who worked night and day to combat cold and rain and get everything running smoothly. Every time we heard "O Canada" sung as a gold medal was awarded to Canada, we sang along with joy in our hearts. We looked on as Joannie Rochette made the decision to skate her short program only two days after the death of her mother, her biggest fan. Through her tears, she won a bronze medal and the admiration of everyone who watched her skate, no matter what country they came from.

Quick Facts about the Vancouver 2010 Winter Olympics

- 17 days of Olympic events
- 2566 athletes from 82 countries participated
- 10 000 media representatives were there to record events
- 3 billion people watched on TV

Kevin Martin's curling team shows off their Olympic gold medals.

- The gold-medal win by Canada's curling team, skipped by Kevin Martin
- The silver-medal win in women's curling, skipped by Cheryl Bernard
- The gold-medal win in women's hockey, our third in a row at the Olympics

- The gold-medal win for Jon Montgomery for skeleton (His exuberance won the hearts of many watchers.)
- Sidney Crosby's overtime goal, which won the Canadian men's hockey team a gold medal and a 3–2 win over the US

COMPREHENSION CHECK

1. Who sang the theme song "I Believe" for the 2010 Olympics?
2. Why did some of the people of Vancouver protest hosting the Olympics before the games began?
3. During the Olympic Games, how did most Canadians feel, and why?
4. How did Joannie Rochette gain the respect of all Canadians?
5. How many people are believed to have watched the Olympics on TV?
6. What kind of game do you think the Canadians had against the Americans in the gold-medal men's hockey game? Was it one-sided or very close? How do you know?

VOCABULARY

grumbling	complaining
get caught up in (something)	become part of something
enchanted	delighted or fascinated by something
grit (one's) teeth	an expression of determination to do something one doesn't want to do but thinks one should
fan	a person who greatly admires the achievements of another
media	television, radio, newspaper, or other communications
luge	a small sled that runs a snow-covered track
exuberance	expression of extreme joy and excitement
overtime	to play beyond the time limits of a game, until there is a clear winner
(curling) rock	a very large rounded granite stone with a handle on top, used in the game of curling
puck	a small black rubber disc that is dropped on the ice in a hockey game; the goal is to get this puck into your opponent's net as often possible in a game
skipped	led a curling team (as its captain)

USING NEW WORDS

Fill in each blank with a word or term from the Vocabulary section.

❶ In curling, while one person is throwing his or her _____ towards the house, two other people are often sweeping the ice with their brooms.

❷ Many athletes showed great _____ when they realized they had won a gold medal for their country.

❸ There were _____ representatives from all over the world recording the events at the Olympics. They were assisted by many volunteers from Vancouver who interviewed the athletes and gave their material to the journalists afterwards.

❹ Nodar Kumaritashvili died while on a training run on his _____ before the competition began. This was a sad and tragic accident for the people of Georgia and for all the athletes preparing to compete in the games.

❺ Sometimes when children do not like to eat a particular food that is good for them, their parents tell them to _____ their _____ and eat it anyway.

❻ It would have been difficult not to _____ all the patriotism that was being expressed with such pride and joy by the Canadians present at these games.

❼ I have always been _____ by the beauty of figure skating, and nowhere is that more true than in the Olympics.

❽ Sidney Crosby is the captain and centre of his team, so it is his job to hit the _____(before the opposing centre can) when the referee drops it onto the ice at the beginning of the game.

❾ Justin Bieber is a young Canadian singer who has a lot of young female _____s.

❿ The Olympics is a time to celebrate the hard work and excellence of athletes from all countries and there is rarely any _____ heard, even when people are disappointed in their results.

FOR DISCUSSION

» In some countries, athletes are given a lot of financial support from their governments so that they can train and compete in events such as the Olympics. In other countries, they only get support after they win major events and, even then, the support they get is nowhere near what is needed to cover the costs of such preparation and competion. How much support do you think world-class athletes should get and at what point in their careers?

» It is extremely expensive to host the Olympic Games. If you were a taxpayer in a community whose leaders wanted to host the Olympics, how would you decide whether to support or not support such a project?

» There is an expression in the introduction to this chapter: *All work and no play makes Jack a dull boy.* How would you express this line in plain English? Can you think of expressions in other languages that are used to teach children the value of work or play?

» Before the 2010 Olympics, many people from other countries did not see Canadians as patriotic because we were very quiet about our feelings about our country. During the 2010 Olympics, however, the whole country was excited and proud of our athletes, our country, and our people. Think about another country you know well. How do people there express their patriotism, or their love of their country?

CHAPTER REVIEW

Match each item on the left with the item on the right that best fits.

1. football	a)	a game played originally by the Algonquians
2. hockey	b)	cross-country ski competition
3. lacrosse	c)	a popular winter game played with a large "rock"
4. golf	d)	sport that is played with clubs and small balls
5. basketball	e)	sport whose athletes compete for the Stanley Cup
6. 14 gold medals	f)	paddle
7. Big Valley Jamboree	g)	a holiday for workers
8. powwow	h)	sport invented by James Naismith, a Canadian
9. farmers' markets	i)	sport whose athletes compete for the Grey Cup
10. Valentine's Day	j)	a place to buy fresh, local produce
11. Labour Day	k)	a day for lovers
12. fringe festival	l)	a gathering of country and western–music lovers
13. Shania Twain	m)	what Canada won at the 2010 Olympics
14. canoe	n)	Aboriginal dancing and drumming celebration
15. curling	o)	artist who sold 39 million copies of *Come on Over*
16. Birkebeiner	p)	a showcase of new theatre work

Chapter Five

The Mosaic of Canada

Quick Facts

» There are well over one million people in Canada who claim Aboriginal ancestry.

» The word *Canada* comes from the Iroquois word *kanata* which means villages.

» Approximately 22 percent of Canadians speak French as a first language while 59 percent speak English as a first language.

» Toronto is one of the largest centres of Italian-speaking people in the world.

» Canada is a multicultural, multiracial country with people from all over the world.

» Some religions are on the decline in Canada as our society becomes increasingly secular; however, many non-Christian religions are gaining more of a presence in the country.

» The diversity of Canada is both a strength and a great challenge as we seek to maintain harmony and identify our common values.

Cultures of Canada

The New Canadian Centre Peterborough's float in the Canada Day Parade 2010

Unlike many countries, Canada does not have one culture. When someone asks, "What do Canadians do when . . . ?" most often the answer is, "Well, it depends . . ." Because Canadians find their origins in so many different countries around the world, there are many accepted ways of doing things. Some people eat meat; others are vegetarians. Some women wear western clothing; others wear saris or other ethnic dress. Some Islamic women cover their heads, while most women do not. Some people play mahjong, while others play bingo.

Who are the people of Canada? Well, you saw in Chapter 1 that the first people of Canada were the First Nations and Inuit. Just over one million Canadians have Aboriginal origins. The Aboriginal population grew by 45 percent between 1996 and 2006 as compared to 8 percent for the non-Aboriginal population. They speak many different languages, but also speak English or French, except for a few (generally older people) who live far from the cities.

Approximately one-fifth of Canada's population does not speak English or French as a first language.

Immigration to Canada

Prior to the early twenty-first century, the largest group of immigrants to Canada had come from the United Kingdom (England, Scotland, Northern Ireland, and Wales). In 1991, more than 15 percent of immigrants to Canada said the UK was their country of birth. The second-largest group at that time was the Italians (8.5 percent of immigrants), followed by the Chinese (7 percent of immigrants were from China or Hong Kong). Now, however, this has all changed. Annually, nearly 15 percent of immigrants come from China or Hong Kong and only 2.3 percent come from the UK. China and Hong Kong now top the list of source countries followed by India (11.6 percent of new immigrants), the Philippines (7 percent), and Pakistan (5.2 percent). Next is the United States, with 3.5 percent of new immigrants coming from our neighbour to the south each year. South Korea, Iran, and Romania each make up roughly 3 percent of our annual immigration total. Our diversity grows.

Does it surprise you that so many people (currently totalling more than one quarter of a million) chose to leave the US to come to Canada? Some chose to leave during the Vietnam War in the late 1960s and early 1970s. (They were called draft dodgers at the time.) Others like the lifestyle in Canada. Safer cities, less pollution, less racism, and better social programs are some characteristics of Canadian society that American immigrants sometimes mention as reasons for coming to Canada.

Most Canadians appreciate the multicultural, multiracial character of the country. Most large Canadian cities have a multicultural festival of some sort during the year. Edmonton's Heritage Festival, for example, draws up to 400 000 people over a three-day period in August.

In the graph below, you can see that Canada's immigration has not been steady through the years. People have come in waves with low immigration levels during the world wars and high levels immediately after the wars and according to other world events.

Typically, we have had several different types of immigrants. In 1978, the Canadian Immigration Act recognized the need for what we today loosely call economic immigrants: those who gain entrance because of the economic contribution they can make to the country. The act also recognized refugees, people to whom Canada offers safety from situations where their lives are in danger. Refugees are most often fleeing either war or governments which severely persecute citizens who do not agree with their views.

The Immigration Act in fact defined three classes: family class (wives, husbands, children under 22, and parents or grandparents of

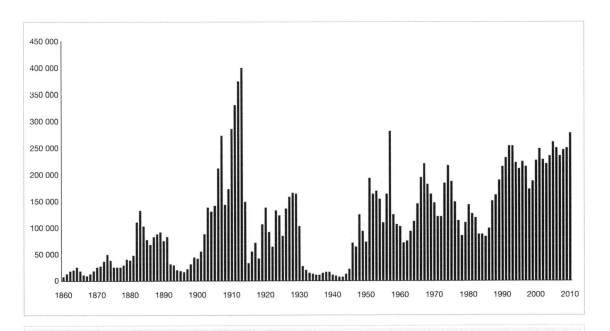

Immigration levels in Canada over the last 150 years

immigrants already here and able to sponsor their relatives); independent class (entrepreneurs and those who gain entry on the point system which varies according to the labour-market needs in the country); and refugee class.

Immigration policy is always changing. In the 1990s, eligibility narrowed to include only close relations such as spouses and dependent children under the family classification. There is also a trend toward allowing more immigrants who have money to invest. Those who are allowed in because of their skills can be required to live in parts of the country where their skills are needed. Before, they could choose where they wanted to settle. There is a processing fee of $550 per adult with each permanent resident visa application, as well as a fee of $490 for the Right of Permanent Residence (excepting refugees and children, who do not pay this fee).

Refugees

Canada has a tradition of welcoming refugees from all over the world. In the 1880s, many people fled from famine. They included potato farmers from Ireland and farmers from Ukraine. They were not called refugees in those days, but they were nonetheless fleeing for their lives. In 1956 Hungarians arrived in large numbers, after the Hungarian Uprising was crushed by the Soviets.

Then, in 1968, Czechs came when Soviet tanks moved into their capital city. In 1972 and 1973, many Ugandans immigrated when ethnic persecution in their country made life difficult, if not impossible. Between 1973 and 1979, people arrived from Chile and other Latin American countries, where many were facing torture and death because of the political situation.

From 1979 to 1980, Canadians opened their hearts to the Vietnamese boat people and to those escaping the horrors of the Khmer Rouge in Cambodia. Other refugee groups have included Poles, Lebanese, Iranians, El Salvadorans, Guatemalans, Sri Lankans, Ethiopians, Somalis, and Bosnians and others fleeing the terrible war in what used to be Yugoslavia.

In the twenty-first century, several large-scale conflicts have led many refugees to seek out Canada as their new home. Wars in Iraq and Afghanistan prompted thousands of refugees from each country to come to Canada. In addition, Canada has welcomed a large number of Burmese refugees who had fled from their government's army and were living in Thai refugee camps for years or, in some cases, decades.

It is important for us to recognize both the difficulties refugees experience making the transition to a new and different country, and the contribution they make to our society.

Canadian Voices

Below is a story written by Vu Nhat Nam, who says, "I am a boat person. I came to Canada on March 9th, 1990. I am working now so I can study English on Saturdays only now."

Because I was born and grew up in a hot country, I had never seen snow before except in movies. But I saw it in the winter of 1990. It was also my first winter in Canada. It was said that the winter of 1990 was the coldest winter in 10 years in British Columbia.

Since I still didn't get used to cold weather, I stayed in my room to see the snow falling. How beautiful it was! The snowflakes were falling down lightly. After about three hours, everything outside was covered with snow. The view looked like a perfect picture of nature.

COMPREHENSION CHECK

1 Who were the first people of Canada?
2 What is the first language of 59 percent of Canadians?
3 From what country did the "boat people" come?
4 In what ways did the family class in Canada's immigration policy change in the 1990s?

VOCABULARY

mosaic	a picture or pattern created by many variously coloured pieces; a diversified thing
racism	treating people differently—usually worse—because of their race or colour
pollution	the introduction into the environment of substances which are harmful to it; dirtying the environment (for example, air pollution or water pollution)
persecute	treat an individual or group unfairly and harshly
entrepreneurs	people who set up and manage their own businesses to earn their livings (make money)
trend	a general direction of events, opinions, or fashion
famine	starvation of a large number of people in a geographic area; a lack of food in an area
transition	a change from one way of being to another

USING NEW WORDS

Fill in each blank with a word from the list above.

1 It is not acceptable in Canada to _____ people for their religious beliefs.
2 The _____ from a tropical country to one with freezing cold winters is a very difficult one for many people.
3 To believe that one group of people will do a job less well than another because they are a different colour is an example of _____.
4 _____ take risks.
5 People who suffer from asthma or other breathing problems are not comfortable in cities which have a lot of air _____.
6 Many Irish people came to Canada when the potato crop failed in the late 1800s and there was a major _____ in Ireland.
7 Most Canadians believe that Canada is not a melting pot in which people from different cultures become like one another; rather, they see Canada as a _____ in which each small piece can keep its identity within the whole.
8 There is a _____ toward greater concern for the environment in the twenty-first century.

ACTIVITY

Newcomers may find it interesting to learn that there are some myths about immigration in Canada. Myths, in this sense, are strongly held beliefs which are not based in fact. See if you can connect each myth on the left below with the statement that refutes (disagrees with) it on the right.

❶ When our economy is weak, immigrants take valuable resources away from Canadians. We should cut the number of immigrants we allow into Canada until our economy is healthy once again.

❷ Immigrants are too often on welfare when they do not need to be.

❸ Fifty percent of immigrants do not speak English when they arrive and therefore can't find work.

❹ Canada's immigration system lets in too many criminals who commit violent crimes here and endanger our citizens.

a) Immigrants who cannot speak English or French often take very low-paying jobs such as cleaning or factory work and study language at night. Many make a great effort, and sacrifice time with their families to fit in to Canadian society and do well here.

b) Criminals come from all classes of society. In fact, immigrants are under-represented in Canada's prison population according to the report "Canada's Changing Immigrant Population 1994." Recently, immigration rules have tightened up to make it more difficult for criminals to enter the country with false papers.

c) According to a study by the Economic Council of Canada, immigration produces a net benefit to the country. More people create the need for more services and therefore for more jobs. Our future depends on immigration to replace retiring workers and to make up for a declining birth rate.

d) An Economic Council of Canada study shows that immigrants are clearly less likely than native-born Canadians to be on welfare.

FOR DISCUSSION

» What do you think is most difficult for newcomers to Canada? What has been the most difficult for you?

A Story of Cross-Cultural Confusion

In Canadian Voices on page 80, we saw how simple everyday things like snow can require some adaptation on the part of new Canadians. More difficult, perhaps, are some of the cultural differences experienced by newcomers and those who get to know them. The following story comes from an ESL teacher.

Three of my Vietnamese-Chinese students had invited me for dinner one Saturday evening. I was looking forward to going. I put on a nice dress, bought some nice flowers for the hostess and arrived promptly at six o'clock as invited. When I got out of my car, the three students in my class came running across the grass of the apartment building eager to greet me.

When I entered the apartment, there were a lot of people, old and young, male and female. Everyone was speaking Chinese so I did not understand what they were saying. One thing worried me, however; the men were wearing their undershirts—white sleeveless cotton shirts. Some wore them with trousers but two men just had on their boxer shorts. I felt very strange and wondered if those two men were sick and had just gotten out of bed to get some food.

I asked one of the students if the men were sick. She looked very surprised and said, "No, why?" I told her my fear and she laughed and said that they were just relaxing because it was the weekend. I felt quite silly, but I had a good time because everyone was very friendly to me. I was especially impressed that everyone took care of a baby with Down's syndrome. The mother was busy cooking but she did not have to worry because everyone took turns with this child, even though he was crying a lot.

COMPREHENSION CHECK

❶ Why did the visiting teacher feel uncomfortable?

❷ What were the men wearing? Why?

❸ Who looked after the baby?

VOCABULARY

adaptation	a change to fit in better or make more suitable for a purpose; an adjustment
hostess	a woman who receives or entertains guests
promptly	right on time

USING NEW WORDS

Write a sentence using each of the words above.

FOR DISCUSSION

» Have you ever felt embarrassed because you misinterpreted something in another culture?

» What do men in your culture wear to relax at home? What do women wear?

» Whose responsibility are the small children when a group is together in your culture?

ACTIVITY

We make everyday decisions based on our cultural values and beliefs. Answer the following questions and then discuss them with people from other countries to see what their answers are. You may be surprised. Try to ask one or two people born in Canada and compare their answers to your own.

❶ You have been invited to a Canadian home for dinner. When you asked what time, your host said, "6:30 p.m." What time is it okay to arrive? What time is it okay to leave? If we tell you that your host was born in Chile or Ethiopia, will that change your answer? Why or why not? Would you take anything with you to the dinner? If so, what?

❷ You are in the store shopping and you meet an old dear friend you have not seen for a long time. You are very happy to see her. How do you greet her? Do you say hello, shake hands, hug her, kiss her on one cheek, kiss her on two cheeks, kiss her three times, or something else? If you kiss her, which cheek do you kiss first? If you are a man, is your answer different than if you are a woman? If your friend is from your country, is your answer different than if she is from Canada?

❸ You are going to the wedding of someone you work with. What do you take for a wedding gift? Do you give money or buy a gift? Are there some gifts that would be considered inappropriate for a wedding?

❹ You are going to the home of someone whose husband died two days ago. You want to take her some flowers and maybe something else. What else would you take? Does it matter what kind of flowers or what colour they are? Does it matter if the woman is born in Canada or if she comes from an Asian country? What colour of clothing would you wear to the funeral, or does it matter?

❺ You have been invited to your boss's house for dinner. Your boss said, "Would you and your husband like to come for dinner this Saturday evening?" You agreed to go. Do you take your two children with you or leave them with a babysitter?

Celebrating Diversity

You may wonder how Canadians feel about having many different cultures in the country. Most feel lucky and find it interesting. Some people do not like it and think that everyone should become the same as English Canadians when they move here.

Canadian Voices

Here is what an Edmonton journalist had to say on Canada Day, July 1st, 1995:

The true meaning of being Canadian, surely, is to embrace and celebrate diversity. People who come to that insight always find reward. Don't take my word for it. Ask Pansy Strange, who celebrated her 90th birthday a few days before Canada turned 128. For the past 30 years, Pansy and her husband George, 92, have offered not just a second home but a new family to dozens of Canadians who first arrived here from India.

When I asked permission to write about her, she hesitated—she does not wish it to seem as though she is seeking to draw attention to herself.

"I've had 51 for Christmas dinner," she told me at a recent gathering which included some of her "children" and "grandchildren." The love within that family does not need to be demonstrated. It is evident in every gesture, in the small acts of kindness people do for those they care about. Pansy and George made the act of becoming Canadian all that much easier for those they adopted, and Pansy says their lives have been filled with a richness in return.

I cannot think of a more affirming symbol of what Canada ought to mean.

COMPREHENSION CHECK

1. How old is Pansy Strange?
2. How old was Canada in 1995?
3. From what country did Pansy and George's adopted family come?

VOCABULARY

embrace (v)	hug or come close to; to accept willingly or gladly
celebrate	be very happy about
insight	a view which goes beneath the surface; a deeper understanding of something
reward	something of value given in return for a deed or service
turn (an age)	become an age (for example, "She turned 21 (years old) last week")
permission	someone's "okay" to do something
hesitated	paused for a short time before acting
demonstrated	shown or showed
gesture	body language; a body movement which has meaning
affirming	supporting of what one says or thinks; in agreement with
symbol	something that represents an idea or quality
ought to	should

USING NEW WORDS

Fill in each blank with a word from the list above.

1. Children normally need their parents' _____ to visit their friends' homes and to stay out later than usual.
2. It feels very _____ to have support for a cause you believe in.
3. You _____ call someone if you are going to be more than 15 minutes late for a dinner invitation.
4. Usually, having a good friend is the _____ for being a good friend.
5. Getting to know people from many different cultures can sometimes give us _____ into our own culture.
6. Many Canadians do not _____ one another when they meet unless they are lovers or very good friends.
7. Holding up the third finger with the outside of the hand facing toward someone is considered a very rude _____ and usually expresses both anger and disrespect.
8. Many people _____ their birthdays with a party, especially when they _____ a significant age such as 16, 18, or 65.
9. A flag is a _____ of a country.

⑩ The woman _____ so that she could think for a moment before explaining her concerns.

⑪ With a hug, the child _____ his affection for his father.

FOR DISCUSSION

» What gesture means "go away!" in Canada? Is that gesture considered rude or acceptable?

» What gesture means "come" in your culture? Is it the same or different from those used by most Canadians?

» What is a friendly gesture that people of most cultures know? What gestures are considered rude?

Aboriginal Peoples of Canada

A powwow celebrating Aboriginal heritage

More than one million people in the most recent census declared Aboriginal origins. Most of these said they were First Nations (sometimes called North American Indian), but 30 percent are Métis and 3 percent are Inuit.

You will hear many different words to describe people of Aboriginal origins. Years ago, people talked about Indians and Eskimos, but today these words are considered inappropriate and most people no longer use them. The term *Indian* was originally used to describe Aboriginals because the Spanish explorer Christopher Columbus thought he had sailed to India and, by mistake, called the first people he saw Indians. That term persisted for many years. Nowadays, we usually refer to people of indigenous origins generally as Aboriginals. First Nations people living in the northern boreal forest and Arctic regions refer to themselves as Dene people and speak Athapaskan languages.

There are also legal terms to describe the status of Aboriginal people. The term *Status Indian* applies to an Aboriginal who is registered with the federal department of Aboriginal Affairs and Northern Development Canada under the Indian Act. A Status Indian in Canada is entitled to free medical care, education, and training. Those whose ancestors signed treaties with the Canadian government also receive a small amount of money each year from the government of Canada (treaty money). All Status Indians have the right to live on special lands set aside for Aboriginals. These lands are called reserves and are found in various regions across the country. Reserve lands are owned by the bands which occupy them.

Métis are people who have at least one-quarter First Nations ancestry together with European ancestry. Many Métis were born as a result of marriages between French-Canadian or Scottish settlers and First Nations people long ago and, as a consequence, the Métis have developed a distinctive culture which combines traditions from their founding cultures. One well-known tradition is the colourful dance called a jig which involves rapid foot movements to the music of a fiddle. Many Métis live in the cities and rural areas of Canada. A few live in communities called colonies in rural areas. Whereas the rights of Status Indians are clear, the rights of many Métis are not. Métis can be Status Indians only if one of their parents was a Status Indian. Other Métis do not enjoy the same rights and privileges that Status Indians do.

The Inuit are the founding people of northern Canada, those who used to be called Eskimos. *Inuit* means *people* in their language. They prefer this term over *Eskimo*, which means *meat eater* in the Algonquian language. The lives of the Inuit, like those of other First Nations peoples, have changed dramatically in the past 200 to 300 years. Whereas Aboriginals once grew crops or followed the animals which provided them with food and other needs, many lost their old ways when European settlers arrived and took over the land. Many Aboriginals lost their livelihoods and their sense of control over their lives. The result was devastation for many communities that now face social problems they did not have before.

The transition to a completely different way of life has been traumatic for many, but the people are resilient and are reclaiming their strengths once again. Thanks in part to the natural resources found on some reserve lands, many communities have developed industries which

The Métis Fiddler Quartet

give jobs to their people. In addition, people from many First Nations are beginning to rediscover the value of their Nations' traditional religions, which had declined after Christian missionaries moved into their communities. Their ancestors lived with an understanding of themselves as part of nature. They had a respect for nature and recognized that they depended on all parts of it. Many people today feel that our modern cultures have neglected and even abused nature. They feel we have much to learn from Aboriginal cultures if we want to save our environment.

COMPREHENSION CHECK

1. Why is the term *Indian* no longer used by many people today?
2. What are the lands set aside for and owned by Aboriginal people called?
3. What are two heritage cultures of many Métis?
4. Where do most Inuit live?

VOCABULARY

indigenous	born in or native to a particular region or area (such as indigenous plants)
persisted	lasted for a long time
status	1. the legal standing or position of a person, allowing him or her certain rights 2. position or standing in relation to others
entitled to	having the right to do or have something
ancestors	one's predecessors; generations of people who gave birth to one's family
treaties	legal agreements signed between two groups or nations, often for peace or land
distinctive	particular to; different from others
founding	original, as in founding cultures, founding peoples
fiddle	a stringed instrument also called a violin (We call it a violin when used for classical music and a fiddle when used for rapid folk music.)
privileges	special rights enjoyed by a person or group
devastation	destruction; upset and shock
traumatic	very upsetting and painful; totally disorienting
resilient	strong and flexible; resistant to decay or destruction
reclaiming	taking back; asserting ownership over something one had lost or abandoned
relevance	meaning, importance
missionaries	people who teach their beliefs to others with the hope that they will adopt those beliefs too; usually associated with religions
neglected	failed to pay attention to something, usually at the cost of its well-being
abused	hurt physically or emotionally

USING NEW WORDS

A The following words have something in common. What is it?

persist   *reclaim*   *neglect*   *abuse*

If you said that all of these words are verbs, you are right! Use each one in a sentence below.

1. The Ethiopian refugees promised that they would _____ in fighting for their country even though they could not safely live there now.

2. It is not acceptable for men to _____ their wives in Canada.

3. He had to _____ his suitcase at the airport when the flight landed.

4. Children who _____ reading do not usually do well at school.

B What do these four words have in common?

distinctive   *indigenous*   *resilient*   *traumatic*

If you said that they are all adjectives, you are right again! Use each one in the most appropriate sentence below.

1. The famous singer has a very _____ voice. No one confuses her singing with that of anyone else.

2. Many immigrants find it quite _____ to leave the country they have known all of their lives and settle in a new country.

3. Even though it is difficult to adapt to living in a new country, those who succeed are _____ and can overcome many obstacles.

4. Grizzly bears and Rocky Mountain sheep are _____ to the Rocky Mountains of Canada; elephants and tigers are not.

C Lastly, what do these words have in common?

status   *ancestors*   *relevance*

Right again if you said that they are nouns. Fill in each blank below with one of these words.

1. Nova Scotia means *New Scotland* because many of the people who first moved to that province came from Scotland. Therefore, people who live there now often say that their _____ are Scottish.

2. Many well-educated immigrants feel that they lose a lot of _____ when they immigrate to Canada.

3. It can be very boring to read material that we think has no _____ to our lives.

D What word is used to refer to each of these groups of Canada's Aboriginal peoples?

1. people who Columbus referred to as Indians, assuming they came from India _____

2. people who speak Athapaskan languages and live either in the Arctic or northern boreal forest _____

3. other people who live in the Far North_____

4. people who were born of mixed blood, some of which was First Nations _____

FOR DISCUSSION

» What do you know about Canada's First Nations? How did you learn this? Do your first impressions tell the whole story?

» How many different races and people have lived in your first country?

ASSIGNMENT

Using a library or an encyclopedia, searching online, or asking someone, find out what the following are and how you could learn more about them.

1. potlatch
2. powwow
3. totem pole
4. moccasins
5. mukluks
6. kayak
7. pemmican
8. bannock

In your notebook, write one or two of the following beside each of the words above.

You can wear these.

You can watch or look at this.

You can eat this.

You can travel in this.

One Aboriginal Voice

To begin to understand the feelings of many First Nations peoples today, we need to try to understand the sense of betrayal many have felt from the time that the first settlers arrived on the land.

Canadian Voices

The following quotation is from a speech given by Dr. Walter Currie, a Potawatomi Ojibwa and educator from Ontario.

As an Ojibwa Indian, one of the many Indian peoples of Canada, one of this country's three founding races, I would like on behalf of my people to officially welcome you to our shores. We hope and expect that your stay here will be pleasant and memorable, that while you are here you will not only take note of our customs and beliefs but will respect and honour them. In turn, we will not try in any manner to impose upon you our ways, nor to change yours.

You smile when I say these words, and yet, over the past few hundred years, my forefathers by word and deed expressed these feelings to your predecessors. As a matter of fact, examine the writings of those early explorers along either coastline, and you will find that my people greeted the newcomers graciously and made them welcome; that in no case were my people hostile. That did not come until later, until after sad experience taught us that all newcomers were not worthy of trust and brotherhood.

Further to this, it was our forefathers who taught the Europeans how to survive and how to live in this land. Now it is true, the Indians accepted and adopted some of the technical advantages of your culture—the killing stick, the iron pot, the steel blade, the steel traps, the blankets ... the liquor—but only to improve upon their physical way of living. It was the Indians' way of life—which animals to kill and how to kill; which plants, fruits, and nuts to eat; which herbs to use for medicinal purposes; how to build the canoe to travel great distances, to make portages easily, to explore around the next bend in the river—it was the Indians' way of life that made it possible for those first Europeans to survive and prosper.

COMPREHENSION CHECK

1. Were relations between Aboriginal peoples and the first explorers usually friendly or unfriendly?
2. Who helped the early settlers to live off the land?
3. What are some examples of knowledge that the early Aboriginals had?

VOCABULARY

memorable	worth remembering
take note of	notice, to pay attention to
impose	force on another that which he or she does not want
forefathers	ancestors
predecessors	those who came before
hostile	very unfriendly, dangerously unwelcoming
worthy	deserving
brotherhood	a close relationship, as between brothers
adopted	took as one's own
liquor	alcoholic beverages with more alcohol than wine or beer
herbs	plants which are used either to flavour foods or to make medicine
medicinal	for medical purposes; for healing
portages	carrying of boats and supplies overland from one body of water to another
prosper	be successful in a material way

Note: The term *brotherhood* is considered politically incorrect because it excludes women. A term more in keeping with our efforts to equalize the relations between men and women and among all races would be *the global community.* The term *ancestors* is also preferred over *forefathers* because it is more inclusive.

USING NEW WORDS

Fill in each blank with a word or term from the Vocabulary section.

① The _____ of the Liberals under Jean Chrétien's government were the Conservatives under Brian Mulroney.

② Some people grow _____ outdoors or indoors, while others buy them from the store.

③ In the days of the early settlers, alcohol was often used for _____ purposes as well as recreational ones.

④ To be _____ of my trust, you must not lie to me.

⑤ A grizzly bear can be _____ to people in the wilds.

⑥ To _____, young children need affection as well as water, food, and shelter.

⑦ For many people, their wedding day is one of the most _____ days of their lives.

⑧ You may _____ on people you do not know very well if you do not call ahead to let them know you would like to visit.

⑨ When you park your car in a large parking lot or parkade, it is important to _____ exactly where you left it.

⑩ The young man does not look like his parents because they _____ him as a baby.

⑪ The group made several _____ on their canoe trip.

⑫ Drinking too much _____ has ruined many lives.

FOR DISCUSSION

» Why do you think First Nations peoples could feel betrayed? Do you think the early settlers always realized the effect they were having on the Aboriginals' lives?

» Have you ever felt betrayed? How did you feel at that time? What did you want to do?

» Have you ever hurt someone without fully realizing what you were doing? How did you feel and what did you do?

» Have you ever had someone try to impose his or her values and beliefs on you? What did that feel like?

» What do you think that the government of Canada can do to solve the problem of alienation and injustice experienced by First Nations peoples?

Resource: If you wish to learn more about Canada's First Nations peoples, you could visit the Aboriginal Affairs and Northern Development Canada website and view some of the available documents and videos. These resources are free and give you an introduction to the topic. To understand the feelings and experiences of the people, however, you need to meet and talk to some. Many communities have a Native Friendship Centre where you would be welcome to talk to people.

The Two Solitudes

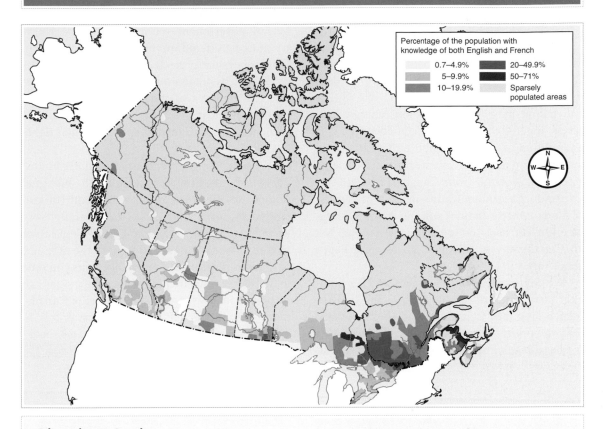

Percentage of the population with knowledge of both English and French

- 0.7–4.9%
- 5–9.9%
- 10–19.9%
- 20–49.9%
- 50–71%
- Sparsely populated areas

Bilingualism in Canada

As you read in the first chapter, two other founding cultures in Canada were the English and the French. Canada is officially a bilingual country. While this has created wonderful opportunities not found in countries with only one official language, it has also created problems. In most of Canada, the anglophone and francophone communities live relatively separate from each other. This is why they are often referred to as *the two solitudes.*

Although there are pockets of French-speakers throughout the country, the majority live in the province of Quebec. People of French heritage in Quebec call themselves Québécois. On the map of bilingualism shown above, you can see that relatively few areas have large numbers of people who are fluent in both languages. There are certainly more bilinguals in Quebec

than there are in the rest of Canada. It has often been difficult for anglophone and francophone Canadians to truly understand one another. The battle on the Plains of Abraham in 1759 may have been a victory for the English, but it did not end the bitterness many French-speaking Canadians felt about their situation.

Many Québécois see themselves as one of two nations in Canada, but they do not feel treated as a nation. They believe they are different from the other provinces. Quebec has its own legal system, language laws, and education system, but the Québécois feel at risk. They believe their culture is threatened by the dominant anglophone culture in North America. This is why some were fighting for a distinct society clause in the Canadian constitution to protect once and for all those institutions which are unique to Quebec and which protect the language and culture of Quebec's French-speaking majority.

For some time now, there has been a separatist movement in Quebec. In 1970, some terrorist activities were carried out by one separatist group called the FLQ (Front de Libération du Québec). The federal government under Pierre Trudeau responded by declaring a national emergency and jailing many people without charge. This action angered many people in Quebec. In a 1995 referendum, a little less than half of the province voted in favour of sovereignty (of becoming a country separate from Canada). In 2006, the Canadian government announced that because of the province's distinct culture, it would recognize Quebec as a "nation within a nation." Not all Canadians—or all Québécois—were happy about this.

While many people celebrate Canada's bilingual status, others resent it. They feel that the French language is irrelevant to their lives and that too much money is spent on preserving the language across the country. Canada has

an official policy of bilingualism, which means that all federal government documents must be published in both French and English and all federal government services across the country must be offered in both French and English. This policy has protected the rights of French-speaking Canadians outside Quebec, but it has also cost a great deal of money. Some Canadians think there must be a better way for English- and French-speaking Canadians to assert their rights in Canada.

Whereas many parents have supported bilingualism by sending their children to bilingual schools so that they could speak both official languages, anglophones were generally very unhappy when, in 1977, the Quebec legislature passed a law saying that all signs in the province of Quebec must be in French. No signs could be in English or any other language. Since signs can be posted in any language in the rest of Canada, many Canadians felt this law was unfair to English-speaking citizens of Quebec and speakers of other languages. This one action cost the

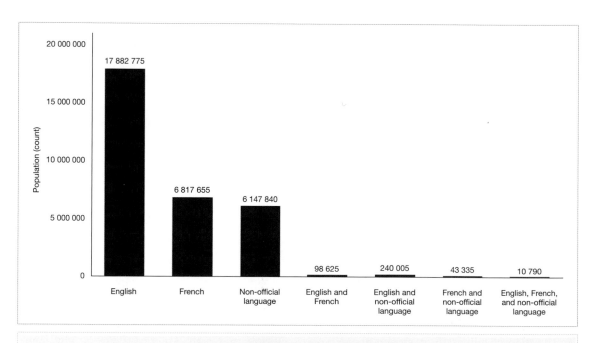

Languages spoken by Canadians (based on information from the 2006 census)

Québécois a lot of support from Canadians who had, up to then, been sympathetic to their cause. Quebec's language law has been changed so that signs can be English as long as French signs are larger, but the issue is still a controversial one.

In the graph shown on the previous page, you will see that although the percentage of people who speak both French and English is low, the number of people who speak a different first language is relatively high.

COMPREHENSION CHECK

1. In which areas of the country do you see the most bilingual (English and French) speakers?
2. Why are the English and French in Canada sometimes called *the two solitudes*?
3. What do separatists want for Quebec?
4. How do you explain an increase over the past several decades in the number of people who claimed a language other than English or French as their mother tongue?

VOCABULARY

solitude	a feeling or state of being alone
anglophone	(adj) English-speaking; (noun) English-speaker
francophone	(adj) French-speaking; (noun) French-speaker
terrorist	a person or group that commits violent actions to gain attention for its beliefs
referendum	a vote held so that citizens may vote on an issue of great importance
sovereignty	legal control over one's own governance

USING NEW WORDS

Fill in each blank with a word from the list above.

1. The people of Quebec have indicated that they do not want another _____; instead, they want the government to do something about the other problems the province is facing.
2. When a person is around people and noise at all times, a little _____ is appreciated.
3. Canada, Australia, India, and the other countries of the British Commonwealth all have _____; none are still colonies of Britain.
4. It was a _____ group that claimed responsibility for the bomb that killed several people in Northern Ireland.
5. The population of western Canada is mostly _____ while the population of Quebec is mostly _____.

Black Culture in Canada

The Caribbean Carnival in Toronto, Ontario

Usually we think of culture as something associated with a country, but sometimes culture can be bigger than a country. Many people who live in Canada but have African or Caribbean origins want to recognize a Black culture in Canada. They feel that what they have in common is more important than any differences they may have. This common culture is especially important for people whose ancestors were Black, but who themselves are born in Canada. These people often do not identify with a particular ethnic community like those who were born in Ethiopia or Jamaica do, for example.

There are Black Canadians living in all parts of Canada. In Toronto there are many people from the various Caribbean islands, in particular Jamaica and Trinidad. Many of these people are active in the Caribbean community there, just as other groups such as the Italians and Portuguese have active communities for their members. Some

Black Canadians, such as those in the Halifax-Dartmouth area of Nova Scotia, come from families that have lived in Canada for generations. Some came as slaves or runaways from American slavery. Others, like many of Canada's immigrants, came in search of new opportunities and freedom. Life here has not been easy for many Black Canadians. In some cases, property owners refused to sell or rent them homes, and government policies made it difficult for them to bring their families to Canada. Segregated schools existed in some parts of the country as late as the second half of the twentieth century.

One of the great Canadian scandals was the destruction in the 1960s of Africville in the north end of Halifax. The centre of this community of 400 was the Baptist Church, which also served as a school in the early years. This community had problems. Factories, a prison, and a garbage dump had been located in the middle of the community and railway tracks ran through it. Although residents paid taxes and in many cases owned their land, houses, and businesses, the city did not provide the water, sewage, and police services which other residents had. The decision was made by the majority of city council to move all Africville residents into public housing and to destroy the community. People were further humiliated by the use of garbage trucks to move them out. They were dispersed throughout the area and the land was cleared. It sits now as a flat, barren park—a national historic site and a cold reminder of this embarrassing and painful chapter in our history.

Canadian Voices

Black Canadians still face problems of racism in many parts of the country, but they are working together to recover their history, to conquer these problems, and to showcase their achievements for the rest of the country. Henry Bishop, curator of the Black Cultural Centre in Dartmouth, Nova Scotia, explains what it means to him to be a Canadian:

Born and growing up as the youngest of fourteen siblings in Weymouth Falls, Digby County, Nova Scotia, I began to develop a keen interest in becoming an artist, cultural worker, and visionary at an early age.

Realizing the significance of African heritage, it became my passport and foundation to security in my future as a Canadian citizen. The contribution and meaningful achievements would be my salvation. I knew by comparison that everyone needs equal opportunity to succeed. My determination would not be destroyed by racism. Pride in my heritage would be an example to all Canadians. I would be an ordinary person doing extraordinary deeds that would reflect the purpose of a positive approach to life in the land where my forefathers settled and died.

We, as Canadians, live in one of the greatest countries in the world. Thus, we must strive to understand the cross-cultural composition around us, learn to appreciate the beautiful mosaic of Canada from sea to sea, and from east to west. Let us join in the spirit of respect and dignity for all thus creating a proud identity as we stand on guard for these principles, O Canada!

Henry Bishop is also an artist and student of Black history and culture. He works hard with other members of his community to teach Black youth that they are a part of history and that they can make a difference, too.

COMPREHENSION CHECK

1. Why did many Black people come to Canada?
2. What was the name of the Black community in Halifax, Nova Scotia, in the 1960s?
3. Does this community still exist today? What happened to it?

VOCABULARY

identify with	feel a sense of belonging to; to feel a lot in common with
segregated	kept apart or separate (Black children went to separate schools)
humiliated	very embarrassed; made to feel very small and unimportant
dispersed	spread out over an area
barren	lifeless
reminder	that which causes us to remember
achievements	things one has done which one feels very proud of; successes
siblings	brothers and sisters
visionary	a person who has an image of the future
identity	that to which one feels a sense of belonging; character or nature
principles	strongly held ideas or truths which guide our decisions in life

USING NEW WORDS

Fill in each blank with a word from the list above. The first letter of each word is given to help you.

1. Sometimes we tend to forget things which are important; we may need a r_____.
2. The Canadian i_____ is not easy to describe because Canadians are a very diverse people.
3. No one likes to feel h_____.
4. Our society needs v_____ people to help us create new and better futures.
5. Most of us have failures which embarrass us, and a_____ of which we can be proud.
6. The p_____ of truth, justice, and freedom are universal.
7. In Canada, men and women work, eat, and socialize together, but in some cultures they are s_____ from one another.
8. To find the missing child, the searchers d_____ over the area where she was last seen.
9. Many people think of northern Canada as a b_____ place, but it is rich in plant and animal life.

ACTIVITY

The following Black Canadians are very famous for their achievements. See if you and your classmates can match the person with his or her accomplishments.

Rosemary Brown   first Black cabinet minister in the government of Canada; first Black Lieutenant-Governor (Ontario, 1985–1991)

Oscar Peterson   first female editor of a North American newspaper (Chatham, Ontario, *Provincial Freeman*, 1853)

Lincoln Alexander   first Black woman elected to a provincial legislature (BC, 1972)

Mary Ann Shadd   a journalist and the 27th Governor General of Canada

Michaëlle Jean   famous jazz musician

(You can find the answers on page 250 at the back of the book.)

FOR DISCUSSION

» What difference, if any, does skin colour make in your first country?

» Do you know of any other groups of people who have been unfairly treated because of their skin colour?

» What do you think that we can do to create a country in which all people feel proud of who they are and can live freely without fear of injustice?

Other Cultures of Canada

English is the first language of nearly 60 percent of Canadians, but there are many different cultural groups living in Canada. Two-and-a-half percent of the population, for example, speak Italian as their first language. Many large Canadian cities have a "little Italy" where you can shop for Italian products like pasta, black olives, gelato, cappuccino, and supplies for making wine. Toronto has by far the largest Italian population of any city in Canada, and in fact has more Italians than any city outside Italy. Italy used to be the largest source of immigrants to Toronto, but in recent years, most immigrants to the city have come from India or China. Approximately 17 percent of people in the City of Toronto claim Chinese as their mother tongue.

There are many Chinese immigrants who now call Canada home. Large cities such as Toronto and Vancouver have lively Chinatowns with restaurants and shops selling fresh vegetables, dried foods used in Chinese cooking, large sacks of rice, and other goods imported from China and Hong Kong. Chinese New Year in February is a popular annual celebration and everyone looks forward to the colourful celebrations at this time. Even many small rural communities have a Chinese restaurant or Chinese grocery store.

Germans have also settled throughout Canada, in both urban and rural areas. Some communities still have large numbers of people who speak German, but others have blended into the English-speaking culture. The children and grandchildren of immigrants sometimes do not learn to speak their heritage language and do not follow all of the cultural traditions of their ancestors. Like several other groups, however, the German people often have their own radio and TV programs, private clubs, and restaurants serving their own community as well as others who enjoy German cooking and cultural events.

Spanish soccer fans in Toronto celebrate their team's World Cup victory in 2010

Cultures and languages from every part of the world form the fabric of Canada. Each cultural group that has come to call Canada home has contributed much of value to this country. Immigrants have opened small and large businesses. They have contributed to the arts and sports communities. The multicultural nature of Canada is seen in every supermarket, school, and government office.

Although people of every origin have blended in with the communities in which they live—working side-by-side with people from other cultures, living in neighbourhoods where they may be the only family on the street that speaks their language—many still find ways to keep their cultures and languages alive in Canada. In urban centres, children can choose to go to bilingual programs where half of their studies are in English and the other half in their heritage language. In other cases, they can attend heritage language classes after regular classes, in the evenings, or on Saturdays. Adults organize huge annual heritage festivals in their ethnic communities and get together regularly to celebrate or discuss issues common to their members.

It is important to understand that many people have come to Canada in search of a better life. Many were refugees running away from religious or political persecution. Others were living in poverty or famine and decided to take a chance in a new, developing land. Many came to join family members who were already here. Few found the transition easy.

COMPREHENSION CHECK

❶ What is a 13-letter word that describes the diverse cultural nature of Canada? (Clue: It starts with an *m*.) _____

❷ What is the name of a colourful celebration in February where Chinese people present their traditional dances and sometimes have fireworks?

❸ What are two things immigrants sometimes do to preserve their culture in Canada?

VOCABULARY

gelato	Italian ice cream
cappuccino	a popular strong Italian coffee served with foamed milk on top
looking forward to	excited about something which is coming
blended in	mixed together harmoniously
heritage	one's ethnic background; the culture of one's ancestors
huge	very large

USING NEW WORDS

Fill in each blank with a word or term from the list above.

1 She is _____ having a good job so that she can sponsor her parents to come to Canada.

2 Learning English can be a _____ problem for many people when they first come to Canada.

3 Many Canadians have a very mixed _____. Monique's ancestors come from England, Scotland, Holland, Ireland, and France, for example.

4 It is fun to meet a friend for a _____ at a café on the weekend.

5 As soon as they went out to play, the new children _____ well with their classmates.

ACTIVITY

In the following puzzle, the names of 21 countries from which people have come to live in Canada are listed. Circle them. The words may appear from right to left, left to right, top to bottom, bottom to top, or on a diagonal (slant). Have fun!

```
F M E Z P C E B O N T C V Z X R
I J A P A N H O P Q K O R E Λ B
U S A C U Y T I N D I A V R F S
X R L E B A N O N Q G E L U T N
N B E P Y T I E B A E S D S C C
M R T P O L A N D N R M X S C A
G R E E C E P G V Y M A I I N R
D Z E B H O R L O V E K I A K G
R A T Y U P B A N M N C H I L E
E M V V I E T N A M Y G M N X N
T B Y Z Q A S D P L R E G Y P T
A I D O B M A C H T A R E S D I
D A C I A M A J N M G H P X F N
E B C S T H A I L A N D L R S A
F P L K Q V E N E Z U E L A B G
P A K I S T A N O P H E I C S Y
```

(You can find the answers on page 251 at the back of the book.)

Religions of Canada

The picture of religion in Canada has changed rapidly in recent decades, in part due to the large number of immigrants from different parts of the world, and in part, due to a growing decline in religious interest in many of the Christian churches. In addition, it is difficult to assess the true picture from census data because people are not asked which religion they practise, but rather with which religion they identify. In other words, growing numbers of people were born into a religion that they no longer practise. The difficulty in assessing religious trends is compounded by the fact that the government has stopped asking any questions about religion on the census.

	2006		2031 (projected)		Percentage Change 2006–2031
	thousands	%	thousands	%	
Roman Catholic	13 830	42.5	15 389	36.6	-13.9%
Protestant	8970	27.6	8973	21.3	-22.8%
Christian Orthodox	566	1.7	978	2.3	+35.3%
Other Christians*	974	3.0	1944	4.6	+53.3%
Muslim	884	2.7	2870	6.8	+151.9%
Jewish	348	1.1	421	1.0	-9.1%
Buddhist	358	1.1	607	1.4	+27.3%
Hindu	406	1.2	1024	2.4	+100.0%
Sikh	384	1.2	906	2.2	+83.3%
Other Religions	122	0.4	185	0.4	+0.0%
No Religion	5680	17.5	8780	20.9	+19.4%

*Includes those who reported "Christian," "Apostolic," "Born-again Christian," and "Evangelical."

Note: 2006 data on religious denomination were projected from 2001, as questions about religion are no longer asked on the census.

Source: Adapted from Statistics Canada, Projections of the Diversity of the Canadian Population, 91-551-XIE2010001, March 2010.

The chart above shows some interesting projected trends in religion in Canada. Most notable, perhaps, is the anticipated increase in the percentage of Muslims. Between 1991 and 2001, the number of Muslims in Canada increased by almost 129 percent; those numbers will continue to rise over the coming decades. This is due to the many immigrants coming from the Middle East and East African countries, as well as the groups' high birth rates. Likewise, Hindus and Sikhs will see large increases in numbers.

The Catholic and the Protestant churches—considered to be the mainstream churches in Canada in generations past—have declined in recent years and will continue to do so. Many of these churches find themselves with pews filled with aging parishioners, and they struggle to understand where all the young people have gone.

Over the last few decades there has been an increase in the number of Canadians who claim no religion, and that trend looks to continue, although at a somewhat slower pace. Many people who no longer attend a church still express a desire to honour their spirituality and are searching for new ways in which they can do that. There is also a growing interest in interfaith studies, as we strive to see our commonalities in various religions and to understand our diverse country better.

COMPREHENSION CHECK

❶ To which religion do most people in Canada belong?

❷ Do all people with spiritual beliefs follow an organized religion?

❸ Which religion is expected to grow the most in Canada between 2006 and 2031?

VOCABULARY

declare	say openly; say that something is true
misleading	not totally true; confusing
synagogue	the building in which the Jewish community worships
temple	the building in which the Buddhist, Hindu, and Sikh communities worship
mosque	the building in which the Islamic community worships
pews	wooden benches for sitting in many older churches

USING NEW WORDS

Fill in each blank with a word from the list above.

❶ When you purchase goods from another country and bring them into Canada, you must _____ their value at the customs office.

❷ The vandalism of a _____, _____, or _____ by those who hate people of religions different from their own are hate crimes and are against the law in Canada.

❸ Salespeople who are not honest will sometimes give you very _____ information about a product so that you will buy it.

ACTIVITY

Try matching each of the religions listed below with the appropriate sentences. You will have to use some religions more than once.

Islam	Hinduism	Buddhism	Christianity
Judaism	Shamanism	Sikhism	

❶ The founder of this religion was known as Jesus, a Jew who lived in what is now known as Israel. _____

❷ People of this religion communicate with their ancestors, asking for their help with problems, and they find much wisdom in using the medicine wheel. _____

❸ Members of this religion were seriously persecuted during the Second World War in Germany. _____

❹ Men of this faith often wear a turban and carry a ceremonial dagger. _____

❺ People of this faith often pray five times daily by kneeling and facing Mecca. _____

❻ People of this faith do not eat beef as they believe that the cow is a sacred animal. _____

❼ People of this religion often burn incense and have a large golden statue representing their founder at the front of their centre of worship. _____

❽ A spiritual leader of this faith is called an imam. _____

❾ A spiritual leader of this faith is called a rabbi. _____

❿ A spiritual leader in this faith is often also a healer. He or she is called a shaman. _____

(You can find the answers on page 251 at the back of the book.)

Religious Practices in Canada

In Canada, we believe in religious freedom. Everyone should feel safe following their own religious practices as long as they do not cause harm to others. What countries do you know of where there is no freedom of religion?

Sometimes, there are problems because someone's religious practices conflict with the practices of the majority, but most people try to find solutions agreeable to everyone. For example, different religions have different feast days. In some cases, people have to work on their religious feast days, but sometimes they are able to negotiate the day off.

Members of Sikhism ran into some problems when they wore their turbans in places where most Canadians remove their headgear. Sikh students faced some difficulties when they wore their ceremonial daggers in high schools because some people felt this practice could be dangerous. Sikh members of the Royal Canadian Mounted Police are now permitted to wear their turbans instead of the usual Mountie hats, and Sikh students in many high schools have been given permission to wear their ceremonial daggers. These religious rights have not come easily to the Sikh community, but many Canadians have supported them in this struggle to have their religious practices recognized.

Sgt. Baltej Singh Dhillon, a Sikh Mountie

Christianity: The Majority Religion in Canada

While all members of the Christian churches express a belief in Jesus as the son of God, there are many different understandings of this belief. Therefore, there are many different kinds of Christian churches in Canada with various beliefs and practices.

The largest denomination, by far, is still the Roman Catholic Church, despite its decreasing membership. The head of the Roman Catholic Church is the Pope, who lives in Rome. Roman Catholics represent more than 40 percent of Canada's population. The second-largest denomination is the United Church of Canada, a union of four smaller denominations including the Methodist, Presbyterian, and Congregationalist churches. Like many of the other Protestant churches such as the Anglicans and Lutherans, the membership of the United Church has been in steady decline over the past years. While the Catholic and many Protestant churches are suffering from general decline, some evangelical Christian denominations are showing strong growth and are expected to continue to do so.

Historically, Canada has seen many groups of religious refugees come to its shores in search of religious freedom. Mennonites, Hutterites, and Doukhobors have settled in various parts of the country, adding richly to the mosaic of our

Hutterites in southern Alberta

cultural makeup as a country. Members of these three groups live in very close-knit communities—in fact, Hutterites live in colonies where all property is communal. Their community-centred way of life is one way that their religion is preserved.

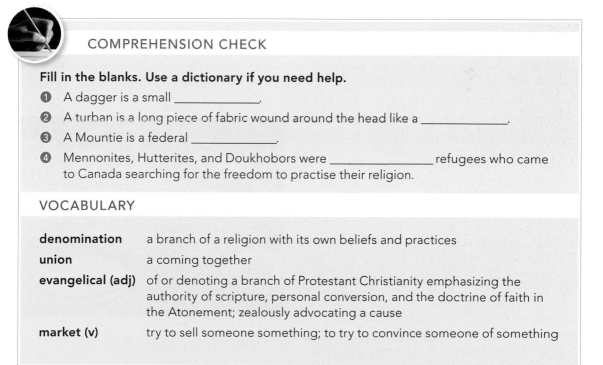

COMPREHENSION CHECK

Fill in the blanks. Use a dictionary if you need help.

1. A dagger is a small _____.
2. A turban is a long piece of fabric wound around the head like a _____.
3. A Mountie is a federal _____.
4. Mennonites, Hutterites, and Doukhobors were _____ refugees who came to Canada searching for the freedom to practise their religion.

VOCABULARY

denomination	a branch of a religion with its own beliefs and practices
union	a coming together
evangelical (adj)	of or denoting a branch of Protestant Christianity emphasizing the authority of scripture, personal conversion, and the doctrine of faith in the Atonement; zealously advocating a cause
market (v)	try to sell someone something; to try to convince someone of something

USING NEW WORDS

Fill in each blank with a word from the Vocabulary section.

1. When you are looking for a job, you have to _____ yourself, your skills, and your attitude to employers.
2. A marriage is sometimes described as a _____ of two people.
3. Each _____ within the Christian church has its own beliefs and practices.
4. The _____ minister was a very persuasive speaker.

FOR DISCUSSION

» Some people believe that it is important to be part of a religious community, while others believe that spirituality is a very personal thing. Which of these views do you think is growing and why?

» It has been very important for many immigrants to Canada to find not only their own religious community, but one which worships in their own language. What are the advantages and possible disadvantages of active membership in a religious community which worships in your first language in Canada?

Celebrations and Holidays

Christmas, Easter, and Thanksgiving are the major holidays. They are traditionally days when family members gather to eat, visit, and relax together. They are also days of religious celebration for active members of the Christian faiths. On Christmas Eve (the night before Christmas), many people go to church and then return home to a feast and open gifts. Others wait until Christmas morning when they gather around the Christmas tree, empty their stockings, and then open their gifts. Then, in late afternoon, the family gathers for a turkey dinner with the traditional stuffing, cranberry sauce, mashed potatoes and gravy, Brussels sprouts, and sweet potatoes, and plum pudding for dessert. Families have their own special menus on these days, but these are menu items which are very common on Christmas for many families. Ukrainian families will add cabbage rolls and perogis to that menu, for example, and other ethnic groups will have their own special items. On Boxing Day, the day after Christmas, many people rush to the stores to shop because there are lots of bargains on this day.

A table set for Thanksgiving dinner

Easter, too, is both a religious celebration for Christians and a secular celebration for everyone. Children love Easter for the treats they get. Small children believe that, just as Santa Claus comes to leave them gifts at Christmas, the Easter Bunny comes to leave them their basket of chocolate eggs at Easter. The traditional meal for Easter Sunday is roast ham with sweet potatoes. Easter Sunday is a special day for Christians who are celebrating the resurrection of Jesus from the dead. Easter, as we experience it in Canada, is actually a mixing of the Christian festival with old pagan rituals which celebrated the spring solstice. In pagan rituals, eggs are the symbol of life and rebirth.

Another traditional meal is served on Thanksgiving when, once again, many families enjoy a large turkey together. The meal is topped off with delicious pumpkin pie and whipped cream. Thanksgiving began in the sixteenth century as a celebration of an explorer's homecoming, and later to celebrate the harvest season. Americans also celebrate Thanksgiving, although their holiday had a different origin. The American holiday falls in November, while the Canadian celebration is in October because the Canadian winter starts earlier.

There are also many other days of celebration for particular ethnic groups and religions in Canada. The Jewish religion, for example, celebrates Purim in March, Rosh Hashanah in September, Yom Kippur in October, and Hanukkah in December. Muslims, too, have special feast days, as do the Orthodox Christians who celebrate Christmas later than the other Christian churches. Muslims have a 30-day fasting period called Ramadan during which they only eat after sundown—much more difficult in our summers with their long days than near the equator when the sun sets about 6 p.m.! The Chinese New Year in February is well-known and is enjoyed throughout the Chinese community. Those who celebrate these holidays often take time off work on these special days.

A Muslim man prays during Ramadan

Other celebrations are an excuse for a party, but not for a day off. On Valentine's Day, lovers and children send heart-shaped cards to those they love. Husbands and wives, boyfriends and girlfriends, and others also exchange flowers or chocolates. The flower shops and candy stores do a big business on Valentine's Day each year.

On Halloween, children dress up in costumes and knock on doors shouting "Halloween Apples" or "Trick or Treat." The homeowner then puts a treat of some kind in their bags. Parents are cautioned to examine their children's treats carefully, however, to make sure they are safe to eat. At school or at home, children carve pumpkins into jack-o'-lanterns with a candle in the middle. The scarier it is, the better!

Remembrance Day in November is a time to remember those who died in wars to defend their countries. Many people wear a poppy as a sign of respect for those who died.

COMPREHENSION CHECK

1 On which two days do many Canadians eat turkey for dinner?

2 On which day do neighbours give out candy to children and how do the children ask for this candy?

3 What is the date of Canada's birthday?

4 How is Christmas celebrated in Canada?

5 What is the name of the special day for lovers? Is this a day off from work?

VOCABULARY

gather	come together
stuffing	a filling (usually for chicken or turkey) made with dry bread crumbs, chopped vegetables, herbs, and sometimes meat or fruit
gravy	a sauce made from meat juices, flour, spices, and water, and served on potatoes and meat
plum pudding	a rich, heavy dessert made from dried fruits and other ingredients (served hot, it is normally eaten only at Christmas by people of British ancestry)
bargains	cheap prices; good value for one's money
rush	go quickly
secular	not religious
bunny	a child's name for a rabbit
sweet potatoes	orange-coloured root vegetables
fast (v)	go without food
topped off	completed
civic	belonging to the people of a municipality (city or town)
excuse	a reason given when one needs a reason and cannot think of a good one
costumes	clothing, out of the ordinary and made for a special purpose, (at Halloween many children wear costumes to look like a ghost or cat)
treat	something unusually nice to eat
cautioned	told to be very careful; informed of danger
examine	check very carefully
poppy	a small, red flower we associate with a battlefield in Europe called Flanders Field

USING NEW WORDS

Fill in each blank with a word from the Vocabulary section.

1. What _____ could the young girl possibly have for coming home at 2:00 a.m.?

2. You should _____ clothing carefully before you buy it to make sure there is nothing wrong with it.

3. If you see a thief breaking into a house, you should _____ to the nearest telephone and call 911 for the police.

4. Even when we have very little money, we all like to give ourselves a _____ sometimes.

5. Some young children like to sleep with a stuffed toy such as a _____.

6. The workers were _____ to wear hardhats and steel-toed boots on the work site.

7. We elect our mayor and city councillors in a _____ election.

8. Boxing Day is a _____, not a religious, holiday.

9. The children made _____ to wear for their school play.

10. Some people _____ for religious reasons, while others _____ for health reasons. (same word used for both blanks)

FOR DISCUSSION

» What holidays does your family celebrate each year? How do you celebrate these?

» When you have a special religious holiday and you do not want to go to school or work on that day, when is it appropriate or not appropriate to take time off? If you don't know, how can you find out?

» Christmas can be very expensive for many Canadians. If you decide you want to celebrate Christmas, what are some ways you can do so without spending a lot of money?

» Fortunately, there are very few people who do not respect the rights of children. Nonetheless, parents have to be very careful with whom they trust the care of their children. Is this a problem in the country you come from, too?

CHAPTER REVIEW

Write a few paragraphs or a letter to a friend telling about some of the people from other cultures you have met in Canada, the experiences you have shared, and what you have learned.

Chapter Six

The Pacific Region

Quick Facts

» British Columbia (BC) joined Confederation in 1871.

» Today, British Columbia is the third-largest province in Canada—in both area and population—after Ontario and Quebec.

» The province's population is more than 4.5 million, with about 2.5 million living in the Greater Vancouver area.

» The capital of British Columbia is Victoria, located on the southern tip of Vancouver Island.

» The provincial flower is the Pacific dogwood; the provincial bird is the Steller's jay.

» The average temperature in Vancouver in January is above zero degrees Celsius, but take an umbrella!

Introduction

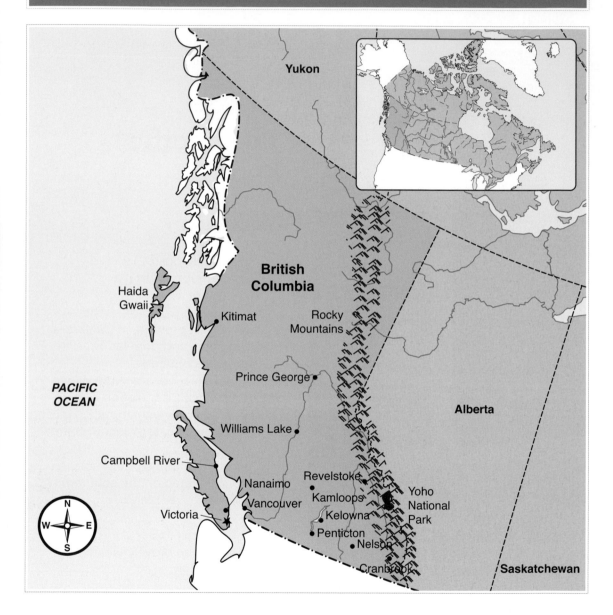

Southwestern British Columbia (BC) is often referred to as the jewel of Canada. It boasts the most idyllic climate, if you do not mind rain, and some of the most spectacular scenery in the country. The hub of British Columbia is Greater Vancouver, a metropolis surrounded by the sea on the west and mountains on every other side. Vancouver is the third-largest city in Canada, after Toronto and Montreal. It is also an unquestionably beautiful city.

Just west of Vancouver are the Gulf Islands and then Vancouver Island, the site of BC's capital city, Victoria. Victoria is a favourite retirement spot for Canadians mainly because of the mild winters. In the summer months, the traffic is unbelievable as tourists come from all over North America and other continents to enjoy the sunshine, the ocean, and the charm of this area.

When Canadians think of BC, they think not only of the mountains and the sea, but also of tall, ancient rainforests, fresh salmon from the rivers, and apples or grapes (which make great wine) from the Okanagan Valley. These are resources of the vast interior, which has a landscape and climate very different from the coast. Or, if they are artists, they may think of Emily Carr or Bill Reid and the beautiful west coast art for which they are famous. Others may think of the mysterious totem poles carved by Aboriginals of the Pacific Northwest. These are carved to tell the stories of a clan or extended family. Each symbol on the pole has meaning and purpose to those who understand it.

Business people may think of Vancouver Harbour filled with ships or downtown office towers soaring into space. Air travellers look forward to stepping off the plane to that unique smell of salt water and damp cedar, a welcome aroma indeed for a traveller seeking to escape from the cold of winter elsewhere in the country.

People of Chinese ancestry may remember the many Chinese who lost their lives building the national railway through the mountains or working in the mines of BC's interior during the 19th century. Others will remember those Canadians of Japanese ancestry who, in the Second World War, were taken from their homes and sent to the interior of BC or to the beet fields of southern Alberta. These events are part of Canada's history, an embarrassing part, but nonetheless important events in our coming of age.

BC has grown and changed. Once mainly British, the province had its first Cantonese-speaking Lieutenant-Governor, the Honourable David Lam, from 1988 to 1995. In 2001, BC's first female Lieutenant-Governor, the Honourable Iona Campagnolo, was appointed. Campagnolo was a Member of Parliament in the Trudeau years (1974 to 1979). In 1991, Rita Johnson became the first female premier in Canada, and served until her party was defeated in an election six months later. In 2011, Christy Clarke became BC's second female premier.

Totem poles in Vancouver, British Columbia

Vancouver, which used to be very Anglo-Saxon, now has a very large and diverse immigrant population from all over the world. In fact, Vancouver's richness is largely due to the numbers of people who have made their home in the city after leaving countries from every part of the globe. Walking through the streets of Vancouver, you have the sensation of passing through a global village, the same feeling you get in Toronto or Montreal.

The Chinese population of Vancouver has always been high, but has risen sharply in recent years due in part to the change of governance in Hong Kong. In 1997, Hong Kong became a territory of China after a long period of British rule. Leading up to 1997, many people from Hong Kong chose Vancouver as their new home. The arrival of so many Chinese-speaking newcomers so suddenly was a little shocking to some Vancouverites, who saw their neighbourhoods changing very quickly. Now, people are used to these changes and most welcome the diversity.

COMPREHENSION CHECK

1. Where do most people in British Columbia live?
2. What geographical features border Vancouver?
3. What is the capital city of British Columbia?
4. Who are Bill Reid and Emily Carr?
5. Which ethnic group was very important in the building of Canada's national railroad?
6. What do we call a person who lives in Vancouver?

VOCABULARY

boasts	is proud of, and likes to tell people so
idyllic	perfect, as if made in heaven
mind (v)	be bothered by; dislike
hub	centre of activity
metropolis	large city
unquestionably	without doubt
retirement	the stage of life when people stop working, usually at about age 65
charm	the power or quality of giving pleasure or delight
ancient	very, very old
interior	the inner part of a region, not near the sea
totem poles	tree-sized wood carvings made by First Nations peoples
soaring	reaching high into the sky
cedar	evergreen tree with very aromatic needles and wood
aroma	pleasant smell
coming of age	growing up; maturing

USING NEW WORDS

Fill in each blank with a word or term from the list above.

1. The person who _____ too often is not usually popular.
2. Penticton and Kelowna are two cities in the _____ of BC.
3. The _____ of old communities is the marketplace.
4. Some people want their _____ to begin at the age of 55 so that they are still healthy enough to enjoy their freedom.
5. A person's _____ can often win him or her many friends.
6. Many people like to store woollen clothing in _____ chests because there, the wool is safe from moth worms.
7. For many people, it is _____ difficult to learn to speak another language well.

⑧ The pyramids of Egypt are _____, as they were built many thousands of years ago.

⑨ Because the cafeteria was very crowded, the young woman approached an older woman who was sitting alone and asked, "Would you _____ if I sat down here?"

⑩ Perfume is not a pleasant _____ if you are allergic to its smell.

⑪ To Canadians, the climate of the Caribbean islands seems _____.

⑫ Like Vancouver, Toronto is a busy _____.

⑬ At the air show, people were watching the planes _____ across the sky.

⑭ Most cultures have _____ ceremonies for their young people when they become adults.

⑮ You can see beautiful Aboriginal _____ at the Museum of Anthropology (MOA) in Vancouver.

FOR DISCUSSION

» Most Canadians are embarrassed at the injustice done to Canadians of Japanese ancestry during the Second World War. Can you think of other examples, in Canada or in other countries, where people have suffered greatly because of their ethnic background?

» Prices of real estate in Vancouver and the Gulf Islands have gone up so much in recent years that it is difficult for young families to buy a home there now. Some people feel this is in part due to the number of people from other countries who buy property as an investment. What do you think? Should Canadian real estate be limited in some way to Canadian buyers, or should anyone be able to buy land in Canada?

» Retirement is the common practice in North America for most people when they turn 65. Is it a common practice in other countries? If not, what is different?

» English speakers use a lot of acronyms (abbreviations where each letter stands for a word) to replace names of things. *BC* is an acronym for British Columbia and *MOA* is an acronym for the Museum of Anthropology. What are some other acronyms you know in English?

Geography, Climate, and Economy

Visitors to Vancouver need to remember to take their umbrellas unless they want to get wet, because it rains a lot in the city. Most people do not mind the rain, though, because the weather is so warm. In summer, the temperature averages 22 degrees Celsius during the day. Even in January, the average daytime temperature is six degrees, while at night, it hovers just above zero degrees. Visitors to Vancouver and the Gulf Islands are amazed to see rose bushes in bloom for six months of the year!

Whereas the coast enjoys a balmy climate, the climate of British Columbia's interior is colder and gets a lot of snow in some parts. Most of the interior is mountainous with deep gorges where rivers run. The northeast, however, is a continuation of the Great Plains found in the prairies. In the southern interior, there are a few valleys which remain warmer than the surrounding mountain areas and provide an ideal climate for fruit farming, an important part of BC's economy. The Okanagan Valley is the best-known area for

Logging trucks transport lumber from BC forests

orchards and everyone looks forward to the cherries, peaches, apricots, plums, and apples grown there, as well as the grapes which support a thriving wine industry in the province. The warm temperatures in this area have also made it a popular retirement area and vacation spot. The communities of Kelowna, Penticton, and Salmon Arm are also popular tourist centres.

The area around Kamloops in the southern interior is hot and dry in the summer and provides land for some of the best ranching in the province. Here, as in the Okanagan Valley, farmers and ranchers depend on irrigation to provide the water needed for successful agriculture.

About 55 percent of British Columbia is covered by forest. The trees that grow in the mild, wet climate on the coast are the tallest trees in Canada. They include the towering Douglas fir, Sitka spruce, and western red cedar. Forests also cover large areas of the interior. Forestry and related industries are a central part of BC's economy. Lumber is used for the construction industry in Canada and is also exported. Pulp and paper are also produced for domestic and foreign use.

Conservation of the forests, however, is a growing concern. Most of the large forestry companies are now making an effort to replenish the forests and are replanting trees in areas where they have been cut down. Many people agree with ecologists that we should be extremely concerned about overlogging Canada's forests, especially the ancient rainforests of BC. People have held demonstrations to protest logging in areas such as Clayoquot Sound on Vancouver Island, one of the largest remaining areas of rainforest in Canada. An infestation of pine beetles in recent years has killed a great many of the trees in the Rockies and is very worrisome to the forestry industry. The only way to kill these beetles is to have sustained and very cold weather.

Mining, tourism, fishing, and manufacturing are the other large industries in BC. As on Canada's east coast where fish stocks have declined, large numbers of salmon in British Columbia have also disappeared. Many fishing industry workers have been concerned that their livelihoods are being changed forever. In 2010, nature rebounded and people rejoiced to see the largest population of spawning salmon in many, many years. Everyone hopes to see this trend continue.

COMPREHENSION CHECK

❶ In which province would a gardener have the longest growing season in Canada?

❷ Which area of BC is most famous for its fruit orchards?

❸ What is BC's largest industry?

❹ What is the significance of Clayoquot Sound?

❺ What has recently concerned people in BC's fishing industry?

VOCABULARY

balmy	mild and pleasant
gorge	narrow opening between hills or mountains, especially with steep walls and a stream or river at the bottom
ranching	raising and breeding cattle
thriving	growing, prospering
irrigation	means of moving water from natural areas (such as lakes and streams) to dry areas for agricultural purposes
domestic	local, in one's own country; as opposed to foreign
conservation	protection, particularly of the natural environment or aspects of it
replenish	put back in abundance that which has been taken away or used
ecologists	people who study the relationship between humans and their natural environment, and who are concerned with the well-being of both
demonstrations	visible political actions by a group of people to make a point for or against an issue
declined	reduced in number
livelihoods	ways of making a living, of being self-supporting

USING NEW WORDS

Fill in each blank with a word from the list above.

❶ Canada put a moratorium (allowed no fishing) on cod-fishing in the Atlantic to help _____ the fish stock.

❷ All of us can participate in _____ by recycling and reusing things such as glass and paper.

❸ Farmers earn their _____ by growing crops or raising livestock.

④ The number of people who stay married to one person all of their adult lives has _____ in Canada.

⑤ Hawaii has a _____ climate, while the Arctic has a harsh climate.

⑥ Canada does not need to import wheat because it has a large _____ supply.

⑦ Vegetable farming in the dry areas of the Fraser Valley in British Columbia and southern Alberta depends on _____.

⑧ Standing on the side of the mountain looking down into the river at the bottom of the _____, the tourist took a wonderful photograph.

⑨ _____ want to put an end to pollution and the wasting of natural resources.

⑩ The students held _____ to protest cuts to education.

⑪ Many farmers combine grain farming with _____ to ensure financial stability.

⑫ Japan and South Korea both have _____ economies that have greatly improved the standard of living in their cities.

MATCHING

Match the words on the left with their opposites on the right. All of the words on the left are used in the text above and some are in the vocabulary list. Refer to a dictionary if you need help.

_____ conservation	a) foreign
_____ domestic	b) narrow; small around
_____ broad	c) waste; destruction of the environment
_____ declined	d) towering
_____ protest	e) cold, harsh
_____ balmy	f) exterior
_____ interior	g) flat, low-lying land
_____ mountainous area	h) support; encourage
_____ short, low to the ground	i) increased

DEBATE

» As we use more of our natural resources, conflicts between those who want to preserve these resources (such as forests and fish) and those who make their living by making use of them (including those in the lumber business and fishing industry) have increased. To examine this issue further, read the following short article and then choose to be either a forestry worker or a conservationist. Make a list of reasons why, from your point of view, large-scale logging should or should not continue in British Columbia.

» Then get together with students who have chosen the same position and prepare for a debate. Discuss your arguments and choose a spokesperson to present them. Some students may wish to be moderators, asking questions of both sides.

Clayoquot Sound

Vancouver Island's southwest coast receives the heaviest rainfall in North America and the woodlands are as dense and jungle-like as the famous rainforests of South America. The old-growth rainforest of Clayoquot Sound has developed over 14 000 years and today is home to a vast variety of plant and animal life. Conservationists are determined to save the complex web of life in this forest.

Logging has been going on in Clayoquot Sound since the beginning of the twentieth century, but the campaign against it has been strongest over the past 20 years. The BC government has set aside some areas as parkland and has limited logging, but this decision pleased neither the conservationists nor the loggers. Immediately after the government announced its decision, people (including students, parents, grandparents, business owners, professionals, and others who rarely take actions against the law) staged demonstrations and blocked loggers' access to the forest along the Pacific Rim Highway. The demonstrators' main concern was clear-cutting, where all the trees in an area are cut down, leaving little of the original forest.

For the loggers, the issue is their livelihood. There are families who depend on the forests of Clayoquot Sound and people who feel they have a right to their jobs. While conservationists want the

Old-growth red cedar in Clayoquot Sound

irreplaceable old-growth trees to remain standing far into the future, forest workers need them today.

Adaptation of "Clayoquot: Where a Hard Rain Falls" from *Beautiful British Columbia Magazine*, Vol. 36, No. 2, Summer 1994, reprinted by permission of Bruce Obee.

Vancouver

Vancouver Harbour at night

Vancouver is a busy, thriving city. Bordered by the Pacific Ocean, the Coast Mountains, and the Fraser Valley, it has an ideal location for many reasons. With its excellent harbour, it is an important port for ships coming in from all over the world. The railroad also brings grain from the prairies, iron ore and coal from mines in various provinces, and lumber from BC and Alberta lumberyards. These goods are then loaded onto ships for transport to Japan, Russia, China, and other destinations.

The same trains load manufactured goods for shipment to the rest of Canada. Vancouver is one of Canada's main centres for exporting and importing.

Vancouver has grown remarkably in recent years. Today Metro Vancouver includes many different municipalities in one large area. Surrounding the harbour to the south is the city of Vancouver itself. To the north is North Vancouver, and to the west of *North Van*, as the locals call it, is West Vancouver or *West Van*. West Vancouver is home to many of the wealthier citizens of the city and has an exclusive area called the British Properties. Immediately east of Vancouver, you find municipalities including Burnaby, Coquitlam, New Westminster, and, further south, Surrey. Some areas to the south of Vancouver are Richmond, White Rock, and Delta. Half the population of the province lives in this Metro Vancouver area.

Culture and Sightseeing

In addition to having a healthy labour market for those in search of work, Vancouver has much to offer its visitors including museums, art galleries, theatres, parks, and unique neighbourhoods. Granville Market in the False Creek area of the harbour is an attractive place to shop or visit. It has many little gift shops and galleries in addition to the market. The market features great quantities of fresh vegetables, fruits, meats, seafood, and baked goods. You may even want to rent a kayak there and see the sights from a different perspective— on the sea. Some people drive their cars into the area, but parking is difficult. Other visitors prefer to come on water taxis, the tiny boats which shuttle back and forth across the harbour to the West End.

Both visitors and Vancouverites like to visit Stanley Park and see the dolphins and whales in the Vancouver Aquarium there, or walk on one of the many trails through the old cedar forests. Many people also stop and have tea at the tea house on Ferguson Point. This is a great place for photographers to take pictures of the Lions Gate Bridge, the swans on the lagoon, or the ships in the harbour. If you want a more active approach to sightseeing, you can go walking or jogging on the seawall which surrounds the park.

Want more shopping? Try Robson Street with its many different shops for tourists and locals alike, or Granville Street which passes through the centre of the city. Some like Gastown with its steam clock and interesting boutiques. Those who cannot afford Gastown go a little further into one of the best Chinatowns in Canada, where there are bargains everywhere and many interesting cultural displays. The Dr. Sun Yat-Sen Classical Chinese Garden in the Ming dynasty style, for example, is the only garden of its kind outside China. The neighbourhood is also lively during the Chinese New Year celebration with the Vancouver Chinese Lion Dance, a parade, and many delicious traditional foods in the restaurants.

If shopping is not your interest, visit the Museum of Anthropology (MOA) on the grounds of the University of British Columbia (UBC). In this very beautiful building, you will see one of the best collections in the world of art and artifacts from various Northwest Coast First Nations. One of the most striking works of art is Bill Reid's *The Raven and the First Men*, a huge wooden sculpture showing an image from a Haida creation myth.

If you like flowers, the Queen Elizabeth Gardens has beautiful gardens planted in and around a restored quarry. When it's raining, you can go into the greenhouse and see the displays there. On Saturday mornings, hundreds of people do their Tai Chi together in the park.

Another attraction is Canada Place, which was originally built for Expo 86. It is a most unusual structure. The architect who designed it modelled it after an ocean liner with a roof of billowing white sails and a docking area. Canada Place houses a hotel, stores, and the Vancouver Convention Centre.

Dr. Sun Yat-Sen Classical Chinese Garden

While Vancouver has as many cars as any large city, many Vancouverites and tourists alike appreciate the SkyTrain system for getting around. These trains fly over the city. The Canada Line was built in preparation for the 2010 Olympics, to carry visitors from the airport to the athletes' village or many other destinations in Vancouver. It is a fast and inexpensive way for anyone to get from the airport into the city.

If you are a skier, Whistler is a very popular spot north of Vancouver that attracts many during the winter ski season. Sailing is another popular sport in this coastal city, and it is a beautiful sight to sit on the beach at English Bay and watch people sailing and kayaking. For a different recreational activity, many places in and around the city have hiking trails and beautiful parks and beaches for all, including the well-known Wreck Beach just below the UBC campus. At this beach, clothing is optional.

Whistler, British Columbia

COMPREHENSION CHECK

1. Name one important export which leaves Canada from Vancouver.
2. What are two locations where tourists to Vancouver might like to shop for gifts?
3. What happens at the Queen Elizabeth Gardens on Saturday mornings?
4. Name some recreational activities Vancouverites and visitors enjoy in and around the city.

VOCABULARY

port	a city where ships can load and unload
exclusive	upper-class
galleries	places where works of art are displayed and sold
perspective	a way of seeing
shuttle (v)	move people or things from one location to another and back again
lagoon	a stretch of salt water separated from the sea by a low sandbank, coral reef, or other barrier
boutiques	small shops which generally specialize in one type of merchandise, such as women's fashions or household decorations

anthropology	the study of humankind, how it developed, its societies, and their customs
artifacts	human-made objects
quarry	an open-air excavation (dig) where stone is removed for use elsewhere
optional	not required

USING NEW WORDS

Fill in each blank with a word from the Vocabulary section.

1. The ferry was used to _____ cars across the small river because there was no bridge.
2. Many conflicts are easily resolved if both people try to see the _____ of the other.
3. _____ are often more expensive than department stores because the goods are unique.
4. Halifax, Montreal, and Toronto are Canada's other large _____ cities.
5. It is more expensive to buy original paintings from _____ than from the artist directly because galleries take a percentage of the sale price.
6. The stones for this old building were taken from the nearby _____.
7. While sunscreen is _____ for sunbathers, it is highly recommended to protect you from UV rays.
8. Every city has at least one _____ (very expensive) neighbourhood. Where is yours?
9. The calm _____ was a perfect place for a swim.
10. Margaret Mead is well-known for her studies in _____.
11. Stone Age tools are a few of the _____ which teach us about our early ancestors.

ROLE PLAY

You work in the tourist information office in Vancouver. A visitor comes in to ask questions about what there is to see and do in the city. The visitor is interested in the following:

» art galleries, especially Northwest Coast First Nations art

» whale-watching

» sampling some fresh Pacific salmon

» photography, especially photos of interesting sites of the city

» gift shopping

Roleplay the conversation. Work in pairs. Find a map of Vancouver online. Use it to point out and discuss some of the interesting sites.

MAKING CONTACT

If you live in Vancouver or you visit there, here are some other suggestions for how you might want to get to know the city and its people a little better.

» Walk the seawall in the west end starting at English Bay and going towards Stanley Park. Sit down on one of the many park benches and talk to others who join you. Ask them what there is to see and do in Vancouver.

» Take a drive out to Steveston Harbour on a Sunday morning and buy fresh fish from the fishermen right off their boats. Ask them what it is like to be a fisherman on the west coast. Try the sablefish (also called Black Cod) if they have it. It is very delicious.

» Buy a cup of coffee at one of the many coffee shops in the city and talk to someone else who is alone. You will see many people sitting outside the coffee shop watching everyone go by. Many will be happy to speak with you.

» Visit the Museum of Anthropology at the University of British Columbia and ask the staff there questions about Aboriginal art, or go to the nearby UBC Botanical Garden and ask about flowers native to the area.

Victoria

Approximately one and a half hours by ferry from Vancouver is the capital city of Victoria. A relatively small but busy city of a third of a million people, Victoria is definitely one of the warmest cities in Canada's cold winters. If you want to be a gardener, enjoy whale-watching, or just plain do not like cold weather, this is the place to be.

The ferry rides to the city are an experience in themselves. The large ferries can take you, your car, and several hundred other people and cars per trip. The ride across the channel is a scenic one as the ferries pass by many of the beautiful Gulf Islands. The ferry ride is also a pleasant way to meet some interesting people. In summer, reservations are recommended for the ferries.

Victoria was originally a British settlement and its British origins are still very evident in the architecture, shops, and polite atmosphere of the city. In the summer, visitors line up to take high tea at the Fairmont Empress Hotel. High tea is an old English custom which includes the serving of tea, dainty sandwiches, scones, and sweets in the mid to late afternoon. The Fairmont Empress Hotel is one of the magnificent old hotels built by the railway companies to attract tourists in the early 1900s. The hotel was built in 1908 and has recently been restored.

It is located near the legislative buildings in the harbour area.

Another aspect of Victoria's British origins are its bed and breakfasts (often called B & Bs). These are homes which rent out bedrooms, many with their own bathroom, and give the guests wholesome and delicious breakfasts in the morning. The homes chosen to be bed and breakfasts are very often large, antique homes with each bedroom decorated in a unique manner, quite unlike hotels. Bed and breakfasts allow you to meet and talk to your hosts and other travellers during your stay. They are a great way to learn about an area as people are generally very willing to share what they know. (Bed and breakfasts are also sometimes less expensive than a hotel and you have the opportunity to share breakfast with some very interesting people.) Bed and breakfasts are also available in many other parts of Canada.

Just to the north of Victoria is one of the city's main attractions, the Butchart Gardens. These may be the most beautiful gardens in Canada and, like the Queen Elizabeth Gardens in Vancouver, have been designed in what used to be an old quarry. While summer may be the best time to see the flowers, the gardens are beautiful at any time of year and are even lit at night for those who

Butchart Gardens

prefer to go in the cool of evening. Midday in July looks like a photographers' convention as busloads of tourists come to this special spot. There are Japanese and Italian gardens, a rose garden, and a spectacular sunken garden.

Near the Butchart Gardens are the Victoria Butterfly Gardens, an indoor tropical garden where birds and butterflies fly about in abundance. They say it is good luck if a butterfly lands on you!

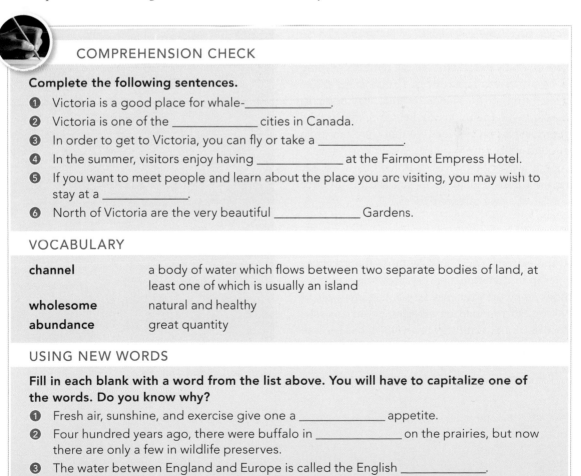

COMPREHENSION CHECK

Complete the following sentences.
1. Victoria is a good place for whale-_____.
2. Victoria is one of the _____ cities in Canada.
3. In order to get to Victoria, you can fly or take a _____.
4. In the summer, visitors enjoy having _____ at the Fairmont Empress Hotel.
5. If you want to meet people and learn about the place you are visiting, you may wish to stay at a _____.
6. North of Victoria are the very beautiful _____ Gardens.

VOCABULARY

channel	a body of water which flows between two separate bodies of land, at least one of which is usually an island
wholesome	natural and healthy
abundance	great quantity

USING NEW WORDS

Fill in each blank with a word from the list above. You will have to capitalize one of the words. Do you know why?
1. Fresh air, sunshine, and exercise give one a _____ appetite.
2. Four hundred years ago, there were buffalo in _____ on the prairies, but now there are only a few in wildlife preserves.
3. The water between England and Europe is called the English _____.

Other Places of Interest

Haida Gwaii (formerly known as the Queen Charlotte Islands)

Just off the coast of central BC are the beautiful Haida Gwaii islands, the home of ancient rainforests and Aboriginal people who have lived in harmony with nature on the islands for centuries. *Haida Gwaii* means *islands of the people*. These beautiful islands are the homeland of the Haida Nation, and you can still see the remains of some of its ancient villages today. Cruise ships make a brief stop at the islands on their way north to Alaska, while many young people prefer to take their bicycles on the ferry so that they can cycle through these lovely islands. Emily Carr, a well-known west-coast artist, painted many of her pictures here and in them you see the ancient rainforest as we can see it today.

The Kootenays

In the extreme south and centre of the province, you can find a number of very interesting communities along the Kootenay Lakes. The small city of Nelson, surrounded on all sides by the majestic Rockies, is an old railway town which has become a chosen home for many diverse groups of people. Nelson, like many other areas of BC, is home to a Doukhobor community. Today's Doukhobors

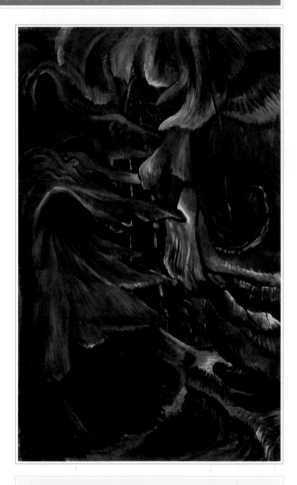

Cedar, by Emily Carr

are descendants of immigrants who came from Russia in search of religious freedom many years ago. Some are very conservative in following their old religious customs, while others are indistinguishable from their neighbours.

At the July 1st Canada Day celebration in Nelson, you can also see ranchers in their cowboy boots and hats, long-haired hippies who settled in the Slocan and Kootenay areas in the 1960s, Wiccans (modern-day witches) in long black cloaks, as well as many other Canadians of all ethnicities. Beside the hamburger stand is an equally busy stand selling veggie burgers to the many vegetarians in the area. There are many New Age communities along the Kootenay Lakes and, as a result, you find not only good vegetarian food but also high-quality bookstores with alternative collections of books and many small industries producing arts and crafts for sale. All in all, this is a very interesting area for a summer vacation.

The Okanagan Valley

Winery in the Okanagan Valley

Further west and north lies the hot, dry Okanagan Valley where so much of western Canada's fruit and wine come from. The communities of Penticton, Kelowna, and Summerland play host to vast numbers of tourists all summer long. The tourists come to frolic on the sandy beaches of the large, cool Okanagan Lake. Local legend says that the Ogopogo monster (a very large marine reptile which has never been proven to exist) lives in the lake and children are warned not to venture too far away from shore!

National and Provincial Parks

BC has a number of beautiful wilderness parks in the mountains. On the province's eastern fringes in nearby Alberta lie Jasper and Banff National Parks. Yoho National Park is just west of Banff. In addition there are several smaller provincial parks with lovely campsites where tourists come early if they want to pitch a tent or park a trailer. And Ogopogo is not BC's only monster. In the mountains, we are all cautioned to look out for the Sasquatch, a large hairy creature said to be a link between human and ape. Although many footprints have been spotted and a few photos taken of this hairy beast, the Sasquatch keeps largely to himself (or herself) and has never been captured!

These mountain areas are famous all over the world and mountain climbers come to challenge their peaks. Less-skilled climbers may still find wonderful hiking areas, as long as they take care to protect themselves from attack by grizzly bears or other wild animals. Overnight campers must register with the appropriate park authorities and are encouraged to handle food carefully so that, at night, all food is well away from their tents, hoisted high into the air over a tree branch. Some hikers wear bells on their ankles to warn animals they are coming. In addition, these hikers never get between a mother bear and her cub!

Campers are also asked to be very careful with fires, as many forest fires are started when campfires are not extinguished properly. Since BC's economy depends on its forest products, these fires can be extremely costly as well as wasteful and dangerous.

COMPREHENSION CHECK

1. Canada's version of Scotland's famous Loch Ness monster is the _____ of Okanagan Lake.
2. Canada's version of the abominable snowman (said to live in the Himalayas) is the _____ of BC's mountain areas.
3. In what community can you find Doukhobors, older hippies, and Wiccans, among others?
4. How do some hikers protect themselves from bears while hiking?
5. Where did the Doukhobors originally come from?

VOCABULARY

indistinguishable	unable to be seen apart from other things around it; the same as its environment
hippies	the name given to people in the 1960s who left traditional working ways to live simply in nature
frolic	play in a carefree manner, like a child
venture	go forth, as in search of adventure
peaks	tops of mountains
hoist	lift up
warn	signal danger to
cub	a baby bear
extinguish	put out

USING NEW WORDS

1. There are three nouns in the vocabulary list. What are they?
2. Here are four verbs from the vocabulary list: *venture, hoist, warn,* and *extinguish.* Fill in the blanks below with the best verb.

   _____ into the unknown.

   _____ that match!

   _____ your neighbours that a storm is coming.

   _____ the sack into the truck.

   All of these can be considered as commands. Make them into full sentences by adding a subject.

3. There is one adjective in the vocabulary list above. Which preposition does this adjective take after it: *in, to, with,* or *from*? Complete the following sentence with the adjective and the correct preposition.

   Salt is almost _____ _____ sugar, unless you taste them!

FOR DISCUSSION

» People have many different ways to travel such as flying, going by train or bus, driving, cycling, or walking. Which ways, in your opinion, best enable you to enjoy the places you are passing through? Why?

» The hippie generation rejected what they saw as the workaday, materialistic lifestyle of their parents' generation in favour of living communally and simply in more natural settings. Can you think of other groups of people who have rejected the traditions of their culture and chosen new ways of living? Have you ever wanted to do something really different from what your parents expected you to do?

» Camping is a recreational activity enjoyed by many Canadians in the summer. Have you camped? If so, discuss your camping adventures with your classmates. If not, what stops you?

CHAPTER REVIEW

Unscramble the following words found in this chapter's vocabulary lists. Clues are given on the right.

1 march _____ (when you have this, you can often get you what you want!)
2 buh _____ (the centre of activity)
3 loocegists _____ (people who want to save old trees)
4 dimn _____ (I don't _____; do you?)
5 darce _____ (an evergreen)
6 aiennct _____ (very old)
7 desticmo _____ (not foreign)
8 shrah _____ (a characteristic of winter on the Atlantic coast)
9 yamlb _____ (a characteristic of winter on the Pacific coast)
10 ropt _____ (Vancouver and Halifax are both called _____ cities.)
11 rawn _____ (you need to _____ someone of danger!)
12 pihieps _____ (These flower children of the sixties sang, "All you need is love!")

(You can find the answers on page 251 at the back of the book.)

Chapter Seven

The Prairie Provinces

Quick Facts

Alberta

» Alberta joined Confederation in 1905.

» The province has a population of approximately 3.8 million.

» The two major urban centres are Edmonton and Calgary.

» Primary industries include oil and gas, agriculture, and pulp and paper.

» The provincial flower is the wild rose; the provincial bird is the great-horned owl.

Saskatchewan

» Saskatchewan also joined Confederation in 1905.

» It has a population of approximately 1 million.

» Primary industries are farming and mining.

» Saskatchewan has two major urban centres, Saskatoon and Regina.

» The provincial flower is the western red lily; the provincial bird is the sharp-tailed grouse.

Manitoba

» Manitoba joined Confederation in 1870.

» The province's population is approximately 1.3 million.

» The capital city is Winnipeg, the only large city in Manitoba.

» Primary industries are manufacturing, agriculture, food production, and mining.

» The provincial flower is the prairie crocus; the provincial bird is the great grey owl.

Introduction

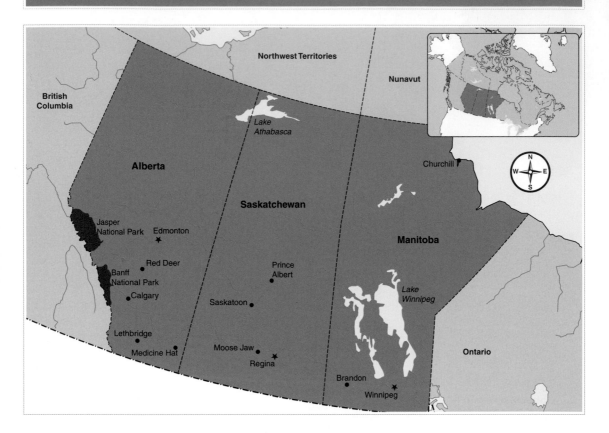

The Prairie Provinces are often thought of as the "bread basket" of Canada because of the amount of wheat and other grains grown in their southern regions. While the word *prairie* calls forth images of dry, flat, monotonous lands, these three provinces actually have a variety of landscapes ranging from the mountains bordering western Alberta, to the tundra in the north, to the forests and streams of the Cypress Hills which straddle the Alberta-Saskatchewan border in the south. The forests in the northern regions have not changed much over time, but the grassy hills of the southern prairies, once covered with buffalo, have been turned to agricultural use.

Alberta is the most populated of the three provinces with two large urban centres, Edmonton and Calgary. These centres, along with Winnipeg in Manitoba, and Regina and Saskatoon in Saskatchewan, are thriving cities with immigrants from every land counting themselves citizens. The rural areas were also settled by people from many different countries such as Germany, Ukraine, Iceland, Denmark, Scotland, England, and Ireland where agriculture had played a large role in people's lives. There are still communities where these cultures remain strong and intact. These immigrants came seeking freedom and opportunity. The prairies of the west gave them both. Recently, immigrants from many other countries have added to the cultural mix.

Alberta

Geography and Economy

Bounded by the Rockies on the west and the plains of Saskatchewan on the east, Alberta is the prairie province that has the greatest variety of geographical features. A visitor can find treeless prairie in the south, spectacular ice-capped mountain peaks in the west, rolling foothills east of the mountains, and parkland of grass and trees in the north.

Alberta's climate is typical of the Prairie Provinces: long, cold winters and short, hot summers. In the southern half of the province, the much-appreciated chinook winds bring warmth in the middle of winter to melt the snow. Spring comes later than in most of Canada, usually not until late April and May. September and October are fall months and are enjoyed for good temperatures, gentle weather, and—after the first frost comes—no mosquitoes!

With the variety of landscapes in the province comes an equally diverse economy. There is grain farming in south and central Alberta. Vegetable farming in southern Alberta includes a large sugar-beet industry. Cattle ranching takes place all over the province, but is on a particularly large scale in the High River area south of Calgary. The pulp and paper industry creates the bulk of the jobs in the Hinton-Edson area west of Edmonton. Lumber is cut from the vast stands of timber in the north and west of the province.

Alberta's most important industry, however, is oil and gas. Since the first major oil discovery at Leduc in 1947, the industry has grown and been a major factor in the prosperity of the province. Today, Alberta still has the lowest provincial income tax rate of any province in Canada and is the only province to remain free of a provincial sales tax. This is a popular factor for tourists who come here from other parts of Canada for holidays and shopping.

The oil sands near Fort McMurray are a significant and controversial feature of today's

Cattle ranching takes place throughout Alberta

economy in Alberta and in Canada. The oil sands contain enough crude oil to make Canada second only to Saudi Arabia in supplying oil to the world. On the one hand, the province receives a lot of income from royalties on the oil extracted in Alberta. Many Albertans have jobs related to this resource and Americans get 15 percent of their oil supply from Alberta, much of which is from the oil sands. On the other hand, many people are concerned about the environmental damage done to the land and to Alberta's water supply due to the process which has been used to extract the bitumen from the oil sands. This is a constant challenge for the industry and for the Alberta government. The industry keeps the public informed as they continue to find and use better ways to protect our water supply and restore our land.

Manufacturing, such as food and chemical processing, and tourism are other important industries in the province. Greater Edmonton is home to manufacturers of many chemicals and plastics made from the material taken from the oil sands, as well as several oil refineries.

Tourism is a major industry for Albertans, too, as millions of tourists come to visit the Rocky Mountain parks, such as Jasper and Banff, and Alberta's cities each year.

The Sister Cities: Edmonton and Calgary

Alberta's two largest cities are Edmonton and Calgary, both healthy communities of similar size. They are sister cities, and like many sisters, they are always competing with each other. Both cities are fiercely supportive of their hockey teams, the Calgary Flames and the Edmonton Oilers. When the Stanley Cup playoffs begin in the spring, Albertans are glued to their TV sets to watch the games and cheer on their favourite team.

Edmonton, located in the centre of the province and divided by the North Saskatchewan River, is Alberta's capital city. It is also the heart of the oil-refining and petrochemical industries in the province. The metropolitan area has a population of 1.3 million and is an ethnic mosaic. People from all over the world have come to live in Edmonton. One of the earliest groups—who came in the late 1800s and early 1900s—the Ukrainians, still have a major presence in the city and its surrounding area. Thanks to them, Edmontonians are all familiar with cabbage rolls and perogis!

Edmonton has many features of a large and thriving centre. It has the largest of Alberta's universities, the University of Alberta, which has a full-time enrollment of nearly 40 000 students. In 2009, Grant MacEwan College, also located in Edmonton, became Grant MacEwan University. The city plays host to the Edmonton Oilers hockey team, which won the Stanley Cup four times in five seasons from 1984 to 1988 with the leadership of the now-legendary Wayne Gretzky or "Number 99." The other team of which Edmontonians have been proud through the years is the Edmonton Eskimos football team, which plays in the Canadian Football League (CFL).

A favourite spot for visitors to Edmonton is the West Edmonton Mall, one of the largest shopping centres in the world. It has an indoor water park, an ice rink for skating, an amusement park, submarines, aquatic animals, a large hotel, and over 800 shops and services with parking for 20 000 cars. If you drive there, you do not want to forget where you parked! This unusual mall is the amazing achievement of an immigrant family, the Ghermezians, who came to Canada from Iran in the 1960s and opened a carpet business.

Visitors to Edmonton in summer can also enjoy the many summer festivals held throughout July and August, including the Edmonton Folk Music Festival and the Edmonton International Fringe Theatre Festival (showcasing alternative theatre). The Art Gallery of Alberta attracts many to the city's downtown with its unique architecture, and Edmontonians enjoy the quality of the frequently changing exhibitions there. The Winspear Centre hosts the Edmonton Symphony Orchestra and many other performers who appreciate a fine concert hall.

Calgary's crowning achievement was the hosting of the 1988 Winter Olympics. Canada watched with pride as thousands of Calgarian volunteers made the world feel welcome. A city of 1 090 000 people, Calgary has a thriving business community with head offices for many American firms doing business in Canada. It is also the location for many Canadian industries concerned with oil and gas or agriculture.

The Art Gallery of Alberta in Edmonton

The people of Calgary still enjoy the excellent sports facilities built for the 1988 Olympics, such as the famous Olympic Saddledome. The National Hockey League's Calgary Flames play in this unique arena, which has a roof in the shape of a saddle to reflect the city's cattle driving history. The Stampeders football team also draws many fans to its CFL games. Visitors interested in history can go to the Glenbow Museum, which has an impressive collection on the history of the Canadian west and its Aboriginal peoples.

Like Edmonton, Calgary boasts two fine universities, the University of Calgary and the newer Mount Royal University, formerly known as Mount Royal College.

For years, a source of celebration and tourist dollars for Calgarians has been the Calgary Stampede, a large, old-fashioned rodeo where cowboys and cowgirls compete for prizes in steer-riding, bull-riding, and chuckwagon racing. Meanwhile, the public welcomes the opportunity to wear cowboy hats (called stetsons) and enjoy country and western music and dancing. The Stampede, as it's called by Albertans, has stood the test of time, and honours the ranching roots of southern Alberta. Calgary's proximity to Banff (it is only one and a half hours by car), as well as its lovely riverside parks, make it a pleasant city in which to live.

Spruce Meadows is an internationally known and very popular equestrian show-jumping facility that attracts the finest riders and their horses from all over the world. It is located on the southwest fringe of Calgary. The track is beautifully laid out and spectators come year round to visit this facility.

Calgarians elected Canada's first Muslim mayor, Naheed Nenshi, in 2010. A former professor at Mount Royal University, Nenshi had a strong message and packaged it in diverse social media, which many feel may have won him the election. He reached out to the younger generation, many of whom had never before bothered to vote, and they said, "Yes!"

Other cities of importance in Alberta are Lethbridge (Alberta's southernmost city and the site of the University of Lethbridge); Red Deer, halfway between Edmonton and Calgary; Medicine Hat in the southeastern corner; and Grande Prairie and Peace River in the northern part of the province. Fort MacMurray joins these smaller centres as a rapidly growing service community for the oil sands industries in Alberta's north.

Rocky Mountain Parks

Alberta is fortunate to have many national and provincial parks, including the world-famous Jasper and Banff National Parks. Jasper is a four-hour drive from Edmonton or a pleasant stop on the train west to Vancouver. Motorists can drive the breathtakingly beautiful stretch of highway between Jasper and Banff and stop at the Columbia Icefield or Lake Louise, only two of many exceptional places to visit. Lake Louise is famous for the lovely green colour of its waters. The Columbia Icefield is 325 square kilometres of glacial ice and snow formed over thousands of years. Visitors to the Icefield take the trip across the large glacier in specially designed buses with gigantic tires. In the winter, the ski slopes of Banff and Jasper attract skiers from all over the world.

Further south near the American border is Waterton Lakes National Park, a smaller but equally lovely park in the Rockies. Waterton borders Glacier National Park in the US, home to a significant number of grizzly bears. Grizzlies are known for their unpredictability and are considered the largest and most dangerous of the bears in Canadian parks.

Prince of Wales Hotel in Waterton Lakes National Park

Dinosaurs, Badlands, and Hoodoos

Archaeologists think of dinosaurs when they think of Alberta. The badlands area in southern Alberta around Red Deer and Drumheller is one of the largest sites of dinosaur fossils in the world. The story of these ancient dinosaurs is told at the famous Royal Tyrrell Museum northwest of Dinosaur Provincial Park. When you see the hoodoos—tall, thin sandstone pillars—in this area, you can easily imagine these large reptilian creatures wandering about the land. Two large valleys in this area also provide spectacularly unusual scenery for tourists.

Dinosaur skeleton at the Royal Tyrrell Museum in Drumheller

COMPREHENSION CHECK

Ask a question that will give you each answer below.
1. oil and gas
2. Ghermezian family
3. the 1988 Winter Olympics
4. Wayne Gretzky
5. a rodeo
6. Dinosaur Provincial Park

VOCABULARY

be glued to (the TV)	watch (the TV) for hours at a time
monotonous	with little variety, boring
bounded by	bordered by; on the boundary of
foothills	low, rounded hills found between mountain and lowland or prairie landscapes
frost	white, frozen dew coating the ground at night and found on windows
on a large scale	in large measure; usually referring to human activity
bulk of	majority of
vast	of very great size, or many in number
timber	trees destined to be cut for lumber
prosperity	state of wealth and success
roughly	approximately, about
straight	without interruption

perogis	small Ukrainian boiled dumplings with a flour pastry on the outside and various fillings such as cottage cheese or potato and bacon. They are usually served with sour cream.
legendary	famous for extraordinary achievements
proximity to	closeness to
breathtakingly	surprisingly, amazingly; enough to take one's breath away
exceptional	unusually good, outstanding
glacier	large, slowly moving, ancient body of ice
gigantic	huge, unusually large in size
slopes	hills and mountainsides with trails for skiing
dinosaurs	very large reptiles of the ancient past which are now extinct (have died out)
badlands	flat, dry, desert-like land in the prairies; often with hoodoo land formations near old, dried-out riverbeds
fossils	the remains or impressions of a plant or animal hardened in rock

USING NEW WORDS

Fill in each blank with a word or term from the list above.

1. During spring break, those high-school students who can afford it often go to the ski _____ in Alberta and BC.
2. There is a lot of ranching done in the _____ of Alberta.
3. Canada is _____ three different oceans to the north, east, and west, and by the United States (US) to the south.
4. Giving birth to a child can be _____ painful.
5. Canada has _____ areas of wilderness.
6. One cabinetmaker can make relatively few cupboards, but a factory can produce them _____.
7. The person who owns the land also owns the _____ growing on that land.
8. The three Prairie Provinces are _____ similar in size.
9. The man had gone 15 years _____ without having a drink of alcohol.
10. Be sure to pick your tomatoes before the first _____.

FOR DISCUSSION

» Why do you think that dinosaurs became extinct?

» What are some advantages and disadvantages of having a mega-mall in your city?

» Most communities have some sort of summer celebration such as a rodeo or a festival. What is the main purpose of these events? Does your community have one? What about the community you used to live in? Compare your experiences of these celebrations with those of your classmates.

» As water becomes a more and more precious commodity, some business people want to bottle water from the glaciers in our parks and sell it. What do you think of this idea?

Saskatchewan

When people think of Saskatchewan, they think of golden fields of grain blowing gently under blue summer skies. They think of peaceful small towns with the inevitable grain elevator beside the railroad track, although the old wooden grain elevators are fast disappearing. Saskatchewan is defined by its farming communities. The number of farms, however, has been declining since the beginning of the century. Falling prices, rising costs, and challenges such as BSE (bovine spongiform encephalopathy, a disease cows can catch) were all difficult and discouraging for farmers. In Saskatchewan, everyone cares about the farmers because, if the farmers have a bad year, everyone has a bad year!

Saskatchewan is one of the largest wheat producers in the world and definitely the largest in Canada. Other seeds and grains of importance to the economy are canola, rye, oats, barley, and flax. These grains are grown on the fertile prairie land in the southern third of the province. Oil and potash, which is used in the production of fertilizers, are also important resources. Saskatchewan is the largest exporter of potash in the world. In the rugged Canadian Shield of the north, valuable minerals such as gold, copper, and uranium are mined. The recent exploration and development of oil fields in Saskatchewan is the new and exciting change in the economy. The government is moving slowly to avoid mistakes, for this huge resource in Saskatchewan promises bounty in the years ahead.

The province has some beautiful parkland area as well. The Qu'Appelle Valley in southern Saskatchewan has some pleasant green hills and lakes, a welcome respite from the flat, dry southern landscape. Various other prairie lakes dot the province and provide pleasant camping areas for city dwellers who want to relax in the country. Most people are surprised to learn that 12 percent of the province's area is covered by freshwater lakes, streams, and rivers.

Like its neighbours, Saskatchewan has a continental climate: hot in the summer and cold in the winter. In the city of Regina, the average daytime temperature in January is minus 11 degrees

The Qu'appelle Valley in southern Saskatchewan

Celsius, while in July it is 26.3 degrees. That is quite a difference! Saskatoon, which is a little further north, is slightly cooler in summer, and one degree colder in the winter.

The seasons on the prairies are very distinct, and Saskatchewan's weather is much like Alberta's, although the south can get hotter in summer, as it is further from the mountains.

In the Prairie Provinces (and across Canada), two temperatures are often given in the weather report during the winter—the temperature on the thermometer and another which includes the wind chill. If there is a strong wind blowing in cold weather, the temperature feels much, much colder than what it says on the thermometer. If the temperature is minus 27 degrees, the wind chill might be minus 32 degrees if it's a little windy. Canadians get used to dressing warmly for prairie winters because, on a cold day, exposed skin can freeze in minutes!

Saskatchewan has a personality all its own. Shaped perhaps by the harshness of the Depression years, when everyone was poor, the people of Saskatchewan learned how to stick together, to help one another. During the "Dirty Thirties," as those hard years were called, the cooperative movement was strengthened by the creation of the Saskatchewan Wheat Pool. Farmers had not been getting fair prices for their crops and so they agreed to sell their wheat to a Wheat Pool at a fair price and then the Wheat Pool would sell it to buyers. This was the foundation for Saskatchewan's election of the Co-operative Commonwealth Federation, the first socialist government in North America, in 1944. Tommy Douglas, premier of Saskatchewan from 1944 to 1961 and then leader of the newly created New Democratic Party from 1961 to 1971, was also the champion of public healthcare and is known by Canadians as the Father of Medicare.

Regina and Saskatoon

Saskatchewan's two main cities are Regina, the capital city, and Saskatoon. Regina has a population of over 215 000 and is the corporate centre of the province. Because Regina is located in such a dry area, a reservoir was deepened to create Wascana Lake. Today the 920 hectares of lake and park area are the heart of the city, and the Wascana Centre includes the Legislative Building, the University of Regina, an arts centre, art gallery, and museum.

All Royal Canadian Mounted Police (RCMP) officers in the country receive their basic training in Regina. Canadians commonly call these police officers "Mounties." The RCMP Musical Ride is famous all over the world. In their scarlet dress uniforms, the officers make a magnificent picture as they put their black horses through their paces to the beat of lively music. Regina also has a museum that traces the history of the RCMP.

Saskatoon is often called the City of Bridges

Saskatoon is the province's largest city with more than 265 000 people. The South Saskatchewan River, which passes through the city, is spanned by seven bridges and so Saskatoon is often called The City of Bridges. In fact, the city gets its name from the Cree word for the delicious wild berries that grow in the area, known as saskatoon berries. (If you have never tasted saskatoon pie and saskatoon jam, you do not know what you are missing!) Saskatoon is also the business and service centre for the central and northern parts of the province. Both the minerals from the north and the farm products of the south pass through the city.

Like Regina, Saskatoon is a cultural centre with theatres, art galleries, music halls, and museums, including two museums dedicated to Ukrainian culture. A museum on the grounds of the University of Saskatchewan celebrates one of the province's most famous citizens, John Diefenbaker. Diefenbaker was prime minister of Canada in the 1950s. An attractive, well-planned city, most residents agree that Saskatoon is a very good place to live.

The Cypress Hills: An Oasis in the South

One surprising little corner of Saskatchewan is the Cypress Hills in the extreme southwest of the province. This is a pleasant oasis of green hills and valleys. The area is home to some species of plant and animal life not found anywhere else in Canada—a small scorpion, for example. Unlike the dry prairies which surround the area, the Cypress Hills region has many fresh water springs which nurture its green slopes.

COMPREHENSION CHECK

1. Why are grain elevators located beside the railway tracks in Saskatchewan?
2. If the farmers have a bad year, why does everyone in the community have a bad year?
3. What happens to exposed skin on a very cold winter today if a person is not dressed appropriately?
4. How did the difficult conditions of the "Dirty Thirties" prompt political change in Saskatchewan?
5. Where does Canada's federal police force receive its training?

VOCABULARY

inevitable	sure to occur; unavoidable
livestock	animals which are raised for food
canola	a plant used for making edible oil
respite	rest or relief
continental climate	climate with wide seasonal variations in temperature
wind chill	the temperature which takes into account the additional feeling of cold created by winter winds
expose	reveal or leave uncovered
put through paces	an idiom which means to require to perform a series of actions
spanned	extended across
oasis	1. a fertile spot in the midst of a dry, inhospitable area 2. a place of calm in the midst of chaos
springs	flows of water rising naturally from the earth
medicare	the name Canadians have for universal healthcare as a right of all Canadians

USING NEW WORDS

Fill in each blank with a word or term from the list above.

1. The first thing John wanted to do on Christmas Day was _____ his new computer _____ its _____. (an idiom)
2. By law, Iranian women must not _____ their hair in public; they must cover their hair.
3. In Banff, there are natural hot _____ which smell like sulphur but are said to be very healthy to bathe in.
4. One's home should be an _____ away from the pressures of the workaday world.
5. In most cities, you are not allowed to raise _____ in your yard.
6. Success is almost _____ for the person who believes in himself or herself, is honest and kind to others, and works hard.

❼ When the mother turned on the radio and heard what the _____ factor was, she quickly put scarves and mittens on her children before they left for school.

❽ Hawaii has a tropical climate while the prairies have a _____.

MIX AND MATCH

Match each seed or grain listed below with one of its common uses on the right.

oats	used for making linen
wheat	tastes great in beef soup
canola	a favourite hot breakfast cereal
flax	used for making whisky
rye	the most common ingredient in bread
barley	used for making cooking oil

FOR DISCUSSION

» How can you protect yourself from frostbite in the cold winter months?

» Read sentence number 6 in the Using New Words section. Do you agree or disagree with this statement? Why?

WHAT'S IN A NAME?

How do places get their names? Often, a name tells us about a place's history, its environment, or its people. How did the Qu'Appelle Valley get its name? *Qu'appelle* is French for *who calls*. The story behind the name comes from an Aboriginal legend. Paddling his canoe across Katepwa Lake, a young warrior heard his dying lover call his name. When he was told of her death, he was so stricken with grief that he drowned himself in the lake. People say their voices can still be heard in the wind that blows through the valley.

» Find out how the following prairie places got their names and then share the story with a partner. The book *Place Names of Canada* and the *Canadian Encyclopedia* website are useful resources for this exercise.

Regina, Saskatchewan	Selkirk, Manitoba
Medicine Hat, Alberta	Prince Albert, Saskatchewan
Winnipeg, Manitoba	Portage-la-Prairie, Manitoba
Moose Jaw, Saskatchewan	

FOR FURTHER RESEARCH

» There is a large First Nations population in Saskatchewan and they have a very interesting history. You may want to go online and research Big Bear (Mistahimaskwa) and Poundmaker (Pitikwahanapiwiyin). Both were highly respected Cree chiefs in the days when the treaties were being signed and the Northwest Rebellion was underway in the late nineteenth century.

Manitoba

Manitoba is the oldest of the Prairie Provinces, and while it is similar to its neighbours in some ways, it is very different in others. The province has a colourful history and is well-known for its Red River settlers and the Red River Rebellion in 1870. Louis Riel is remembered as a hero by the Métis people for standing up for their rights. He was hanged as a traitor by the Canadian government, but is remembered with respect for gaining Manitobans rights they might not otherwise have had: the official use of French and English, the right to Catholic and Protestant schools, and the right of the Métis people to vote.

Prairie landscape makes up only about one-fifth of Manitoba and is found in the south and southwest. Much of the north is Canadian Shield, and there is tundra in the far northeast. Agriculture, while still significant, is perhaps a little less important in the province than people may think.

Statue of Louis Riel in Winnipeg

Manufacturing is Manitoba's largest industry and products include foods, transportation equipment, clothing and textiles, and machinery. Agriculture is the second-largest industry, followed by the food industry, mining, and construction.

Manitoba has a population of 1.2 million, with 760 000 people living in Winnipeg, the capital city. Located only a short distance from the United States border, Winnipeg is nonetheless the heart of Manitoba.

Winnipeg: Heart of Manitoba

Like Canada's other large urban centres, Winnipeg is an ethnically diverse city. More than 38 000 people of Filipino origins live in the city, for example, and the Filipino community is not the only one in Winnipeg to maintain a strong sense of its ethnic heritage. Approximately 40 000 people in the Winnipeg region identify themselves as francophone. The Mennonites, a religious group originally from Germany, are another strong community in southern Manitoba and have their national Mennonite Central Committee offices in Winnipeg.

Many countries have consulates in the city, and there is strong support for learning heritage languages. The University of Manitoba offers credit courses for teachers wanting to learn how to teach heritage languages. In many schools, children can participate in heritage language programs after regular school hours.

The city supports two dynamic universities, the older University of Manitoba in the south of the city, and the newer but very successful University of Winnipeg located in the downtown area.

Like Regina, Winnipeg has very hot summers and very cold winters. The average temperature in January during the day is minus 13.2 degrees Celsius, while at night it is minus 23.6 degrees—and that is without the wind chill! In addition, it is often very humid in Winnipeg due to the presence of Lake Winnipeg to the north. The humidity makes it seem even hotter in summer and colder in winter than it actually is.

Lake Winnipeg is a popular place during the summer months when thousands of Winnipeggers escape the heat to go to their cabins on Grand Beach or just drive up to spend the day at the beach. Some people say you will not see nicer fine, white sand dunes anywhere. The park there gets so crowded that it sometimes has to be closed to additional visitors. There are many other lakes and parks in Manitoba for summer recreation.

The city of Winnipeg also has many parks and three rivers passing through it. Unfortunately, most of the land around the rivers is privately owned with no public access. The city's largest park is Assiniboine Park, which has a zoo, botanical gardens, and bike trails. Older than other prairie cities, Winnipeg has some wonderful historic architecture.

A favourite gathering place for Winnipeggers year-round is The Forks. This downtown spot has been a gathering place for over 6000 years. Archaelogists have found evidence of Aboriginal encampments and there is an interpretive centre onsite for those interested in this early history. There is also a marketplace, hotel, restaurants and coffee shops, a children's museum, and year-round attractions of interest to the whole community.

Winnipeg has gained recognition as a major cultural centre in the country, though it is smaller in population than Canada's other large cities, including Edmonton and Calgary. Winnipeg has not only Canada's Royal Winnipeg Ballet, but also an active symphony association, a thriving theatre community in both English and French, and a lovely concert hall. Folklorama is a summer festival celebrating the diverse cultures which make up the city.

Have you ever wondered where Canada's money is made? The Royal Canadian Mint in Winnipeg makes the coins we use every day. Winnipeg also has the distinction of being at the geographical centre of Canada, in spite of the fact that most people think of Ontario as "central" Canada.

One other very interesting feature of Winnipeg is the large floodway that diverts water excess from the Red River and channels it back into the river east of the city. Winnipeg sits flat at a low elevation, and has suffered major spring and summer floods many times at a cost of billions of dollars in rebuilding. The 1950 flood caused a state of emergency to be declared and led to the building of this spectacular engineering feat. It extends a distance of 47 kilometres and cost 63 billion dollars to construct when completed in 1968. It is estimated that the floodway has saved over 10 billion dollars since it was built. It is second only to the Panama Canal in terms of the amount of earth that needed to be moved to build it. In 2008, an expansion project was begun to widen the floodway and dramatically increase the level of flood protection.

Other Areas of Interest

Manitoba's second-largest city is Brandon, located on the Assiniboine River in the south. The city is a service centre for the fertile farmlands of southern Manitoba, has a small university, and is close to many lakes and parks in the surrounding region. To the south of Brandon on the Canada-US border is the International Peace Garden, which is meant to symbolize good relations between the two countries.

A community of special interest in the north is Churchill, a port on Hudson Bay. This is Canada's only seaport on the Arctic Ocean and is open for navigation just three months of the year. Adventurous tourists who go there may see polar bears, beluga whales, and other interesting wildlife. The beluga whales feed at the mouth of the Churchill River, and the polar bears gather in the fall to wait for the bay to freeze before they go out onto the ice to hunt.

Polar bears in Churchill

COMPREHENSION CHECK

1. Louis Riel was a member of what community?
2. What is the primary industry in Manitoba?
3. What major project was completed in 1968 and has saved over 10 billion dollars since its completion?
4. What is the name of the place where Canadian coins are manufactured?
5. What is the name of a port in Manitoba and how many months of the year is it open for ships?

VOCABULARY

traitor	a person thought to have betrayed the government or the people
Mennonites	a religious group which originally fled persecution in Germany
dynamic	very alive and active
humid	warm and damp; humidity describes the degree of moisture in the air
access	a means of approach or entrance
shifting	moving
fertile	productive
symbolize	represent
navigation	the activity of setting a course, as for shipping on water

USING NEW WORDS

Fill in each blank with a word from the list above.

1. Only the bank manager and her assistant had _____ to the safe.
2. Once a person is known to be a _____, people do not trust him or her.
3. The air was so _____ that his glasses became steamy.
4. The _____ land produces vegetables and fruits, which are not only tasty but also healthy.
5. A _____ individual is more likely to succeed in a job interview than a person who shows no energy at all.
6. There is usually a _____ of values from generation to generation because the world is always changing.
7. The colours of a country's flag are always meant to _____ things that will inspire citizens to patriotism (love of country).

FOR DISCUSSION

» Louis Riel was hanged as a traitor and yet most people today regard him as a hero. Why was he regarded as a traitor in the past? Can you think of other situations where time has changed public opinion about a person or event?

» Do you think that lakeshore and riverside property should belong to private individuals or be available for use by all the people in a community? Why?

RESEARCH AND WRITE

» The following people are all famous Canadians from Manitoba. Choose one and do some research to find out more about the person and why he or she is famous. Write a short profile about the individual's life and accomplishments.

Evelyn Hart   Margaret Laurence   Ovide Mercredi

Gabrielle Roy   Arthur Meighen   Edward Shreyer

CHAPTER REVIEW

What is an animal you might find in Alberta's Rocky Mountain parks? Find the answer by completing the following puzzle.

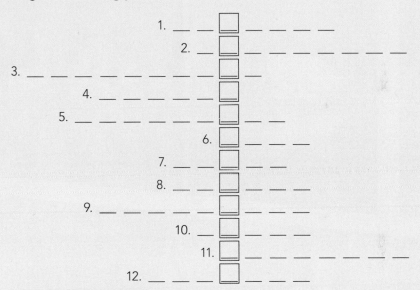

Clues

1. Canada's westernmost Prairie Province
2. ancient extinct reptiles
3. a university town in southern Alberta
4. Saskatchewan's most important export after wheat
5. a prairie city named after a wild berry
6. a Métis hero
7. Canada's oldest national park
8. another popular Rocky Mountain national park
9. a popular place for polar bears in Manitoba
10. animals that campers need to beware of
11. the hometown of the Oilers hockey team
12. a popular pastime of Canadians in the wilderness

(You can find the answers to this puzzle on page 251 at the back of the book.)

Chapter Eight

Central Canada: Ontario

Quick Facts

» Ontario was one of the original four provinces in Confederation in 1867.

» With over 13.5 million people, it is the most heavily populated province in Canada.

» The capital and largest city is Toronto.

» The Greater Toronto Area has a population of 5.8 million, making it the largest city in Canada.

» In 2010, 50 percent of the population of Toronto had been born outside Canada.

» Toronto produces more than half of the country's manufactured goods.

» The provincial flower is the white trillium; the provincial bird is the common loon.

Introduction

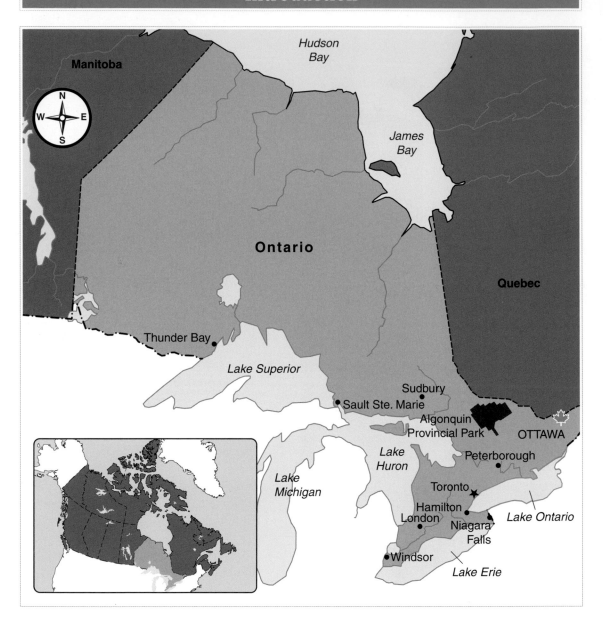

Ontario may not be at the geographical centre of Canada, but in other ways we can say that it deserves to be part of the region called Central Canada. It was one of the first parts of Canada to be settled, after Quebec, and has a rich history. From its early days, when it was known as Upper Canada, to the present, southern Ontario has been at the economic and political centre of the country.

Landscape and Climate

Although Ontario has the second-largest area of any Canadian province, only one-third of the land is considered truly hospitable. The remaining two-thirds is the rough terrain of the Canadian Shield with its great forests and rocky outcroppings, including some of the oldest rock on the face of the earth. While this rocky landscape is not good for agriculture, the land in the small southern area of the province is rich and fertile. The majority of Ontario's population of over 13 million people lives on the fertile plains in the southern part of the province around the Great Lakes.

One great dilemma in this area is the continual pressure the ever-growing population places on the valuable agricultural land. With more than a third of the country's people squeezed into this relatively small area, it is increasingly difficult to protect the farmland against the demand for more housing and services.

Ontario actually enjoys tremendous variation in its climate and landscape from north to south. In addition to the Canadian Shield, there are the Hudson Bay Lowlands in the far north. This is a strip of flat, marshy lowland around Hudson Bay and James Bay. Although very few people live in this area now, Moose Factory, the first English settlement in Ontario, is located there. First Nations peoples also still inhabit the area. South of the Canadian Shield is the region known as the Great Lakes–St. Lawrence Lowlands. This is a beautiful area with rich farmlands, orchards, forests, and lakes. Also in the south is the Niagara Escarpment, a steep limestone ridge which runs northwest from the Niagara River to Lake Huron.

Given the size of Ontario, it is not surprising that the climate varies greatly from place to place. Southern Ontario is a gardener's delight with a longer growing season than either the Prairie or the Atlantic provinces enjoy. Needless to say, the north is colder and has more snow in winter. When spring blossoms have come and gone on trees in the south, the ice is just beginning to break up on the rivers flowing into Hudson Bay and James Bay. Like most of the country, Ontario has four distinct seasons: winter, spring, summer, and fall. Many people would argue that fall is the most beautiful, when the maple leaves turn their awesome red colour.

Some Famous Artists

The beauty of Ontario's landscape has been captured by some of the artists in the famous Group of Seven. Many of these artists' paintings now hang in the McMichael Collection outside Kleinburg, a small community north of Toronto.

The Group of Seven is a very significant group of artists who did most of their work in the 1920s and early 1930s in Canada. The following words come from a 1920 catalogue of their work:

> The Group of Seven artists, whose pictures are here exhibited, have for several years held a like vision concerning art in Canada. They are all imbued with the idea that an art must grow and flower in the land before the country will be a real home for its people . . . . The artists invite adverse criticism. Indifference is the greatest evil they have to contend with.

Tom Thomson, who painted the beautiful fall scene shown below, was not actually a member of the group. He died in 1917 before the group was formed, but he was one of the first to paint the rugged northern Ontario landscape in a bold style. The picture by A.J. Casson shown on the next page expresses with eloquence the windswept loneliness of the great Canadian Shield that covers so much of Ontario. Like the others in this

Algonquin, by Tom Thomson

White Pine, by A.J. Casson

group of painters, his art is expressive of the land in which we live. In addition to Ontario's landscape, the Group of Seven painted scenes from many other areas of the country.

The original members of the Group of Seven were Lawren Harris, A.Y. Jackson, J.E.H. MacDonald, Frederick Varley, Arthur Lismer, Frank Johnston, and Frank Carmichael. Four others later joined the group. Not everyone liked the work of these painters when they began, but they are now very famous and well-respected. They formed the beginning of a larger group called the Canadian Group of Painters, which took in artists such as Emily Carr from the west coast. Canadians are proud of these early artists who took it upon themselves to forge a distinctly Canadian style of painting.

COMPREHENSION CHECK

1. Why is Ontario often called Central Canada?
2. What landform region covers two-thirds of the province?
3. What problems does the rapidly growing population of southern Ontario create?
4. Was Emily Carr a member of the Group of Seven artists?

VOCABULARY

hospitable	welcoming
terrain	landscape
outcroppings	large sections of rock that have broken through the surface of the earth
dilemma	a problem in which a choice has to be made between two equally strong alternatives
ridge	a long, narrow hilltop
awesome	awe-inspiring, amazing, wonderful
imbued	filled with feelings or qualities
adverse	negative
indifference	not caring; not paying attention to; apathy
eloquence	a highly effective manner of communicating reason or emotion
forge	shape or make

USING NEW WORDS

Fill in each blank with a word from the Vocabulary section.

1. The parents had just enough money for the new roof they needed for their house, but they also desperately needed a new car. What a _____!

2. Canada has traditionally been very _____ to refugees.

3. No politician who is running for office wants any _____ publicity at election time.

4. My friend's mother-in-law, penniless refugee that she is now, is nonetheless _____ with an air of quiet dignity which hints of a time in which she enjoyed much wealth and was held in high esteem.

5. Canadians are often accused of being apathetic because of their _____ to politics.

6. Pierre Elliott Trudeau, Canada's controversial former prime minister, spoke with _____ of the need for Canada to see itself as part of a global community.

7. It is truly _____ to realize that an artist of many beautiful paintings painted with his feet because he had no arms.

8. Many people feel it is necessary to _____ a lasting peace in areas such as the Middle East and Northern Ireland.

FOR DISCUSSION

» Why do you think a maple leaf was chosen for Canada's flag?

» Do you see anything in common between the two paintings shown on pages 149 and 150?

MAKING CONTACT

» Go online and search The Group of Seven, or go to your public library and look for a book on them. Examine their paintings and see how their images compare to your own images of nature in Canada. In your opinion, do the paintings represent the Canada you see? If not, how are your images different? Why might they be different? Discuss your answers with your classmates or with a Canadian you know.

Past and Present

A Peek into the Past

Ontario has a fascinating history, and if you leave the freeways of southern Ontario and choose instead to drive along the picturesque country roads, you can see clearly the signs of the past: the old brick farmhouses built by United Empire Loyalists who left the United States in great numbers following the American Revolution, the covered bridges, and the quaint shops with their architectural details from another time. To go back even further, reconstructed Aboriginal

The West Montrose covered bridge near Waterloo, Ontario

villages—such as Sainte-Marie among the Hurons near Midland—remind us of the times when the First Nations peoples lived on these lands.

Whereas the prairies of western Canada were not cultivated until the European settlers came and plowed the land, the rich earth of southern Ontario was first cultivated by the Algonquian and Iroquoian peoples. French explorers were the first visitors to the area, but settlement was not widespread until the United Empire Loyalists arrived. Most Loyalists were of English, Scottish, or Irish origins.

A descendant of the United Empire Loyalists, who was born in Toronto in 1917 and lived there until his death in 2009, was asked what influence he felt the Loyalists had on the development of the Canadian identity. His name was Len Black and this is what he had to say:

> The United Empire Loyalists had a major influence on this country. They instilled in their descendants a pride of family, a standard of morality, and a sense of being responsible citizens, all of which have become an important part of what it means to be Canadian.

He believed that the most important change in Ontario, and one he very much celebrated, was the ethnic diversification of the population. He felt that the city of Toronto was a much richer, more interesting place because of all the different people who now live there. What he did not like was the tremendous crowding he experienced, which had resulted in pollution, among other things. People of his generation recall with fondness the days of swimming in Lake Ontario and in the Don River. The Don Valley now has the Don Valley Parkway (a freeway for north-south traffic in Toronto) running through it, and Lake Ontario is much too polluted for swimming. For men and women of older generations, the changes have been tremendous. Most younger Canadians cannot begin to imagine how it must feel to experience such changes in the space of one lifetime.

Maple trees in North Bay, Ontario, in the fall

The Economy and the Environment

The heart of Ontario's economy has traditionally been its manufacturing industry, and while that remains very important, technological innovation is taking on increased importance as well. One example is the Waterloo-based Research in Motion company (RIM) which markets the well-known BlackBerry smartphone and PlayBook tablet. Industries such as steel and automobile production are very important to the economy of the province and the country. The factories of Toronto, Hamilton, and other areas, while highly successful, have also produced a number of the environmental problems which now plague Ontario. The destruction of ecosystems in the Great Lakes is an example.

Further north and west in Ontario, the mines of the Canadian Shield contribute much to the Canadian economy. The nickel mines near Sudbury, the silver mines at Cobalt, gold in the Red Lake area, and iron ore at Wawa have all been important in Canada's economy, but not without a price. Mining, massive hydroelectric plants, and other industrialization have all taken their toll on Ontario's environment. We need only look in vain for the clear skies we see further west to realize that air pollution is becoming a serious problem in Ontario's urban areas.

While of growing concern, the problems of air and water pollution have not completely marred the beauty and charm of Ontario. Our Canadian flag with its large red maple leaf in the centre is a reminder of the beautiful red maple leaves which cover Ontario's countryside in the fall, stunning all who see them. The maple trees in both Ontario and Quebec provide much more than beauty. Wood from the trees is used in producing fine handcrafted furniture, kitchen cabinets, and flooring. The sap is used for the delicious maple syrup that Canadians love to put on their pancakes!

COMPREHENSION CHECK

Ask a question that will give you each answer below.

1. Algonquian and Iroquoian peoples
2. United Empire Loyalists
3. nickel, silver, gold, iron ore
4. maple syrup
5. Blackberry smartphone

VOCABULARY

peek (n)	a quick look at (something)
fascinating	extremely interesting
picturesque	scenic, pleasant to look upon
quaint	pleasantly old-fashioned
cultivated	used to grow crops
instilled	introduced with the intention that it will stay present; usually referring to a feeling or idea
fondness	affection, happy feelings
plague (v)	trouble, torment, create big problems for
ecosystems	the systems of natural, biological life
take a toll on	cause damage to
look in vain for	look with no success for; to fail to find
marred	spoiled, damaged

USING NEW WORDS

Fill in each blank with a word or term from the list above. In one, you will have to add the -ed ending for the past tense.

1. The young man was terribly upset about the used car which continued to _____ him with one problem after another.
2. The community _____ for the lost child. Unfortunately, she was never seen again.
3. The car's shiny surface was _____ in the accident.
4. Anytime we are really interested in something, we find new information about that subject to be _____.
5. The young men who had _____ marijuana in their basement were sent to prison for five years.
6. Most of us have _____ in our children the same or similar values as those which our parents taught us.
7. The landscape of Canada's Rockies is very _____.
8. She felt a real _____ for her new friend.

FOR DISCUSSION

» When the nature of the population changes rapidly in an area, what kinds of problems can arise between the original population and the new population? What steps can be taken to understand and deal with these problems?

» What difference does it make whether the Great Lakes are polluted or not? Why is it important?

» What can ordinary people do to reduce air pollution in industrial centres?

ACTIVITY

» It is one thing to talk about what we can do to make our world a better place and another thing to make the necessary changes. After discussing the last question above with your classmates, choose one thing that you will do differently from now on to improve the environment. You may want to make a chart on which you each list your commitments to change. When you put your commitments all together, you may see that each individual does make a difference.

Toronto: Canada's Largest City

Produce for sale in Kensington Market

Skating at Nathan Phillips Square

Toronto is a vibrant, exciting city where it is hard to believe that anyone with an ounce of curiosity could ever be bored! With nearly 6 million people, it is a world-class centre of finance, sports, and culture, as well as a true multicultural mosaic. More than two million people in the last census identified themselves as belonging to a visible minority. It is also home to Canada's largest university, the prestigious University of Toronto, or U of T as most people call it.

You could start your explorations with Kensington Market on a Saturday morning. This is a large marketplace reminiscent of old-style European markets. People of various cultural origins sell their produce, meats, seafoods, and breads to crowds of customers of equally diverse backgrounds. When you have completed your shopping, you can sit down in a small café and enjoy a cappuccino, which may be served by the smiling daughter or son of the shopkeeper.

Or maybe you would rather go shopping for something other than food. The stores seem endless in Toronto. One popular shopping area, especially in the winter, is the covered, multi-level Eaton Centre in downtown Toronto. Eaton's department store used to be the keystone of this mall, but this popular and uniquely Canadian store closed its doors for the last time in 2002, the end of an institution. Timothy Eaton started this large chain of department stores in Toronto in 1869, and left a legacy of quality products and service now missed greatly by older Canadians.

If shopping is not for you, and it is winter, then perhaps you would like to take a pair of skates to Nathan Phillips Square. Many Torontonians enjoy the freshness of winter by skating in front of the distinctive curved buildings which are City Hall. At other times of the year, this popular square becomes the setting for concerts, art and cultural festivals, and a large New Year's gathering. When it gets too cold for skating, you could travel a few blocks south and take an elevator to the top of the CN Tower. It is a pricey trip but one which gives you a great view of the city, at least on a clear day. The CN Tower was, until 2007, the tallest free-standing structure in the world.

Next, you might enjoy the Royal Ontario Museum. If so, you will need more than a couple of hours. It is a huge, beautiful building in the downtown area with many regular and special displays. Another popular attraction is the Ontario Science Centre, where children and adults alike discover how much fun it can be to experience the wonders of science and technology firsthand. Visitors are encouraged to participate in the demonstrations and play with the objects in many of the exhibits. Bring a camera—you may want someone to take a photo of you when your hair stands on end!

At dinnertime, you might want to take a streetcar to one of Toronto's many excellent ethnic restaurants. There is great Greek food along the Danforth, Indian and Pakistani foods in Little India on Gerrard, and excellent Chinese food at the many restaurants on Dundas or Spadina in Chinatown.

In Chinatown, Little Italy, Little India, or the Greek neighbourhood along the Danforth, you can see store and street signs in the heritage language of the community. Even more impressive to the casual tourist is the fact that the shoppers on these streets are just as likely to be speaking their first languages as English!

Evening has come and there are many opportunities to go to live theatre or one of the other performing arts centres. You may choose something at the luxurious Sony Centre or the Royal Alexandra Theatre. Or, if it is summer, you may be able to catch an outdoor ballet or other dance or theatre production down at the Harbourfront or Yonge-Dundas Square.

If you are not all that interested in the arts, then you might be interested in seeing one of Toronto's professional sports teams play. The Toronto Maple Leafs of the NHL (National Hockey League) have been popular for many years. The Toronto

The Rogers Centre, home of the Toronto Blue Jays

Argonauts are a well-known football team, the Toronto Raptors are Canada's only professional basketball team on the NBA (National Basketball Association) circuit, and the Toronto Blue Jays are Toronto's professional baseball team.

Depending on when you are in the city, you may want to visit the famous Canadian National Exhibition (CNE) in the summer or the Royal Winter Fair later in the year.

Most of all, Toronto is about people—people from all over the world. When you ride the subway, you see people of every race, religion, and culture. Each brings something special to the quality of life in this city.

COMPREHENSION CHECK

1. Name two kinds of public transportation in Toronto (government-owned transportation you pay to ride on).
2. Danforth and Dundas are the names of two _____ in Toronto.
3. Who was Timothy Eaton?
4. What kind of display do you think could make a person's hair stand on end?
5. What is the name of Toronto's professional (NHL) hockey team?

VOCABULARY

vibrant	lively, filled with life
reminiscent of	which reminds us of, which makes us think about
legacy	inheritance, that which has been passed on from someone in the past
pricey	expensive
firsthand	directly
stands on end	sticks straight up
streetcar	a form of public transit which runs on railway tracks and is powered by electricity from an overhead cable

USING NEW WORDS

Fill in each blank with a word or term from the list above.

1. Staying in a hotel is too _____ for many young travellers.
2. Those who fight against oppression anywhere leave their descendants with a _____ of respect for freedom and dignity.
3. The _____ young woman attracted attention wherever she went.
4. Romantic love cannot be experienced by reading a book; it must be experienced _____.
5. _____s have automated announcements that call out the name of the streets as they come to them so that people know where to get off.
6. The scent of that perfume is _____ roses in the springtime.

Around the Province

Ottawa

Ottawa, a city of 900 000 people, is our nation's capital. It is a pleasant, well-planned community with a number of distinctive features. Needless to say, the Parliament Buildings are one of the first images that come to mind when Canadians think of Ottawa. These beautiful, old, and elegant structures remind us of our heritage and our proud origins. The city is divided by the steep banks of the Ottawa River and the lovely Rideau Canal. The canal system is one of the more delightful features of Ottawa and is enjoyed by boaters in summer and skaters in winter. When the canal is frozen, it is one of the longest skating rinks in the world. Some citizens even skate to work on the canal in the winter season.

Close to the Parliament Buildings, but across the river in Gatineau, Quebec, you find the unique Museum of Civilization. This museum is a national treasure house, designed by Douglas Cardinal, one of Canada's finest architects. Cardinal's designs often feature smooth curves and circular movement, and this beautiful building is no exception. The circle is a very important shape and symbol in Aboriginal cultures, and Cardinal brings this to his work from his indigenous origins.

We also cannot think of Ottawa without thinking of tulips. In the spring, this city is splendid

The Ottawa Tulip Festival

with its thousands of tulips. Canadians owe these colourful spring flowers to Queen Juliana of the Netherlands, who arranged to have tulips sent to Canada every year in appreciation for the Canadian soldiers who helped free her country from the Nazi occupation during the Second World War.

Other tourist attractions in Ottawa include the Canada Science and Technology Museum and the National Gallery of Canada, with its excellent collection of paintings by Canadian artists. In addition, no visit to Ottawa is complete without an afternoon in the ByWard Market. This is located in Lower Town, just below the gracious

Fairmont Chateau Laurier Hotel. It features an open-air market as well as boutiques and a variety of restaurants.

One of the most wonderful aspects of Ottawa is its truly bilingual nature. About 40 percent of the city's population said they were bilingual in the 2006 census. When you walk down the streets in the downtown area, you are likely to hear people speaking in French and in English.

Hamilton

This city of 700 000 people is Canada's major steel producer, accounting for 60 percent of the country's total steel production. Hamilton is a major industrial centre and has many factories in addition to those which produce steel. Located on the western end of Lake Ontario, its real growth began with the development of a farm-equipment industry in the 1850s.

The city is also home to McMaster University, a stately campus well-known for its innovative medical school among other things. Mohawk College is one of the country's larger community colleges and offers a variety of programs to the adult learning community of the region.

One truly lovely part of Hamilton is the Royal Botanical Gardens, over 1200 hectares of garden spread over 15 kilometres of shoreline along Lake Ontario. The gardens are well worth the visit in the summer season, but wear comfortable walking shoes!

Niagara Falls

Many tourists who come to Canada from other countries make a point of visiting Niagara Falls. From kilometres away, you can hear the sound of these falls, a sound which becomes a deafening roar as you get close. More than 14 million visitors per year come to this site, which straddles the Canadian–American border. The Horseshoe Falls, as they are called on the Canadian side, are three times the width of the American Falls. If you do not mind getting wet, the Maid of the Mist boat tours venture out into the Niagara River and go close to the bottom of the falls during the

A rainbow over Niagara Falls

tourist season. Niagara Falls is also a popular destination for honeymooners.

Other Parts of Ontario

Ontario is a huge province with a large population. It would be difficult to describe all of its attractions. The Trans-Canada Highway passes through southern Ontario and, if you have the time and the money to travel, this is a journey worth taking. You can experience the rugged beauty of the Canadian Shield on this route and also visit other cities in the province, such as Sault Ste. Marie and Thunder Bay. For those who can travel by boat, there is a series of locks extending up the St. Lawrence River. This 306-kilometre section of the St. Lawrence Seaway is regarded as one of the most challenging engineering feats in history, enabling large ships to lift to 75 metres above sea level.

One destination for many tourists in the summer months is the small town of Stratford, home of the famous Stratford Festival, a drama festival that takes place in theatres throughout the town each summer. (Stratford is also the home of Justin Bieber!)

Others head for the Kitchener–Waterloo area where they can experience firsthand the Mennonite culture of the early settlers in that area. You can still see horse-drawn carriages and enjoy the cooking of these people, many of whom choose to keep their old lifestyle as much as possible.

Those who live in Ontario's large cities also like to get out into the country on weekends. Some go to the many beautiful parks of Ontario, the largest of which is Algonquin Provincial Park. If you wish to experience a camping adventure, reserve your space early because the campsites fill up quickly. Others may have cottages in the scenic rural areas such as the Muskokas north of Toronto and the Kawarthas northeast of Toronto around Peterborough. Those who escape to cottage country may go to ski, skidoo, or ice-fish in the winter. In the summer, cottagers swim, waterski, go boating, or just relax.

Paddling in cottage country

COMPREHENSION CHECK

1   Why does a visitor to Ottawa see a lot of tulips in the spring?
2   Where might a visitor go to learn more about the history of Canada?
3   What are the two languages most often spoken in Ottawa?
4   Which city is Canada's major steel producer?
5   Which city has long been called the honeymoon capital of Canada?

ACTIVITY

Rather than give you definitions of new words, here are some clues to help you find them:

1   Find a verb which rhymes with *paddles* and means *to be situated on both sides of something*. Clue: Check the Niagara Falls section.
2   Find a four-syllable adjective which means *new and different* and contains the root *nov*. Clue: Check the Hamilton section.
3   When older people are surprised about something, they may say, *Goodness _____!* Clue: Check the Ottawa section. The word could also be used to describe Queen Elizabeth II.
4   This three-syllable word starts with *d* and means *very special*. Clue: Check the Ottawa section.
5   This noun means *an exciting experience*. The three-syllable word is made by adding a prefix and a suffix to the root *vent*.

(You can find the answers on page 251 at the back of the book.)

FOR DISCUSSION

» If you had three days to spend in Ontario, where would you spend your time and what would you do?

» Most immigrants settle in the urban areas of Canada. Why do you think that is? What advantages might there be for those who choose to settle in smaller communities?

CHAPTER REVIEW

Here is a brief review of some of the vocabulary used in this chapter. Match each of the words below to its *synonym* (a word with the same or a similar meaning) on the right.

1.	legacy	a)	unusual
2.	firsthand	b)	dynamic
3.	vibrant	c)	costly
4.	pricey	d)	heritage
5.	hospitable	e)	friendly
6.	indescribable	f)	directly

Match each of the words below to its *antonym* (a word with the opposite meaning) on the right.

1.	distinctive	a)	ugly
2.	cultivated	b)	boring
3.	dilemma	c)	wild
4.	fascinating	d)	ordinary
5.	picturesque	e)	solution

Chapter Nine

Central Canada: Quebec

Quick Facts

» Quebec was one of the original four provinces in Confederation in 1867.

» It has a population of 8 million, making it the second-most populated province, after Ontario.

» 88 percent of the population was Roman Catholic, compared to 49 percent of the country's population as a whole, in 2001. (Religion questions were not included in the census after 2001.)

» 59 percent of Quebec's population speak French only; 35 percent are bilingual, and only 6 percent speak English only.

» The capital is Quebec City.

» The largest city is Montreal, Canada's second-largest city, with a population of 4 million.

» The provincial flower is the white garden lily; the provincial bird is the snowy owl.

» Manufacturing, hydroelectric power, and mining top the economy.

» Separatism has traditionally been a controversial topic in Quebec.

Introduction

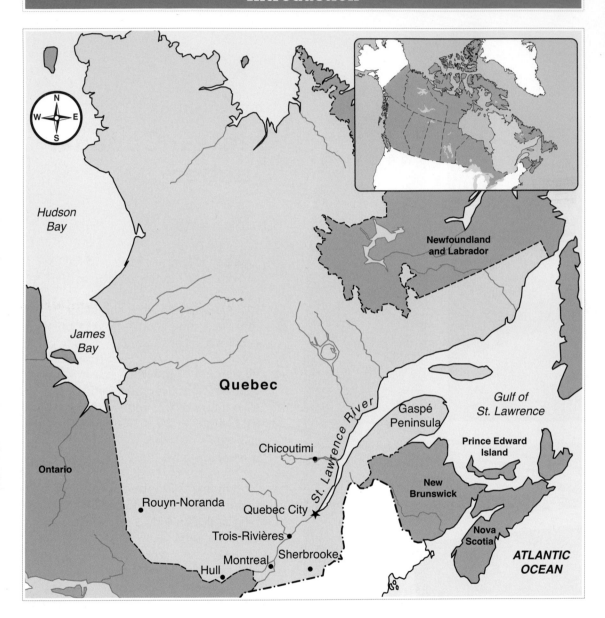

La belle province (the beautiful province), as Quebecers like to call their province, is rich in Canadian history. Quebec is the site of Canada's beginnings. A walk through the old parts of Quebec's largest cities, Montreal and Quebec City, gives us a glimpse of what life must have been like in earlier times: cobblestone streets, horse-drawn carriages, fiddlers playing their music, and old stone buildings.

The Québécois Identity

The majority of Quebec's population is French-speaking and Roman Catholic. This dates back to Quebec's beginnings as a French colony. As a result of this history, the Québécois, as they prefer to be called, have a culture quite distinct from that of other Canadians. The Québécois feel strongly about preserving their language,

Cobblestone streets in Old Montreal

religion, and heritage because they have long feared assimilation by the dominant anglophone culture of North America. A look at Quebec's licence plates tells us how strongly the Québécois feel about their history. The plates say *Je me souviens*, which is French for *I remember*. They remember their culture, and many Québécois struggle to ensure that the rest of the country also remembers.

This strong desire to preserve their distinct identity has led to tensions between French and English Canadians. Some Québécois feel that, in remaining part of Canada, they will lose their French heritage. Some therefore wish to separate from Canada. If Quebec were ever to separate, many Canadians feel that it would be a very sad day for Canada because, not only would it hurt the country economically, it would be a great loss to Canada's identity as a country with two dominant founding cultures. Most Canadians have a strong desire to see these tensions resolved in a way that does not destroy the country.

Geography, People, and Economy

Geography and Climate

Quebec has a total area of 1 540 680 square kilometres, making it the largest of Canada's ten provinces. The major cities, Montreal and Quebec City, lie along the St. Lawrence River, which empties into the Gulf of St. Lawrence and eventually the Atlantic Ocean. These cities are therefore very humid. It is very hot and wet during the summer and very cold and damp in the winter. You may be surprised to know that Quebec City is as cold in January as Murmansk in Russia, which is north of the Arctic Circle. Quebecers would say it feels even colder, because of the humidity. The far northern part of Quebec, which stretches up to Hudson Bay, is subarctic. This area gets very cold in the winter and the winters are long.

Mont-Tremblant, in the Laurentians, is a popular destination for skiers

The vast majority of Quebec (80 percent) is covered by the Canadian Shield with its lakes, rivers, forests, and mineral deposits. There are also two mountain ranges in the province: the Laurentian Mountains north of the St. Lawrence River and the Appalachian Mountains south of the river. The Laurentians are home to some of North America's best-known ski resorts as well as many other tourist resorts that are open in both summer and winter.

The St. Lawrence River is important not only for Quebec, but also for the rest of Canada. It is a major route for shipping goods between the Atlantic Ocean and the Great Lakes. Grain from the prairies travels by rail to Thunder Bay and is then placed on large ocean-going vessels for transport to Europe, Russia, and other parts of the globe.

Population

Quebec has the second-largest population of the Canadian provinces. Seventy-nine percent of Quebecers speak French as their first language. In fact, only Montreal has a significantly large number of people whose first language is not French. Therefore, people immigrating to Quebec who do not speak French tend to settle in Montreal, where they can choose English as their working language. All immigrant newcomers, however, are given their language training in French, and their children are automatically sent to French schools.

Quebec's population also includes 10 First Nations, the majority of whom live on reserves. Aboriginal grievances are especially strong in Quebec because most of the Aboriginals speak English, not French. They are particularly anxious about the desire of some Quebecers to separate from Canada because they fear their rights may be ignored in an independent Quebec. First Nations people are also concerned about their unresolved land claims, which still cover a large area of Quebec in the north and east. Slowly, agreements are being reached, some giving land to the First Nations claimants and others giving them fishing and hunting rights and involvement in the areas' development.

Economy

Quebec has one of the most diversified economies in Canada. Both primary (natural resources) and secondary (manufacturing) industries are strong. The area along the St. Lawrence River in southern Quebec and Ontario is the industrial heartland of Canada.

Mining and electric power are major industries in the province. There are iron-ore deposits in northern Quebec that geologists believe to be among the largest in the world. Metals refined in Quebec include bauxite (the source of aluminum), copper, zinc, and iron.

Quebec is also the only province in Canada which has no fossil fuels (coal or gas) and is therefore dependent on hydroelectricity for power.

In 1963, all electric power was nationalized in Quebec. Hydro-Quebec then became the leading producer of hydroelectric power in North America. With this power, Quebec produces about one-quarter of all manufactured goods in Canada.

Forestry and pulp and paper are other major industries. Forests cover about one-half of the province. Many of these trees are used in Quebec's pulp and paper industry. The province is one of the North American leaders in the manufacture of paper.

Also important to Canada is Quebec's aerospace industry, the fifth-largest in the world. Annual sales from this industry top 12 billion dollars. Originally concentrating on the manufacture of planes and aviation equipment, several companies are now expanding into satellite technology.

COMPREHENSION CHECK

1. What do Quebecers call their province? (Hint: It's a French phrase.)
2. Nowadays, we have pavement on our streets and roadways. What covered the streets of old Quebec long ago?
3. What do many Québécois fear most of all?
4. Do the majority of First Nations peoples in Quebec support Quebec separatism or not? Why?
5. Quebec is the leading North American producer of what type of power?

VOCABULARY

separatism	a political movement in which people want to separate from a larger body and become independent
glimpse (n)	a short look at, or a brief view of, something
cobblestone	a smooth, rounded rock used for road surfaces in the days of horse-drawn carriages
assimilation	absorption into a larger whole, thus losing one's own distinctive characteristics
anglophone (adj)	English-speaking
resolved	settled; no longer a problem
damp	slightly wet
grievances	serious complaints of injustice
nationalized	changed from private to government ownership

USING NEW WORDS

Fill in each blank with a word from the Vocabulary section.

1. Canadians have seen multiculturalism as a way in which there could be integration rather than _____ of the cultures which make up Canada.

2. The children forgot to take their umbrellas to school and, when it rained, they came home feeling very _____.

3. Those who support _____ want Quebec to have its own government independent of the federal government in Ottawa.

4. Where there are _____ streets, you can expect a very bumpy ride!

5. The opposite of privatized is _____.

6. The couple _____ their problems and no longer considered getting a divorce.

7. The settling of the Nisga'a people's land claim in northwestern British Columbia is a sign that the federal government is making a serious attempt to resolve the _____ of Canada's First Nations.

8. Devout Roman Catholics are extremely happy to catch a _____ of the Pope when he visits their community.

9. Montreal has many _____ as well as francophone citizens.

FOR DISCUSSION

» What would Canada miss economically if Quebec separated?

» What might Quebec miss economically if it separated from the rest of Canada?

» The Aboriginals of Quebec voted against sovereignty in the 1995 referendum. Now, some are saying they will separate from Quebec if Quebec separates from Canada. If you were the premier of Quebec, what would you say to convince the Aboriginals to stay with Quebec if it separated?

The Cities

Montreal

If British Columbians can argue that Vancouver is the most beautiful city in Canada, Montrealers can possibly claim their city is the most exciting! Montreal is a modern, bustling metropolis with old and new side by side. While highrise office towers reflect the important role the city plays in finance and business, old limestone houses, cobblestone streets, and quaint old shops and hotels remind us that it is one of the oldest cities in the country. It is a beautiful city and popular with both Canadians and foreign tourists.

Montreal is Canada's second-largest metropolitan area with 4 million people. Two-thirds of the population is French-speaking, making Montreal the second-largest French-speaking city in the world! The other third of the population is made up of native English-speakers and various ethnic groups (including Chinese, Greek, Italian, and Arab), most of whom speak English. Montreal is one place in the province of Quebec where someone who speaks English, but not French, can go and not have difficulty communicating. Many Quebecers who live in Montreal and whose first language is French also speak English.

In the city of Montreal, there are so many different things to do that it is difficult to know where to begin. If you like history, you can visit Old Montreal or one of the museums in the city such as the McCord Museum of Canadian History.

If you are interested in Catholic churches, they are everywhere in the city. You can visit the Notre-Dame Basilica or the impressive St. Joseph's Oratory. The basilica is one of the largest and most beautiful churches in North America. Its outstanding architecture adds to the magic people experience when they attend symphonies and other concerts there throughout the year. St. Joseph's Oratory is a pilgrimage site that people visit from all over the world in the hope that they will be healed. St. Joseph is the patron saint of healing.

If you like shopping, St. Catherine and St. Denis are both good streets to visit. At night, St. Catherine Street is a favourite place to go dancing at one of the many nightclubs. St. Laurent Boulevard is also a popular place for nightlife, with its many cafés, bars, and clubs. St. Laurent is where many of the young, trendy people of Montreal go to "see and be seen."

Montreal is also home to four different universities, two French and two English. The French universities are the Université de Montréal and the Université de Québec à Montréal (UQAM). The Université de Montréal is located in the Mount Royal area. Mount Royal is a mountain in the centre of the city with a beautiful park at the top. It is a popular spot for Montrealers in both summer and winter. The English universities are McGill and Concordia. Many Canadians and Americans attend McGill University, a very prestigious university with high entrance requirements.

Montreal is also famous for its summer festivals. In late June, the Montreal International Jazz Festival is held downtown. This is North America's largest jazz festival and jazz musicians come from all over the world to play here. Many of the concerts are free. In July, Montreal hosts the *Juste Pour Rire* (French for *Just For Laughs*) festival. This is the largest comedy festival in North America and is held in charming Old Montreal.

Montreal is also a city which takes its sports seriously. It is the home of the famous Montreal Canadiens, one of the country's oldest professional hockey teams. Other sports fans speak with pride of the Grand Prix auto and bicycle races held annually and of the Montreal Marathon, in which runners from across the country and around the world compete.

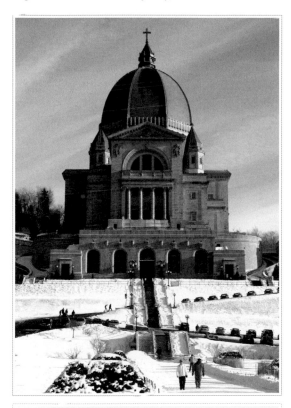

St. Joseph's Oratory in winter

Place Jacques-Cartier

Many people like to come to Montreal to shop because there is so much choice in clothing, furnishings, and art, to name a few. In fact, Montreal is considered the fashion capital of Canada. One of the most popular centres for shoppers is the glamorous Place Ville Marie. The nearby Latin Quarter on St. Denis Street attracts students, artists, and tourists to its many coffee shops and bookstores. Also popular with tourists is Place Jacques-Cartier, the location of one of the city's oldest markets. Now surrounded with hotels and restaurants, the square is filled on summer evenings with street musicians, people selling flowers, and outdoor cafés where people come to enjoy the all-too-short summers in the outdoors.

Quebec City

Quebec City is unique in that it is the seat of the only French-speaking government in North America. The Quebec Legislature made French the province's official language in 1974. Quebec City is home to more than 700 000 people.

Even more history can be found in Quebec City than in Montreal. Quebec City is the oldest city in Canada. A good place to begin a tour is on the Plains of Abraham. This is where the French and the English, in 1759, fought over what was then New France and is now Quebec. The battle was one of the most significant events in Canadian history. Today, the Plains of Abraham are not only a beautiful park area in the centre of Quebec City, but are also the site of many large gatherings such as concerts and political demonstrations.

L'Université Laval is a respected university in the city where many students from other countries, in addition to Quebec students, study. As well, it has a large summer program for English-speaking Canadians who are eager to improve their French and enjoy the ambiance of this lovely city while they learn.

Old Quebec is so distinct that the United Nations Educational, Scientific and Cultural Organization (UNESCO) has made it a World Heritage Site. It is a most interesting part of the city with 400-year-old stone buildings, houses with their characteristic steep roofs, narrow winding streets, and *calèches* (horse-drawn carriages) taking tourists through the streets. There are several museums as well where you can learn more about Canada's early history. A walk through the old part of Quebec City reveals a lot about what life must have been like in New France. Parts of the old fort walls that guarded the city still stand. Quebec City is the only walled city in North America. It is a very beautiful, romantic place to visit and, as a result, has a thriving tourist industry especially in the summer months.

For those who love shopping, la Rue du Petit-Champlain in the Lower Town is a must. Crowded during tourist season, the street is filled with beautiful boutiques and quaint little cafés. Many of the shops sell good-quality local or

The walls of Quebec City

international arts and crafts at reasonable prices. And when you get tired, you can take the funicular up to the Fairmont le Chateau Frontenac Hotel, which towers above the street.

For those who enjoy fine dining, Quebec City offers many quality restaurants including several with excellent French and Québécois cuisine. And, for people who love the nightlife, the city's Grande Alleé has many lively bars and nightclubs.

Carnaval de Québec

Cold winters do not stop Quebecers from enjoying life! Every year in February, Quebec City puts on the Carnaval de Québec. It is a wonderful winter festival attended by people from all over the world.

Huge ice sculptures are built and contests are held to judge whose sculpture is the best. A character named *Bonhomme*, which is French for *good man*, is the mascot for the festival. He looks like a large human snowman and wears a red *ceinture* (a sash worn by the voyageurs) and a red toque, both of which are characteristically Québécois.

During the carnival, people enjoy Québécois treats such as tourtière (a meat pie made with pork, vegetables, and spices), habitant pea soup, and maple syrup. The *habitants* were the original French farmers in what is now Quebec. You can go online and find recipes for these delicious foods.

Have you ever tasted maple syrup? It comes from the sap of sugar maple trees. The trees have exceptionally beautiful red leaves in autumn. A red maple leaf is on our national flag. In the late

Bonhomme, the mascot of the Carnaval de Québec

winter or early spring, maple trees are tapped and pails hung on the side to catch the sap as it slowly drips out. Then, this sap is collected and cooked to make maple syrup, a sweet, tasty treat used on pancakes or for candy. Delicious!

Some people working at *cabanes à sucre* (sugar shacks) pour the hot maple syrup over snow contained in a trough. They then roll wooden sticks into the syrup as it cools on the snow and eat it off the sticks. If you like sweets, you will love this Quebec specialty! Quebec is famous for its maple syrup.

COMPREHENSION CHECK

① What two languages can visitors feel comfortable speaking in Montreal?

② Which city is known as the fashion capital of Canada?

③ Name one university in Montreal that has an excellent reputation throughout the country and high standards of enrolment.

④ Who is Bonhomme?

⑤ Name three foods that are distinctly Québécois.

VOCABULARY

pilgrimage	a trip or journey made to a sacred place as an act of devotion
patron saint	the saint which Roman Catholics believe gives a person or group special protection
trendy	modern, contemporary, popular
prestigious	highly respected
cuisine	the French word for cooking, usually used in English to describe fine cooking or ethnic cooking
mascot	a thing, animal, or person supposed to bring good luck to an event or group of people, such as a sports team
sash	a wide, cloth belt
voyageurs	travellers (from the French word *voyager*, meaning to travel); in Canada, refers to the early French explorers who travelled by canoe
toque	a knitted winter hat often with a long wide "tail" which can be used like a scarf to keep your neck warm
trough	a long, narrow, open container, usually used for water or animal feed
funicular	a mode of transportation for carrying passengers up and down a mountain or large hill; similar to a tramway except the ascending and descending cars are pulled on counterbalanced pulleys

USING NEW WORDS

Five of the words above have a word within a word. See if you can find them. For one of the new words, you will have to add an *e*. Here are some clues to help you find the new words within the words.

1. _____ a person who goes on a long trip of special meaning
2. _____ great respect
3. _____ something which is popular now but probably will not be in the near future
4. _____ a long trip on water
5. _____ not easy or not smooth

Bonus Questions: Which of the vocabulary words describe two pieces of clothing? Which one is commonly worn in winter?

(You can find the answers for this activity on page 251 at the back of the book.)

FOR DISCUSSION

» Ask two of your classmates how they would spend two days in either Quebec City or Montreal and share with them how you would spend those same two days. Which city would you choose to go to and why?

» Imagine that you are a small child from the prairies visiting Old Quebec or Old Montreal. What are five questions you might ask your parents about the unusual sights you are seeing?

Other Interesting Attractions

Saint-Jean-Baptiste Day

Carnaval de Québec is one big festival in Quebec. Another famous Quebec festival is held on Saint-Jean-Baptiste Day, on June 24. For many Québécois, this day is a more important celebration than Canada Day. People parade the streets with provincial flags and paint fleurs-de-lys on the roads and sidewalks. Four fleurs-de-lys are portrayed on Quebec's provincial flag. They represent the coat of arms of the French King and have come to stand as a symbol for Quebec and its French identity.

Saint-Jean-Baptiste Day has been a legal holiday for the people of Quebec since 1922. It began as a religious festival celebrating Saint-Jean-Baptiste as the patron saint of Quebec. In the second half of the twentieth century, it came to be strongly associated with Quebec nationalism and the separatist movement

Celebrating Saint-Jean-Baptiste Day on the Plains of Abraham

Around the Province

The Montmorency Falls are a scenic place to visit in summer or winter alike. These waterfalls are located not far to the northeast of Quebec City. They are actually 50 percent higher than the world-famous Niagara Falls in Ontario. In the winter, they freeze and create an interesting

loaf-shaped ice cone known to Quebecers as the *pain du sucre* (French for *sugarloaf*).

Basilique Sainte-Anne-de-Beaupré is also a very popular attraction. It is located in a town of the same name, 40 kilometres from Quebec City. Many people from all over the world visit this basilica each year because it is known as a place of miraculous healing. Inside the church many crutches and braces hang on the walls, left there by people who no longer needed them because they had been healed.

Percé Rock, located on the coast of the Gaspé Peninsula, is one of Canada's most famous natural sites. It is almost 500 metres long and rises 100 metres out of the water—an impressive sight. Indeed, the entire Gaspé Peninsula is one of the most charming areas of Canada and is popular with tourists during the summer months. The shores of this mainly agricultural area are dotted with small, old villages, each with a church spire rising into the sky. The spire marks the local Roman Catholic Church, at one time the centre of village life in each community.

Percé Rock (or *pierced rock*) on the coast of the Gaspé Peninsula

Quebec's Relationship with the Rest of Canada

Many Québécois have long felt misunderstood and undervalued within the broader context of Canada. At Confederation, they believed they were a nation joining together with another nation, English-speaking Canada. While many people in the rest of Canada accept that Quebec has its own language and culture, some resent the tension created by Quebec's demands to be treated differently from other parts of the country.

To improve French-English relations in the country, the federal government has supported many young people who want to participate in exchange programs. In these programs, junior and senior high school students from Quebec go to another province for one to two weeks and then take their partners back to Quebec with them for the same length of time. These programs have provided participants with a wonderful opportunity to see the country from a totally different perspective. In addition, bursaries have been widely available for university students to take part of their studies in Quebec, either in the summer months or for longer periods. This is but one aspect of the tremendous effort and money which has gone into supporting bilingualism in Canada.

In many ways, the province operates according to its status as a nation within a nation, as opposed to a province. In Quebec, the provincial government is called not a legislature, but a national parliament. Saint-Jean-Baptiste Day is called a national holiday, not a provincial one. School history and geography textbooks refer to Quebec *and* Canada, not to Quebec as part of Canada and teach these subjects very differently from the way they are taught in the rest of the country.

Whereas many Canadians are supportive of Quebec's unique position in relation to the rest of the country, the National Assembly of Quebec took a step in 1977 which cost it a great deal of support in the other provinces. It decided to make it illegal for anyone to display signs in any language other than French. Shop owners could not have English signs on their shops and were fined if they did so. At this point, many anglophone Canadians began to wonder if the much-promoted federal policy of bilingualism was a one-way street which applied to the rest of Canada but not to Quebec. There was a sense of unfairness in this action. Since that time, the government of Quebec has changed the law so that signs can be in English as long as French signs are more noticeable, but the issue remains very controversial.

In October of 1995, the government of Quebec held a referendum asking the people of that province if they wanted sovereignty association. In effect, did they want political separation from the rest of Canada while still keeping economic ties with the country? By a very, very small majority, the people of Quebec said *no*, but almost half said *yes*. Some groups who were against the idea included the anglophone community of Montreal, many of the newly arrived immigrants in the province, and the First Nations peoples. Since that time, the separatist movement has weakened, and Quebecers appear to be more interested in achieving other goals while remaining a distinct part of Canada.

COMPREHENSION CHECK

1. What do most Québécois consider the most important holiday of the year?
2. Why do you think the people of Quebec call this a national holiday when it is celebrated only in Quebec?
3. Which saint is said to work miracles in a large church near Quebec City?
4. What has the government of Canada done for many years to increase understanding between the young people of Quebec and the rest of Canada?
5. What was the purpose of the referendum in Quebec in October 1995?

VOCABULARY

fleurs-de-lys	lilies which symbolize the French people; found on the Quebec flag
miraculous	supernatural, incredible, astonishing; beyond what we understand to be natural and possible
bursaries	gifts of money for study purposes
tremendous	great, requiring a lot of energy or power
referendum	the process of referring an important political question to the general electorate (the people) for a vote
context	the surrounding environment in which something finds its meaning

USING NEW WORDS

Fill in each blank with a word from the list above.

❶ After a long and serious illness, the woman made a _____ recovery which the doctors could not explain.

❷ In the past, students could more easily get _____ to help them with their studies; now, they are more likely to get loans.

❸ There must be a _____ amount of co-operation if those of all races and ethnicities are to live and work together to make Canada a great country for all.

❹ The flag of Quebec has a blue background with a white cross and four white _____.

❺ Politicians are generally hesitant to hold a _____ if they think the people will not support their view.

❻ We can sometimes understand the meaning of new words from their _____.

FOR DISCUSSION

» If you were living in Quebec and were asked to vote in a referendum on the question of separation from the rest of Canada, how would you vote and why?

» What can Canadians do to indicate that they understand the Québécois' fear of assimilation and their desire to remain a distinct and vibrant culture?

» Should Quebec have a different status and different rights and privileges from the other Canadian provinces? Explain your views.

» What can all Canadians do to learn more about the French-English realities in Canada?

CHAPTER REVIEW

» Imagine that you have just come back from visiting the province of Quebec. Write a letter to a friend describing your activities and your impressions of the province and its people.

Chapter Ten

The Atlantic Provinces

Quick Facts

» Canada's Atlantic provinces include the three Maritime provinces (New Brunswick, Nova Scotia, and Prince Edward Island) and Newfoundland and Labrador. (*Maritime* means *having to do with the sea*.)

» Newfoundland and Labrador includes the island of Newfoundland and the mainland territory of Labrador.

» New Brunswick and Nova Scotia were two of the four founding provinces at Confederation in 1867; Prince Edward Island (PEI) joined Canada in 1873; Newfoundland was the last province to join Canada, and did so in 1949.

» The populations of the provinces are New Brunswick 750 000, Newfoundland and Labrador 510 000, Nova Scotia 950 000, and PEI 145 000.

» New Brunswick is the only province of Canada that is officially bilingual and has a large proportion of people fluent in English and French.

» Prince Edward Island is Canada's smallest province with a land area of 5660 square kilometres.

» The capital cities are Fredericton, New Brunswick; St. John's, Newfoundland and Labrador; Halifax, Nova Scotia; and Charlottetown, PEI.

» The provincial flowers and birds are New Brunswick—purple violet and blackcapped chickadee; Newfoundland and Labrador—pitcher plant and Atlantic puffin; Nova Scotia—mayflower (no provincial bird); and Prince Edward Island—lady's slipper and blue jay.

Introduction

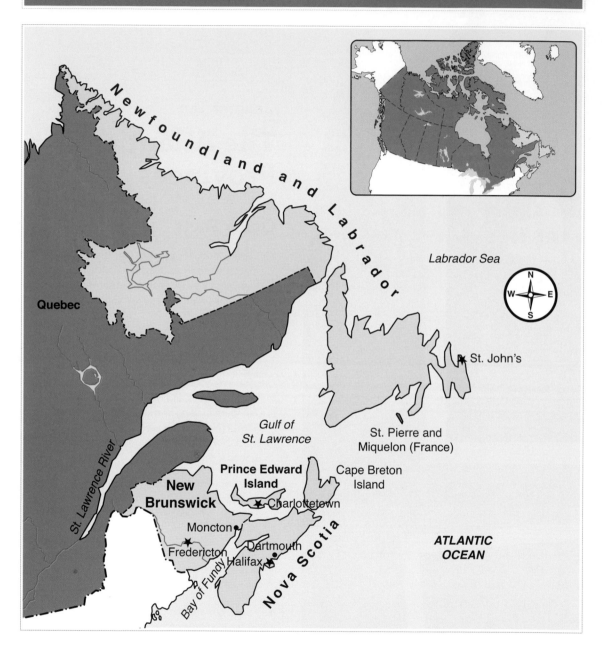

The four Atlantic provinces on Canada's east coast without doubt make up one of the most appealing areas of the country. When we think of Atlantic Canada, we think of lobster traps and fishing boats, singers Anne Murray and Rita MacNeil, the Cabot Trail, and Peggys Cove. These are only some of the interesting people and sites from Canada's east coast. Maritimers and Newfoundlanders have a reputation for warmth and *joie de vivre* that makes most *come from aways* mildly envious.

New Brunswick

The People and History

If you walk into a tourist office or visit a market in New Brunswick, you are likely to hear both English and French being spoken, sometimes both in the same conversation! While over half of the province's population speak English only and about one-tenth speak French only, many are bilingual. In fact, New Brunswick is Canada's only officially bilingual province. Like the city of Ottawa, this province gives you the experience of both French and English cultures.

The French-speaking Acadians are an important part of the province's history and still make up a vital community in New Brunswick today. They were the first European settlers in the region. The Mi'kmaq and Maliseet had already been there for centuries. In 1755, after the British took over the region, the Acadians were asked to swear an oath of allegiance to the British king. When they refused, they were deported. Some fled to the American colonies, to France, and to Quebec. Many later returned in the 1770s and 1780s and re-established themselves in different parts of the country. Some resettled in New Brunswick, along with British and American settlers, including thousands of United Empire Loyalists who came from the United States (US) after the American Revolution. Later, many Scots and Irish settled in the province.

The Acadians are a proud, independent people and have not only succeeded in maintaining their cultural identity, but have in fact increased in number. New Brunswick's French population rose from 16 percent of the total population in 1871 to a high of 40 percent in 1961. That percentage has since decreased. When tourists visit the many reconstructed forts and villages throughout New Brunswick, the guides often tell you proudly of their ancestors, the Acadians, and their achievements.

On the other hand, if you walk the streets of the province's capital city, Fredericton, you may

The old mill in the historic village of Kings Landing, New Brunswick

be surprised by the lack of visible minorities. New Brunswick has one of the lowest levels of immigration in Canada. For example, in 2005, only 3.1 percent of people living in the province had immigrated there. Of those, 40 percent come from the US or the United Kingdom (UK).

New Brunswick still has many reminders of its rich history. Kings Landing on the St. John River is a charming reconstructed Loyalist village from the 1850s with a sawmill, pub, general store, theatre, and traditional musicians. To the north at Hartland you can see the longest covered wooden bridge in the world, dating from the days of horses and carriages. About an hour's drive farther north is Grand Falls, a town with an impressive waterfall at its centre. At Caraquet on the northeast coast is Acadian Historical Village, recreating early Acadian life.

The Picture Province

New Brunswick is known for its vast forests, scenic coastline, and Bay of Fundy tides. In Moncton, a city near the Nova Scotia border, you can join the tourists in watching the daily ritual of the tidal bore. Moncton is located on the Petitcodiac River, sometimes called "the chocolate river" because at low tide, it looks very much like chocolate milk. However, when the tide comes in, a wave up to a metre high rushes upriver. This wave, the tidal bore, brings the water level of the river up to 8 metres. When the tide is out in the Bay of Fundy, you can see the flowerpot-shaped rock islands, watch the birds come to feed, or walk on the wet sands and search for the remains of interesting sea creatures.

Another wondrous phenomenon in Moncton is Magnetic Hill, where you drive to the bottom of what seems like a hill, put your car in neutral, and enjoy the sensation of gradually falling *up* the slope. You are not really being pulled up. In fact, you are experiencing an optical illusion created by the contours of the surrounding hillside, but you certainly feel like you are going up!

In Fredericton, known for its tree-lined streets and nineteenth-century mansions, you can visit the famous Beaverbrook Art Gallery, see a play at the Fredericton Playhouse, or admire the interesting Legislative Assembly Building, constructed in 1882.

The Economy

New Brunswick's economy is largely dependent on forestry and forestry products. Fish and shellfish including lobsters, crabs, and scallops are also

The Hopewell Rocks, in the Bay of Fundy, were shaped by tidal erosion

important products, but overfishing has caused serious concerns and fish farming is becoming more popular. The province is also rich in minerals and there is some agriculture, with more emphasis on livestock than crop farming. A lot of money has gone into developing hydroelectric power plants. Recently, the province has also benefited from a fast-growing telecommunications industry. The three small urban centres have different economies. Saint John has heavy industry. Fredericton is dominated by government services, universities, and the military; and Moncton is a commercial, retail, and transportation distribution centre.

COMPREHENSION CHECK

❶ Which of the Atlantic Provinces is not part of the group called *The Maritimes*?
❷ Which of the Atlantic Provinces has a relatively large French-speaking population and what does that group call themselves?
❸ How are immigration patterns in New Brunswick different from those in other provinces?
❹ What happens during the tidal bore phenomenon?
❺ What are three important industries in New Brunswick?

VOCABULARY

joie de vivre	a French phrase meaning joy of living
come from aways	a Newfoundland expression for people who come to Newfoundland from elsewhere
envious	jealous; desiring something that someone else has
oath of allegiance	promise of loyalty

deported	sent out of a country or region
influx	a continuous entry of people
marked	noticeable
consistent	in the same pattern as previously; in agreement with
ritual	a sequence of actions followed repeatedly without change
phenomenon	an event we can observe, but for which we don't always know the cause; an extraordinary event or fact
optical	having to do with the eyes
illusion	an appearance which is not real, but which seems real
contours	outlines, especially of a natural feature such as a hill or mountain
mansions	large houses

USING NEW WORDS

Fill in each blank with a word from the list above.

1. When Newfoundlanders hear the accent of someone from outside the province, they often smile and say, "Oh, you're a _____."

2. Some newcomers feel obligated to create the _____ that they are very happy in Canada when, actually, they may be experiencing a lot of difficulty and pain after leaving their first country.

3. Heritage language education is _____ with the desire of minority groups to preserve their cultural identity.

4. Many visitors to Canada from smaller, heavily populated countries are _____ of Canada's large, open spaces and relatively small population.

5. After returning from a vacation in Hawaii, the couple had _____ suntans.

6. The _____ of European settlers to North America marked the end of a way of life for the Aboriginal peoples of the continent.

7. The freezing of water is a simple, commonplace _____ that still fascinates us, adult and child alike.

8. The criminal was _____ from the country to stand trial in the country where he had committed the crime.

9. Her morning _____ was to get up, take a shower, dress, and eat breakfast— always in that order.

FOR DISCUSSION

» Their cultural identity is very important to the Acadians. What steps can cultural minorities take to protect their cultural identities? How important is cultural identity to you?

» Do you think that people who belong to visible minorities would feel more comfortable settling in a province with few visible minorities or in a province with people from many racial backgrounds? Explain your reasoning.

» New Brunswick attracts many tourists who want to see the tidal bore and Magnetic Hill. What other unusual phenomena do you know of in Canada or in other parts of the world?

» Communities need to attract industry and small business owners to create employment. What do you think a community needs to be attractive to new industries?

Nova Scotia

Nova Scotia has retained a relaxed, comfortable atmosphere unusual for a modern, industrialized province. The hustle and bustle you would expect in a busy seaport like Halifax is just not there. Instead, you find friendly people who still think it is important to take the time to "shoot the breeze."

Culture and Heritage

Settled largely by Scots in the 1800s, Nova Scotia actually means *New Scotland*. The Scots, however, were not the first Europeans to reach the province's shores. Like New Brunswick, Nova Scotia has a large and thriving Acadian community. Most are the descendants of French peasant families who arrived in the 1630s and now live in

A bagpiper celebrates Scottish tradition in Peggys Cove

the Annapolis Valley of Nova Scotia. They experienced the same deportation order as the French-speaking Acadians in what is now New Brunswick when Acadia was taken over by the British. When some Acadians returned in the 1770s and 1780s, they found that their farms had been given to British settlers and they had to start all over again. It is not surprising that they have worked so hard to preserve their heritage. Many of the British settlers were United Empire Loyalists, who were followed by Scots in the 1800s.

Today, you can find the province's Scottish heritage in the bagpipers, fiddlers, and highland dancers who perform in communities around the province. Acadian festivals also include traditional Acadian dancing and other events. In celebration of days gone by, Nova Scotia has also developed thriving cottage industries with craftspeople producing and selling items such as quilts, handmade clothing, household linens, soaps, and candles. These goods are sought after in many parts of the country for their quaint beauty and high quality.

Halifax

Though it still has some beautiful historic buildings, the city of Halifax was largely rebuilt after the famous explosion of 1917 during World War I. Two ships collided in Halifax Harbour. One of those ships was carrying 227 000 kilograms of TNT, a powerful explosive, as well as other munitions. The explosion was so forceful that 2000 people were killed instantly and over 120 hectares of the city were flattened. Fires destroyed much of the remainder. Windows were shattered in Truro, over 80 kilometres away. The Halifax explosion goes down in history as one of the worst human-caused disasters.

Halifax is a significant port for ships crossing the Atlantic. On the streets and in the bars, you can meet sailors from all over the world enjoying a few days of shore leave in this relaxing and picturesque city. During the Halifax International

Halifax Harbour

Busker Festival in the summer, part of the fascination in watching these entertainers from all over the world lies in their backdrop: a parade of ships slowly passing behind them. The sailors on the ships are as fascinated by the entertainment as the crowds on the waterfront are.

Halifax boasts more universities than any other city in Canada. It has five universities and three colleges. Some are world-famous for their highly specialized programs. One such university is NSCAD, the Nova Scotia College of Art and Design. Students come from all over the world to study at these fine institutions. Many of these universities began with religious affiliations and have survived because they had the quality to attract students from far beyond the borders of their communities.

Across the harbour from Halifax lies Dartmouth, the second-largest community in Nova Scotia with 90 000 people and several manufacturing industries. Dartmouth is also home to many Black Canadians, some of whose families were forced out of Africville as we saw in Chapter 5. The Black Cultural Centre for Nova Scotia in Dartmouth is an interesting place to visit. Its exhibits help visitors understand the important role Black Canadians have played in our country and the obstacles they have faced.

There is also a large Black community in Halifax and racism has been a problem in this city, as in many large urban areas in the country. In the past, members of the Black community have not had the same opportunities as their white neighbours. Partly as a result of that reality, a Black culture has emerged complete with a different dialect of English that is not easily understood by many other Haligonians. Efforts are being made by many people to create equal opportunities for members of this community in the school and in the workplace.

The colourful town of Lunenburg

The Cabot Trail gives tourists a scenic trip around Cape Breton

Around the Province

While relatively flat in its geography, Nova Scotia's forests and interesting shoreline provide some of the most beautiful scenery in Canada. Tourists like to take the secondary highway southwest of Halifax and travel along the coast stopping at such well-known sites as Peggys Cove, Lunenburg, and Mahone Bay, a scenic town which reminds passersby of what Canada was probably like a century ago.

Another popular destination for tourists and the home of many of Canada's best-known folk artists is Cape Breton. Cape Breton is actually an island linked to mainland Nova Scotia by a causeway. The people of Cape Breton Island are very rooted to their homeland and have remained relatively distinct in their dialect and customs. Their Scottish heritage may be found in the lively fiddling music and dancing which are trademarks of the area. Alexander Graham Bell, the creator of the telephone, spent his summers at Baddeck on the island and a museum there is named after him.

The Cabot Trail makes a 300-kilometre circle around the island and provides tourists with some of the best scenery in Canada. The trail follows the coastline through fishing villages, farmlands, and rugged headlands. Cape Breton Highlands National Park would remind a visiting Scot of the highlands of Scotland.

Nova Scotia has a proud history as a ship-building centre. If you look at a Canadian dime, you will see an image of the *Bluenose*, one of the most famous schooners ever built. While the original *Bluenose* no longer exists, you can see a replica (copy) of the original ship in Lunenburg Harbour or at festivals in other ports around the province.

The Economy

Fishing has always been an important industry in Nova Scotia. The decline in cod stocks on the Grand Banks, however, has created major concerns for fishery workers. The federal government has spent a lot of money to provide retraining programs, but unfortunately unemployment remains high, especially in the rural areas.

Coal mining is another important industry in Nova Scotia. When Canadians think of this province, some will remember the Springhill mining disaster which claimed the lives of several men in 1958. Springhill also calls to mind the ever-popular Anne Murray, a folk and country singer from this small town. Originally a physical education teacher, Anne Murray sang on national television and from then on soared to the top of the charts. Her recordings are now sold all over the world. The many gold albums she has earned attest to her popularity.

Eager to find new ways of stimulating a slow economy, the province is promoting tourism and filmmaking. It would also like to attract high-tech industry to the area.

COMPREHENSION CHECK

1. What disaster destroyed most of Halifax in 1917?
2. Name three ethnic groups from Europe whose members settled in early Nova Scotia.
3. What is one way in which Halifax is quite different from other urban centres in Canada?
4. Why is Anne Murray famous?
5. What problem do people who have gone through retraining programs in Nova Scotia face at this time?

VOCABULARY

retained	kept the same
hustle and bustle	busyness; a lot of activity
shoot the breeze	an idiom meaning to converse casually, to chat
cottage industries	industries which can be operated out of a home, usually arts and crafts of some sort
collided	bumped into each other
munitions	ammunition; explosives to be used with weapons
shattered	broken into small pieces
affiliations	relationships or connections
dialect	a version of a language used by one group of speakers but not others
Haligonians	people who live in Halifax
causeway	a raised road across a stretch of water
headlands	points of land extending out into the water
attest to	offer proof or evidence of

USING NEW WORDS

Fill in each blank with a word or term from the list above.

1. When her husband left her and their new baby, her heart felt as if it had been _____ into a million pieces.
2. The Gulf Islands off British Columbia are also noted for their strong _____ such as pottery, weaving, and soap-making.
3. The expression *blood is thicker than water* means that the _____ you feel with members of your family are stronger than the loyalty you feel to people outside your family.
4. When the young couple did the renovations on their old house, they _____ the style of the original.
5. His fine reputation would _____ to his good character.

6. Sometimes, when people hear someone speak a _____ of English they are not familiar with, they think English is not the speaker's first language.

7. It's great fun to _____ if you are not too busy.

8. The man's insurance rates went up a lot when his car _____ with a bus.

9. Rush hour in Toronto is a good example of the _____ one finds in most big cities in Canada.

10. _____ are lucky to have a large number of small universities and colleges located in their city.

FOR DISCUSSION

» What advantages and disadvantages can you see to living in Halifax rather than some other capital city?

» Some people look for high quality of life in deciding where to live, while others look for the best economic advantage. What is most important to you in deciding where you want to live?

» The explosion of 1917 was a terrible disaster caused by human error. What other disasters do you know of which were caused by human beings, either on purpose or in error?

» The rise of cottage industries is often a response to the fact that other kinds of employment aren't available. If you could not find a job, what skills do you or you and your friends have which could be used to create a cottage industry?

FOR FUN

People from Halifax are called Haligonians. What do you think people from these cities and provinces are called?

Toronto	_____
Calgary	_____
Alberta	_____
Edmonton	_____
Quebec	_____
Montreal	_____
Winnipeg	_____
Newfoundland	_____
Vancouver	_____
Prince Edward Island	_____

(You can find the answers for this activity on page 251 at the back of the book.)

Prince Edward Island

The setting for *Anne of Green Gables* is a National Historic Site

A Visitor's Delight

When we think of PEI, as Canadians often call the country's smallest province, two things most often spring to mind: *Anne of Green Gables* and potatoes. While there is much more to this province, there is no doubt that Anne and potatoes are the driving forces behind the local economy. *Anne of Green Gables* is a novel written by Lucy Maud Montgomery. Canadians and people in many countries of the world fell in love with the red-haired orphan named Anne who, adopted by a rather strict older couple, captured their hearts and ours with her simple but humorous ways. *Anne* has become a multi-million dollar industry in PEI. Every year tourists come by the thousands to visit Cavendish, the home of the author and the setting for her novels. The Japanese have a particular affection for this freckle-faced character. Before *Anne* became so popular, potatoes were virtually the mainstay of the economy. They grow in abundance in PEI's unique red soil.

Anne of Green Gables may be the centre of the tourism industry, but that industry is also well-supported by the scenic shoreline, delicious seafood, and quaint accommodations on the island. Some tourists return annually to the same bed and breakfast and find there people they met in previous years. The owners are often happy to open the kitchen to their guests, who happily cook up a kettle of lobsters and eat them with a nice white wine as they chat into the evening. Many bed and breakfasts overlook the waves of the Atlantic Ocean washing over the coastline. There is also Prince Edward Island National Park which runs along the north shore and offers warm, white, sandy beaches in summer. From the beaches you can see the spectacular red cliffs which are especially picturesque at sunrise and sunset. The lobsters from PEI are well-known throughout the country for their tastiness, as are the oysters from Malpeque Bay.

As in Nova Scotia, some strong cottage industries have sprung up to meet the demands of tourists who want souvenirs of their visit to the province. Tourists have been especially impressed with some of the fine woodwork done by local craftspeople. The dyed porcupine quills and strips of ash used by the Mi'kmaq to make baskets in the same beautiful designs of their ancestors are another valued craft.

Culture and Heritage

Islanders know their roots. At one time, the Acadians formed the majority of the population, but now make up a small percentage. Nevertheless, the Acadians' language, literature, music, dance, cooking, and crafts are enjoying a popularity which is growing rather than shrinking. The Celtic roots in the area are also apparent in the number of redheads you can see staffing the shops on the island. Eighty per cent of the island's population trace their heritage to the British Isles. We see that connection still in the popular highland dancing from Scotland, the Irish folk songs, and the English architecture throughout the island's capital city. There are also some people of Lebanese origins on the island. Most of their ancestors came in the late 1800s and early 1900s as peddlars who travelled from house to house selling their wares or who opened small corner stores. The success of the Lebanese merchants led to their playing a significant role in the economy and politics of the island. Most Canadians today would recognize the name of Joe Ghiz, who was premier from 1986 to 1992. In 2007, Robert Ghiz, following in his father's political footsteps, was elected premier of PEI.

The capital city of the province is Charlottetown, best known historically as the place where the first conference on Confederation was held. Now, it is a growing city, the seat of government for the province, and the centre of hospitality for visiting tourists. A place popular with residents and guests alike is the Confederation Centre of the Arts. Not only does the centre house one of Canada's finest museums, but its art gallery hosts a number of important Canadian works of art along with visiting exhibitions which change regularly. The centre's production of *Anne of Green Gables* in the summer months is a popular one with tour groups and sells out well in advance.

How do you get to the island? In the past, people flew in or came by ferry from Nova Scotia. Now, they can drive across the Confederation Bridge which links the mainland with the island. This 12.9-kilometre-long bridge is considered a feat of modern engineering. It was completed in 1997 after four years of work at a cost of one billion dollars. Travellers are advised to check the status of the bridge in bad weather because it is closed in high winds or storm conditions.

Charlottetown City Hall

COMPREHENSION CHECK

Are the following statements true or false?

1. Lucy Maud Montgomery was the character in a famous book written by Anne Cavendish.
2. The shoreline of PEI is rugged and beautiful in places, with red cliffs and white sandy beaches.
3. There are no indigenous peoples living on PEI.
4. There is a large cottage industry (local handicrafts) on the island.
5. Joe Ghiz is a famous baseball player from PEI.

VOCABULARY

orphan	a child whose parents have died
freckle-faced	having small brown spots on the cheeks, often as a result of being in the sun a lot
virtually	as far as the essential facts are concerned
mainstay of	the most important support to
souvenirs	objects you buy to remind you of a vacation or place you visit (from the French word for *to remember*)
porcupine quills	the needle-like protrusions covering the skin of the porcupine
Celtic	of the Celts, an ancient people whose descendants include the people of Scotland and Ireland, among others. Red hair was common in these people.
peddlars	people who sell things from door to door or on the street
character	the unique and special qualities of a person, place, or thing

USING NEW WORDS

Fill in each blank with a word or term from the list above.

1. _____ all people feel the need to be treated with respect by others.
2. A strong _____ is a valuable asset for anyone to have.
3. Agriculture is the _____ of Saskatchewan's economy.
4. It seems rather strange to buy _____ in one country, only to find that they were manufactured in another country.
5. The very name of Nova Scotia tells us that many of its citizens are descended from _____ roots.
6. An _____ in Canada seldom has difficulty finding an adoptive family.

FOR DISCUSSION

» The Anne books, as they are often called, are so popular that they have become part of our Canadian identity and culture. Can you think of books in your own culture that most people think of with affection? What is it about such books that makes them so popular?

» What do you think of the practice of buying souvenirs when you go on holiday to a special place?

Newfoundland and Labrador

To Join or Not to Join

Newfoundlanders are a proud people who clung to their independence for a long time before they agreed to join the rest of Canada. Many Canadians recognize Joey Smallwood, long-time premier of Newfoundland, for the role he played in bringing Canada its tenth province. He was premier from 1949 until 1972, a total of 23 years. The words of the following anti-Confederation song speak poetically of the strong feelings pre-Confederation Newfoundlanders had towards Canada:

> Hurray for our own native isle, Newfoundland!
> Not a stranger shall hold one inch of its strand!
> Her face turns to Britain, her back to the Gulf,
> Come near at your peril, Canadian Wolf!

> Ye brave Newfoundlanders who plough the
>   salt sea
> With hearts like the eagle so bold and so free,
> The time is at hand when you'll all have to say
> If Confederation will carry the day.

> Cheap tea and molasses they say they will give,
> All taxes take off that the poor man may live;
> Cheap nails and cheap lumber our coffins to
>   make,
> And homespun to mend our old clothes when
>   they break.

> If they take off the taxes how then will they meet
> The heavy expense of the country's upkeep?
> Just give them the chance to get us in the scrape
> And they'll chain us like slaves with pen, ink,
>   and red tape.

> Would you barter the rights that your fathers
>   have won,
> Your freedom transmitted from father to son?
> For a few thousand dollars of Canadian gold,
> Don't let it be said that our birthright was sold.

> Then hurrah for our own native isle,
>   Newfoundland!
> Not a stranger shall hold one inch of its strand!
> Her face turns to Britain, her back to the Gulf,
> Come near at your peril, Canadian Wolf!

COMPREHENSION CHECK

1. What are the main feelings behind this song?
2. What is Canada compared to in the first verse of this song?
3. What is the chief benefit in joining Confederation, according to the song?
4. What are the main disadvantages in joining?
5. What expression is used in the fourth verse which refers to bureaucracy?
6. Explain how verse four expresses a distrust of the Canadian promises.

VOCABULARY

clung to	held on tightly or closely to
strand	shore; land bordering the sea
peril	acute or serious danger
molasses	a thick, brown, sweet substance made from either sugar cane or sugar beet and which comes before granular sugar in the refining process; normally used for flavour and sweetness in baking

homespun	a rough, inexpensive cotton fabric
in the scrape	an expression which means in difficulty
red tape	an idiom which refers to the bureaucratic delays often experienced in dealing with government
barter	exchange
transmitted to	passed on or given to

USING NEW WORDS

» Working with a partner or in groups of four, see if you can come up with a fictional story using at least six of the words and expressions above. Then, read your story aloud to the rest of your classmates and listen to their stories. Which group wrote the best story? How did you decide?

FOR DISCUSSION

» From what the song says, which ethnic group do you think was primarily responsible for settling Newfoundland?

» Newfoundland has one of the highest rates of unemployment in the country today and has had one of the highest rates for some time. Why do you think that Newfoundland finally did join Confederation?

» Do you know of other countries where people did not believe it was in their best interests to join others around them and become or remain one country?

» What are the advantages in unity? What are the advantages in independence?

Newfoundland and Labrador Today

Newfoundlanders have retained a distinct identity. Their Irish-like accent is well-recognized across the country and there are in the *Newfie* dialect many expressions which other Canadians do not understand. People, for example, fall into one of three groups: *townies* if they live in the city, *baymen* if they live in the outports, and *CFAs* or *come from aways* as strangers are called.

People raised in Newfoundland and Labrador are often identified by their family relationships, as they are in many other cultures outside Canada. For example, instead of introducing a stranger to someone in the community by saying,

"This is Michael O'Flaherty, the manager of our local bank," Newfoundlanders would be more likely to say, "This is Michael O'Flaherty, the son of John O'Flaherty and Molly Malone, you know."

More than in any other part of Canada, people take time to visit with one another. Some still consider it quite rude to pass a person on the street without having a little chat. People will even stop their cars on the street for a brief "how are you?" and few get upset at the temporary halt in the traffic. In the outport communities, it is beyond understanding to lock your door since people drop in unannounced on a regular basis.

Perhaps it is this strong sense of community which has enabled Newfoundlanders to

Unique architecture in St. John's, Newfoundland

triumph over adversity through the years. Where unemployment in other parts of the country has sometimes led to depression and all its ugly consequences, you do not have that sense in Newfoundland. Rather, people celebrate their blessings, share with one another, and make do in the time-honoured tradition of strong communities everywhere.

Newfoundlanders enjoy a wealth of folk music, like their neighbours in Nova Scotia. Their folk music tells stories of their lives at sea and in the harsh Atlantic climate. Their songs of struggle with survival as well as the joys and humour of romance are reminiscent of old English and Irish ballads, the ballads of their ancestors. Played with a fiddle and a button accordion, the ballads were never written down. They were passed along orally and thus varied from village to village. Two very popular groups in the province today are Great Big Sea and the Irish Descendants, both of which have revived the old music and given it new life for younger generations.

Today's Newfoundland and Labrador, in spite of a strong pulp and paper industry and some mining, is not as prosperous as many of its neighbouring provinces, a fact which some Newfoundlanders blame on their decision to join Confederation by a narrow majority in 1949. The land is mostly rocky Canadian Shield and the sea, which sustained the people so generously for centuries, has lost its abundant stocks of cod. The situation is so serious that the people are no longer allowed to fish off the Grand Banks. The closure of the cod fisheries has brought much hardship to the people of Newfoundland and Labrador, many of whom were dependent on the cod for their livelihoods. They are very angry at foreign fishing boats which come close to their waters and deplete the ocean of cod even further. Unemployment rates in the province remain high, and some Newfoundlanders have chosen to look elsewhere in Canada for jobs. Albertans, for example, all know of Newfoundlanders who have come to Alberta for work in places such as

Fort McMurray or Edmonton. Most plan to return home when they retire.

Even the climate of this province is distinctive. While moderated by the ocean, the weather is nowhere near as mild as that of our western province by the sea, British Columbia. The Labrador current brings the Arctic cold to Newfoundland and Labrador. Spring comes late because of the ice brought south by the current. It is also the windiest of the four Atlantic provinces. Winds can reach up to 180 kilometres an hour and have been known to blow trains off their tracks. Newfoundlanders brag that you can experience all four seasons in one day on their island because the weather can change so dramatically in a short time. Freezing rain and frequent fog are commonplace in this province.

Newfoundlanders have two unexpected neighbours to the south: the tiny islands of Saint-Pierre and Miquelon. These islands are still under the jurisdiction of France, yet are but a short ferry ride from Newfoundland!

The Toll of the Sea

The people of Newfoundland and Labrador have lived for centuries from the bounty of the sea, but it has not been without a price. The following poem by E.J. Pratt expresses this fact.

Erosion

It took the sea a thousand years,
A thousand years to trace
The granite features of this cliff,
In crag and scarp and base.
It took the sea an hour one night,
An hour of storm to place
The sculpture of these granite seams
Upon a woman's face.

Source: Pratt, E.J.: "Erosion" from *E.J. Pratt: Complete Poems*, ed. Sandra Djwa and R.G. Moyles, © University of Toronto Press, 1989. Reprinted with permission of the publisher.

The Atlantic is a wild, cold ocean and both fishermen and sealers lead a hard life. Many folk songs have been written about those who were lost in storms or fogs, or who were killed by shifting ice.

There have been over 700 documented shipwrecks off the coasts of Newfoundland and Labrador. The most famous of these was the *Titanic* which sank on its first voyage from England in 1912. More recently, Canadians recall when the oil rig *Ocean Ranger* sank in 1982, killing over 80 people.

Building a New Economy

Newfoundlanders realize how important it is to find other sources of income for the population, especially in light of the moratorium on cod fishing. The Institute for Marine Dynamics shows leadership in marine research and many new companies are manufacturing goods which range from metal products to satellite communications equipment. There is also a lot of interest in the production of computer software, medical care innovations, and aerospace equipment. Business people are also looking for ways to create markets

Many Newfoundlanders made their living from the ocean, but fish stocks have declined

for sea products which are not well-known, such as seaweeds and less popular kinds of fish and shellfish. Newfoundlanders are open to adapting to a changing world.

St. John's, Capital by the Sea

St. John's is a small but interesting city to visit. Built on the hillside rising up from the harbour, old and new buildings host businesses, shops, and government offices. The city has its own university, called Memorial University of Newfoundland. Visitors like to go to the park at Signal Hill from which the first trans-Atlantic wireless signal was received by Guglielmo Marconi in 1901.

Visitors to the city can stay in a first-class hotel if they choose or in one of the lovely old bed and breakfasts overlooking the harbour. The weather is extremely variable in this city so, regardless of the time of year, dress in layers and take a good raincoat!

COMPREHENSION CHECK

❶ In what ways do many Newfoundlanders sound different from other Canadians when they speak?

❷ What are the roots of Newfoundland and Labrador's folk music?

VOCABULARY

outports	small, remote fishing villages
triumph (over)	conquer or overcome
adversity	difficult, sustained problems
make do	use what you have and make the best of it, even if more would be desirable
revived	brought back; given new life
sustained	maintained continuously over a long period of time
moratorium	a temporary ban or suspension
deplete	reduce in number or quantity
moderated	made less extreme
toll	something paid, lost, or suffered; a charge for or cost of using something
granite	a hard rock
sealers	those who hunt seal
documented	proven and written about
delicacy	something very special to eat; sometimes appreciated by those who are accustomed to it but not by strangers
jurisdiction	authority or administration

USING NEW WORDS

Fill in each blank with a word or term from the list above.

❶ Many people living in Newfoundland and Labrador's _____ have known one another for generations.

❷ You can _____ over _____ if you have faith, hope, and determination.

❸ The city charged a _____ of 50 cents to cross the new bridge.

❹ The city placed a _____ on new commercial developments until it had completed its new development plan.

❺ The people on the beach thought that the child had drowned until she was _____ by a lifeguard.

❻ There are few of us who have not had to _____ when money was scarce.

❼ _____ is very good for use in the construction of small buildings because it is very hard and lasts a long time.

❽ When life is _____ by artificial means, it is difficult to know when to allow a person to die without further interference.

❾ Snake meat is considered a _____ in many parts of the world.

❿ His kind, gentle words _____ her anger.

⓫ The man was a convicted thief and his crimes were well _____.

FOR DISCUSSION

» What are the advantages and disadvantages of living in small communities where everyone knows everything about you? Which do you prefer—life in a small community or in a large city?

» Newfoundlanders seem to have found, for the most part, a way to be happy in spite of their economic woes. How do you think they do this? What can you learn from them?

» What is the function of folk music in a society?

CHAPTER REVIEW

Divide your class into four groups. Each group represents one of the four Atlantic Provinces. Now, imagine that your group has been selected by the provincial government to participate in a regional development think tank. It is your job to argue on behalf of your province and to work cooperatively with the rest of your class to decide how 100 million dollars can best be spent over the next five years for the economic development of your province.

Consider

» your province's natural resources and human resources
» your history of employment
» your relationship to the other provinces, which also want and need this money
» your values as a people
» the location of your population
» the needs of the global and national communities
» your commitment as a province to becoming fully independent economically

11

Chapter Eleven

Canada's North

Quick Facts

» Canada's North includes Yukon, the Northwest Territories (NWT), and Nunavut.

» The NWT joined Confederation in 1870; Yukon joined in 1898. Nunavut was carved out of the eastern NWT in 1999.

» The capital cities are Whitehorse, Yukon; Yellowknife, NWT; and Iqaluit, Nunavut.

» Canada's North is often called The Land of the Midnight Sun.

» The estimated population of Yukon is 36 000; the population of the NWT is 44 000; and the population of Nunavut is 33 000.

» The flower of Yukon is the fireweed and the bird is the common raven; the flower of the NWT is the mountain avens and the bird is the gyrfalcon; the flower of Nunavut is the purple saxifrage and the bird is the rock ptarmigan.

» Nunavut has three official languages: English, Inuit (Inuktitut and Inuinnaqtun), and French. (Inuinnaqtun is written in roman letters like English while Inuktitut is written in syllabic symbols, each of which represents a syllable.)

Introduction

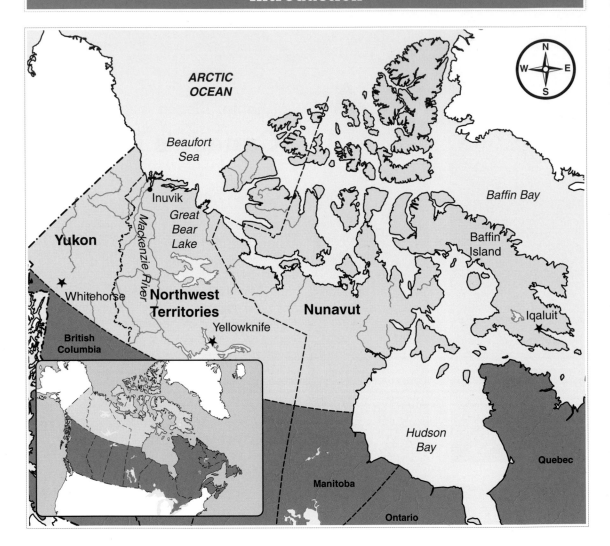

Considering the relatively small population of Canada's northern territories, there is a remarkable interest in Canada's North and a great deal of folklore about the area. Many Canadian school children have studied the challenging lifestyle of the early Inuit, formerly called Eskimos. Their old way of life was unlike any other in the country. In addition, there are numerous poems and sagas telling of the gold rush days in the 1890s, when the discovery of gold in Canada's North sent many people scrambling to find their fortunes.

Today, because of the harsh climate and the relative isolation of the area, most people who live in the North year round are the Native people and those serving the needs of miners and tourists in the communities. With long hours of winter darkness and bitter cold, life is seldom easy in Canada's northlands.

Miners, geologists, and construction workers often venture temporarily into the North for employment. The pay is excellent and the normal work routine is to spend a period of time in the

North, followed by a rest period in the South. For example, workers may spend one month in, two weeks out. There is little recreation in these work camps, so people tend to work long days and take no days off until they leave the area for their break.

Edmonton has often been called the *Gateway to the North* since flights into Yukon and Northwest Territories (NWT) most often come from that city, and off-duty workers frequently take their leave there. Ottawa and Montreal, meanwhile, are the main departure points for those heading to Iqaluit. Perishable supplies are often flown into northern communities, while non-perishables are driven in over the two main highways serving much of this vast area. All supplies are flown in to Iqaluit, as there are no roads connecting it with the South. The distance makes supplies very expensive to buy in the North. That is one reason salaries tend to be much higher there than in other regions of Canada. Due to the cold, it is also very expensive to heat the homes. In other words, the cost of daily living in the North is high. While there are doctors and nurses to serve the everyday healthcare needs of the people, the small size of the population means that people often have to fly out to Edmonton or Montreal if they need specialists or other services not available in their communities.

Small airlines such as First Air serve a growing interest in tourism in the North. In winter, tourists travel to Yellowknife and other centres to view the Aurora Borealis or ride in a dogsled. In the long days of summer, they may choose to experience the vast and beautiful scenery or attend a festival where they can listen to throat singers and watch some of the unique Inuit games which traditionally are co-operative rather than competitive. Other activities include kayaking, canoeing, rafting, and seeing some of the gigantic icebergs whose rapid melting is thought to be contributing to rising water levels all over the world. Yearlong, tourists enjoy the warm hospitality of their northern hosts and the storytelling abilities of the Inuit elders.

The animals unique to the North are also of

Tourists view an iceberg up close

interest to many who come from the South to visit. These include walruses, polar bears, caribou, muskox, beluga and bowhead whales, and the famous narwhals with their long tusks protruding up to three metres from their upper-left jaws. The narwhal is the source of some controversy. The Inuit have hunted it for years for its meat and also exported the long tusks for as much as $450 per metre. The federal government has made it illegal to export the tusks in order to protect these animals that are said to be overhunted.

Nunavut

In 1999, Canada's newest territory was created in what used to be the eastern part of the Northwest Territories. This territory, Nunavut, covers about 14 percent of the total land area of Canada. *Nunavut* means *our land* in Inuktitut. It is home to approximately 17 500 Inuit. In exchange for direct ownership over 18 percent of the territory and 1.15 billion dollars over 14 years, the Inuit gave up any other land claims in what remains of the territory. In some ways, it seems to be a very good arrangement for the Inuit; in others, it may not be. The Inuit used to have hunting, fishing, and trapping rights over a much larger area, but mineral rights over only 22 500 square kilometres of the 219 000 square kilometres in question. The creation of Nunavut made the Inuit the largest single landowning group in the world. On the other hand, the Inuit still do not have full self-government. The territorial government remains under the jurisdiction of the federal government in Ottawa, like the governments of Yukon and the Northwest Territories. Still, the Inuit have more control over their land and resources than they did previously.

COMPREHENSION CHECK

Ask a question that will give you each answer below.

1. gold
2. Inuit
3. miners, geologists, and construction workers
4. Iqaluit
5. 44 000 people (Hint: Check the Quick Facts at the beginning of the chapter to help you with this one.)
6. Nunavut

VOCABULARY

remarkable	worthy of notice; unusual
folklore	the traditional customs, beliefs, songs, and stories of a people preserved in primarily oral form
sagas	narratives or stories of heroic achievements
scrambling	struggling hastily in competition with others for something
venture	risk loss or injury in pursuit of some advantage
perishable	naturally subject to speedy decay (for example, fresh foods which spoil quickly)
specialist	doctor who specializes in one kind of medicine (pediatricians work with children; obstetricians work with pregnant women)
throat singing	a type of singing unique to the Inuit cultures

USING NEW WORDS

Fill in each blank with a word or term from the list above.

1. Only the top student would win the scholarship, so everyone was _____ to get the best mark on the final examination.
2. _____ foods are normally kept in the refrigerator until they are to be eaten.
3. When the boy was young, he loved to sit with his grandfather and listen to him tell _____ of the old Norwegian heroes.
4. Canadians are familiar with some of the _____ of many different cultures because people in Canada come from so many different places.
5. An orthopedic surgeon is a _____ who operates on bones.

6 Terry Fox is considered a Canadian hero because of his _____ feat of running across much of Canada with cancer and an artificial leg.

7 Children are urged not to _____ outside after dark by themselves, especially in the cities.

FOR DISCUSSION

» Why do you think the North is often called the Land of the Midnight Sun?

» Why do you think most Inuit choose to stay in the North rather than move south?

» Have you ever considered living and working in Canada's North? What do you think some of the advantages and disadvantages would be?

» Is the deal between the Inuit and the government of Canada regarding Nunavut a good deal for both? Why or why not?

Land of the Midnight Sun

A lake along the Ingraham Trail in the Northwest Territories

When Canadians who have never visited the North think of it, images of snow, ice, and the Northern Lights most often come to mind. While those are all part of the northern experience, they are not all of it. For people who fly over the North for the first time, the almost overwhelming impression is of the vast size of the forests and lakes, uninterrupted by towns, roads, and other signs of people. It is so very beautiful and so peaceful. It makes you imagine what the earth may have been like thousands and thousands of years ago before humans began to dominate the planet.

The North covers one-third of Canada's land mass and has a great variety of landforms. In addition to vast stretches of forest and even more vast areas of ice and snow, you can also find mountains, lowland plains, and the rocky Canadian Shield. One of the most interesting areas is the lowland tundra. People who live there say they live above the treeline because there are no trees. It is too cold for trees to grow, but there are lichens, mosses, grasses, and low shrubs. The permafrost ensures that everything deeper than half a metre in the ground stays frozen all year long.

One of the most amazing spectacles to outsiders is the splendour of flowering meadows during the short but intense summers in the North. Because there is so much sunlight in the summer months, gardens grow quickly and the wildflowers show off their brilliance, as if they know they have little time to do so. In the summer it is truly the land of the midnight sun—areas near the Arctic Circle and northward experience 24-hour daylight during part of the summer months—whereas in the winter it feels like the land of endless darkness.

The Aurora Borealis

The North is well-known for this unusually beautiful phenomenon, otherwise known as the Northern Lights. In the cold of winter, Canadians can look up and see dancing ribbons of coloured light rippling across the sky. The colours vary from

The Aurora Borealis

almost fluorescent blues and greens to intense pinks, mauves, and other colours. Whereas Edmontonians and other southerners can see these lights from time to time, they are best observed in the North between December and March. Many theories have been advanced to explain them, but the currently popular theory is that they are caused by radiation. Scientists believe that light is given off when atoms in the upper atmosphere are hit by fast-moving electrons and protons. The lights are most active two days after intense activity on the surface of the sun.

COMPREHENSION CHECK

1. What is remarkable about the northern landscape in the summer?
2. What do we see when watching the Northern Lights?
3. What do scientists believe causes these lights?
4. Can people living in the cities of southern Canada see them?

VOCABULARY

lichens   small, short plants which spread over the surface of land, rock, or trees; many lichens have small flowers

spectacle   an unusual or dramatic event or presentation

splendour   beauty on a large scale

fluorescent   describes colours with an unusual sense of light in them

atoms   the smallest particles in any element which still contain all the properties of that element

USING NEW WORDS

Fill in each blank with a word from the list above.

1. Physicists have learned to divide _____ into protons, electrons, and neutrons.
2. Clothing with _____ stripes is used for safety reasons because these stripes can be seen in the dark.
3. What can compare with the _____ of a summer sunset over the lake with a loon calling in the background?
4. We are often surprised to see _____ growing on rocks with no visible soil to nourish them.
5. The sight of 10 000 people cheering for Gilles Vigneault, the Québécois folk singer, was a _____ the students will never forget.

FOR DISCUSSION

» What do you think that the ancient Aboriginals may have believed about the meaning of the Northern Lights?

Aboriginal Peoples of the North

Inuit hunting for walrus

There are three groups of Aboriginals in the North. The Inuit are the people of the tundra. *Inuit* means *the people* in their language, a term they prefer to *Eskimo* which means *meat eater* in the Algonquian language. The Dene are the people of the inland forests and river valleys. There are also many Métis living in the North. In contrast to the cold land in which they live, the people generally have warm hearts and welcome visitors with great hospitality. They have survived their harsh environment because they understand the importance of community. They share what they have with one another.

The Inuit have lived in the Arctic for a very long time. Before people interested in developing the natural resources came to the area, the Inuit lived in harmony with the animals and the seasons. Their homes were igloos, small domed houses made from blocks of ice cut to size. The seals and whales, as well as the occasional polar bear, provided their food and clothing, and the blubber they used to heat and light their homes. They travelled over the icy land by way of dogsleds and hunted in the cold waters of the Arctic Ocean in kayaks made from the skins of animals. Even the bones of animals were used to make weapons and tools. Communities were small and people took care of one another. A seal or whale caught by one meant sustenance for all. Shamans served not only as spiritual leaders and healers of the community, but also as dreamers who "dreamed" the location of the next day's catch at sea or on land, in the tradition of shamans everywhere.

The Dene people live in the forests of the Mackenzie Valley, which stretches from the Alberta border north to the Beaufort Sea. These people speak seven different languages and share a cultural heritage with people as far away as New Mexico. While many are hunters and trappers, others—like many Métis—are joining the professions and trades which serve their communities.

In the past, caribou were the main source of food for the Dene. They followed the herds in much the same way as the Aboriginals on the prairies followed the buffalo herds. When pipelines and highways were built in the area, however, they interrupted the natural path of these herds and disrupted the lives of the peoples who depended on them.

Trapping was also important to the Dene. Even today, many depend on their traplines to catch small animals whose pelts are valued for fur coats, in spite of the increasing awareness that such luxuries are driving some of these animals close to extinction. Beaver, mink, lynx, and fox are still made into very expensive coats, though they are less popular than they once were. Some people now consider it politically incorrect to wear fur coats.

Life for Aboriginals in the North has changed, and not always for the better. Many people died from tuberculosis, a disease brought in by whalers, trappers, and other workers at the beginning of the twentieth century. Like First Nations peoples south of them, the Inuit also lost many of their old spiritual ways when Christian missionaries came north to teach the Christian faith. The missionaries built schools and hospitals and believed they were helping the Inuit, but they disrupted the way of life the Inuit had always known. Later other schools were set up in the North, but few teachers would stay beyond their two-year contract period. Curriculum was often irrelevant as textbooks were about the history and geography of the South, not of the North. Formal education reflected the values of European cultures, not the values and beliefs of the Aboriginals. In short, the Aboriginal cultures were being decimated by their collision with a larger dominant culture. With such drastic changes, the Inuit lost control over their lives. Some turned to alcohol or drugs, and crime increased. There is no going back, but Aboriginals are working to find their identity once again.

Fortunately, the people of the North are resilient and the events which have threatened their traditional ways have not destroyed them. They are learning new skills and adapting to a new way of life. Many have started new businesses and formed co-operatives in which they work together and share the profits. Some Inuit artists, for example, create the soapstone carvings, distinctive prints, and weavings sought by collectors and museums all over the world. Educators look with deep respect to the games of the Inuit, which are based not on competition but on co-operation. The Aboriginals of the North survived because they understood their interconnectedness with one another and with the earth. Many people believe that this is something the rest of Canada today must relearn.

Soapstone carving by an Inuit artist

COMPREHENSION CHECK

1   Which two animals were very important to the Inuit and why?
2   How did the people know where to find the animals when they were hunting?
3   A very serious disease killed many of the Aboriginals in Canada's North. What was that disease?
4   How are the Aboriginals of the North adapting to a new way of life today?

VOCABULARY

domed	in the shape of a half-sphere or half-ball
blubber	the fat of a large sea animal such as a whale
sustenance	that which enables life to continue; nourishment
pelts	the skins of fur-bearing animals used for making clothing or other items
extinction	the end or cessation of life of a species
irrelevant	having no meaning; not important within a particular context
decimated	destroyed; killed on a large scale
collision	the abrupt and unsettling coming together of two opposing forces
resilient	able to recover from a shock or other difficult experience
politically incorrect	a term used to describe language or behaviour which is no longer commonly supported by the majority of people in a society

USING NEW WORDS

Fill in each blank with a word or term from the list above.

1   _____ structures are generally stronger than rectangular ones.
2   The value of _____ is dependent on their condition; those without holes or tears are worth the most.
3   Many people throughout the world are fighting the _____ of various species in the rainforests, partly because these plants provide us with medicines that are not available elsewhere.
4   School textbooks with pictures and information about American plants, trees, and animals are somewhat _____ to Canadian students who have not yet learned about their own plants, trees, and animals.
5   Food which is fresh and locally grown normally provides healthier _____ than food which is frozen, canned, or dried and imported from elsewhere.
6   The people of Ethiopia were _____ by both famine and war for many years.
7   The unexpected _____ of the two cars on the icy road resulted in one death and two people being seriously injured.
8   The whale _____ burned in the small lamps provided both light and heat in the igloos.

9 People knew the woman would recover from the shock of her sister's death because she was very _____.

10 Many people now think it is _____ to drink from paper cups instead of using china or metal cups.

WORD FAMILIES

Fill in the blanks. There are three columns: one for nouns, one for verbs, and one for adjectives. Do you know which column goes with each?

	sustainable	
collide		
extinguish		
	1. distinct 2.	

(You can find the answers on page 251 at the back of the book.)

FOR DISCUSSION

» In the Inuit languages, there are many words for *snow*. Why do you think they have so many words for what we call snow in English?

» Seldom do people own the mineral rights on their land. Usually, the mineral rights are sold separately. What do you think of this practice?

» How would you feel if someone gave you a beautiful fur coat? Do you think everyone would feel the same as you would? Why or why not?

» Do you know of other countries in which people's lives were completely disrupted when other people moved onto their land? Does this still happen today? Why do you think this happens?

The Klondike Gold Rush

In 1896, the cry of "gold" was heard in the Yukon. A prospector from Nova Scotia discovered 8 cents worth of gold when he was panning just north of Dawson City. He and four friends kept on panning until they had about 750 dollars worth of gold before they returned to town for supplies. (In those days, five dollars would buy a piece of land big enough to build a house on.) This was the beginning of a gold rush into the area that would see about a million people leave their homes for the Yukon, hoping to make their fortunes.

Try to imagine how difficult this journey was. To get to the gold fields, prospectors had to hike through difficult and icy mountain passes with no roads. They had to carry heavy supplies both for mining and for living. Some built boats, only to get swept away in dangerous rapids. Out of the million who tried, about 20 000 actually did

Discovery Day celebrations in Dawson City in memory of the gold rush

pan for gold. Some became very wealthy; others did not. Nonetheless, it was an exciting time in Canada's history. The real significance of this period was probably the effect that the gold rush had on Edmonton and Vancouver. The population of Vancouver almost doubled in a short time, while Edmonton likewise grew rapidly as the prospectors stocked up on supplies before they headed north.

While people are seldom lucky enough to find gold nuggets lying on the creek beds of Yukon nowadays, we have little idea just how rich the North really is in mineral deposits. In spite of the harsh climate, multinational corporations continue to send in their geologists to search for more mineral wealth. (Nowadays, it is Canadian diamonds that are valued worldwide for their high quality.)

Dawson City has a summer festival in memory of the Klondike Gold Rush. Men have beard-growing contests, women put on the old long dresses of the time, and young people flock to the lounges to drink beer and watch cancan dancers singing and kicking up their heels. They pay to pan for tiny gold nuggets in artificial creeks and hope—like the prospectors of those early days—to strike it rich!

COMPREHENSION CHECK

Are the following statements true or false?
1. Most of the people who left their homes to look for gold became rich.
2. Edmonton and Vancouver increased in size because of the gold rush.
3. Dawson City in Yukon was the supply centre of the gold rush.
4. Many people still find gold nuggets in creek beds of the North today.

VOCABULARY

prospector	a person who explores an area for minerals and hopes to make money by finding them and claiming mining rights to the area
panning	a method of looking for gold by scooping sand from a river or creek bed into a round pan with a screen at the bottom; the water passes through while heavier substances such as gold nuggets are left in the pan
nuggets	small lumps of gold or other precious metals found in nature; small lumps of something precious embedded in something larger
creek	a narrow stream of water
cancan	a lively dance of French origins in which women kick their heels very high, hold their skirts, and dance on stage in a line
strike it rich	get wealthy suddenly

USING NEW WORDS

Fill in each blank with a word or term from the list above.

❶ While they will probably never get rich doing it today, some people still like to go _____ for gold in the mountains while on their vacations.

❷ In the innocent words of children, we often find many _____ of truth and wisdom.

❸ During heavy spring runoff, a mountain _____ can be dangerously fast and overflowing its normal banks.

❹ Today many people hope to _____ by winning a lottery such as the Lotto 6/49.

❺ The well-educated city woman was an unlikely _____ in the mountains of the North, but she loved the outdoors and believed there was gold in those mountains.

❻ Many people still enjoy watching _____ or other dances on stage.

FOR DISCUSSION

» What do the Klondike Gold Rush, the search for pirate treasure, and the lottery all have in common?

» Try to imagine what a saloon (beer parlour) during the gold rush would have looked like. Who was there? What were they doing and talking about? Was it an atmosphere in which you and your friends would feel comfortable? Why or why not?

» There are many sayings in English about gold. Here is one: *All that glitters is not gold*. What do you think this expression means? How is gold valued in your culture? Do you have any sayings in your first language about gold?

Other Points of Interest

The Alaska Highway

The Alaska Highway is the major route to the North from the United States and the rest of Canada. As you can imagine, building a highway through isolated mountains and frozen tundra was neither easy nor cheap. The reason for building this highway was actually for self-defence! The first Alaska Highway was built in 1942 during the Second World War when the Japanese began bombing the Aleutian Islands and the United States wanted to get planes and other war supplies into Alaska. The American government made a deal with the Canadian government to co-operate on the project, and 20 000 American soldiers were brought in to help with the work. They started building the highway in March of that year and reached Fairbanks, Alaska, in October of the same year.

It was a truly amazing feat of engineering and hard work. The workers not only had to deal with icy rivers, semi-frozen bogs, and rocky mountainous terrain, they also had to deal with swarms of voracious mosquitoes and blackflies. The bites of these insects have made them infamous with travellers in the North.

The Alaska Highway, which now gives tourists access to some of the last unspoiled wilderness in the world, was built at a cost beyond dollars. Many Aboriginals along the route died of epidemics as a result of diseases brought in by the workers. Many animals were killed by soldiers. In fact, several species were virtually eradicated. (That was one reason for the founding of the Kluane Game Sanctuary, which later became Kluane National Park and Reserve.) Furthermore, many of the worst sections of road were assigned to Black soldiers. These men have never been given credit for their work and their sacrifice on this monumental project. The road also made it possible for some unscrupulous industries to come in and dump their poisonous waste along the roadsides.

Starting in north-central Alberta, west of Edmonton, the highway goes through the northeast corner of British Columbia, and then through Yukon to Alaska. This remarkable highway provides a route for Americans and Canadians alike to see the northern parts of their countries.

National Parks of the North

A surprising number of tourists take the time to visit the beautiful piece of wilderness known as Kluane National Park and Reserve each summer. Hiking trails allow tourists to reach the icefields and many other unspoiled areas in the park. Located in the southwest corner of Yukon, this park is easily accessible to travellers on the Alaska Highway.

Perhaps the most valued treasure of the North is not the gold which may still be found by tenacious gold-diggers, but the beauty of Nahanni National Park Reserve. The river gorges there are deeper than those found in the famous Grand Canyon, and the Virginia Falls are twice the height of Niagara Falls. Daring canoeists in search of whitewater rapids can test their skills. Anyone who has gone there has found it to be one of the most beautifully wild areas in the world. There is, however, one small disadvantage: you cannot drive into the park. You cannot even realistically hike in, as the terrain is too difficult and the distance too far. You can only fly in or venture in on the tricky waters of the South Nahanni River.

Camping in Kluane National Park and Reserve

COMPREHENSION CHECK

1. Which two countries co-operated to build the Alaska Highway?
2. Who suffered when this roadway was being built?
3. Why was the Kluane Game Sanctuary established?
4. How do the waterfalls in Nahanni National Park Reserve compare to the famous Niagara Falls?
5. How do the Nahanni gorges compare to those found in the famous Grand Canyon in the United States?

VOCABULARY

made a deal with	reached an agreement with
feat	a remarkable accomplishment
bogs	low-lying wet areas difficult to travel through
swarms	large groups of insects flying together
voracious	extremely hungry
mosquitoes	insects whose bites are very itchy (they may also carry disease)
infamous	famous in a negative way; having a bad reputation
epidemics	diseases which kill many people in an area at one time
eradicated	completely destroyed; wiped out
monumental	of great size and importance
unscrupulous	dishonest; without morals or ethics concerning the well-being of others
tenacious	determined

USING NEW WORDS

Fill in each blank with one of the words or terms from the list above.

1. Farmers and loggers can be _____ diners because they work very hard in the fresh outdoors.
2. The acrobats at the circus performed one amazing _____ after another.
3. Robin Hood was an _____ hero of Old England who robbed the rich to give to the poor.
4. The _____ landlord refused to do needed repairs to his rental properties and never gave back damage deposits unless ordered to do so by the courts.
5. There have been many _____ of cholera, a tropical disease which kills people who do not have access to clean drinking water and proper sanitation.
6. The teenager _____ with his mother: he would paint the fence and she would give him the money to get a new bicycle.
7. If there are too many _____, it is not fun to sleep outdoors.

8   The Irish tell their children scary stories about people being lost in the _____ to frighten them from wandering off and getting lost there.

9   _____ of killer bees have killed many people in Africa and the southern United States.

FOR DISCUSSION

» You have read about some of the negative effects of building the Alaska Highway. Can you think of other examples of progress for one group of people that caused significant problems for other people or other living things?

» What do you think is a suitable punishment for an industry that knowingly pollutes the environment?

» Why do you think that the worst sections of the Alaska Highway were assigned to Black soldiers?

» Why is it important to set aside national parks where development is restricted? Do you agree or disagree with this policy?

» Why do you think people go rafting in whitewater rapids knowing that this is a dangerous practice? What other sports do you know where people risk their lives?

FOR RESEARCH

» An inuksuk has come to symbolize many things in the lifestyle of the Inuit people. Find out what they mean, why they are built, and who builds them. Search online for information.

CHAPTER REVIEW

» Choose one of the pictures in this chapter and use it as the basis for a story about the North. Use your imagination and include some of the new words you have learned in this chapter. You could write this from the perspective of an observer, or as if you were in the picture.

Chapter Twelve

Noteworthy Canadians

Quick Facts

» The following are some of the noteworthy Canadians mentioned in this chapter. Do you recognize any of them? Can you identify some of them and their achievements before reading the chapter?

Alexander Graham Bell
Nellie McClung
James Cameron
Sandford Fleming
David Suzuki
Joseph Tyrrell
Frederick Banting
Dr. Norman Bethune
John A. Macdonald
Louis Riel
Lester B. Pearson
Lucy Maud Montgomery
Pierre Berton
Margaret Atwood
Oscar Peterson
Terry Fox
Ryan Gosling
Wayne Gretzky
Silken Laumann
Pierre Elliott Trudeau
Céline Dion
James Naismith
Sarah Polley
Tom Thomson

Featured in these photos are (top) Terry Fox, (bottom left) Sarah Polley, and (bottom right) Sandford Fleming

Introduction

Canadians are justifiably proud of those individuals who have made major contributions to many fields of endeavour. You may be surprised to discover that some of the following achievements are indeed Canadian! It is difficult, however, to decide who to include in such a chapter and who to leave out. We hope that you will decide to talk to a few Canadians and ask them who they think are noteworthy Canadians.

In Science and Technology

What would we do without the telephone? In 1870, **Alexander Graham Bell** immigrated to Canada from Scotland. While most Canadians believe he was still living in Canada when he invented the telephone, he was not. As an adult, he had moved to the United States (US) where he became a teacher of people with hearing disabilities. He got the idea for the telephone while visiting his parents in Ontario, however, and did actually place the first long-distance phone call from his parents' home to a telegraph office a few kilometres away. Thus, we have a telephone company named after him: Bell Canada.

Bell's inventive mind did not stop with the telephone! He bought land in Nova Scotia and continued his experiments there. One of his inventions was a breathing mechanism that eventually led to the development of the artificial lung and enabled many polio victims to stay alive. He found a way to turn fog into fresh water and was very interested in flying. His experiments alone could fill a very interesting book.

Another Scot to whom we can be grateful is **Sandford Fleming**, a railway surveyor and construction engineer. As recently as the late nineteenth century, time was not standardized throughout the world and this created much confusion. Time was determined in those days by the movement of the sun. When it was directly overhead, it was noon in that place. In 1879, Fleming suggested that the world be divided into 24 equal time zones, with a standard time in each zone. By 1885, several countries around the globe had adopted this system. There are 40 time zones today, and Canada occupies six of those time zones!

More recently, Canadians were proud to send two astronauts into space. **Marc Garneau**, born in Quebec in 1949, was Canada's first astronaut. He was aboard the American space shuttle *Challenger* in 1984. **Dr. Roberta Bondar**, from Ontario, was the first Canadian woman to travel into space. On her voyage in 1992, she performed many important experiments on how space travel affects the human body.

A well-known Canadian scientist is **Dr. David Suzuki**. Dr. Suzuki is a geneticist from Vancouver

Dr. David Suzuki, scientist and environmentalist

who has popularized science, making it understandable to a wide variety of people. Known internationally for his dedication to environmental causes, he is well-recognized by Canadians from his many appearances on Canadian Broadcasting Corporation (CBC) television.

If you are fascinated with dinosaurs, you may have heard of **Joseph Tyrrell**. He is the geologist who discovered the large dinosaur bed in southern Alberta near Drumheller. This site has attracted scientists from all over the world who are interested in learning about these large ancient beasts that disappeared suddenly from the planet's surface so long ago. The wonderful museum located in Drumheller is called the Tyrrell Museum.

You may be familiar with Research In Motion (RIM), the company that created the BlackBerry smartphone. RIM is a Canadian company located in Waterloo, Ontario, and was founded by **Mike Lazaridis** in 1984. After the BlackBerry was introduced in 1999, RIM became well-known worldwide for its innovative technology. In addition, Lazaridis has contributed hundreds of millions of dollars to help fund future research in science and technology.

COMPREHENSION CHECK

Who did each of the following?

1. invented the telephone
2. invented a system for standardizing time
3. invented the BlackBerry smartphone
4. popularized science
5. discovered the huge dinosaur bed near Drumheller in Alberta
6. was the first Canadian woman to travel in space

VOCABULARY

justifiably	with reason
fields of endeavour	areas of work and achievement
standardized	made the same everywhere
astronauts	people trained to travel in space
geneticist	a scientist who studies genetics, the science of heredity and the origins of living things
beasts	animals, often very large animals

USING NEW WORDS

Fill in each blank with a word or term from the list above.

1. Children often think that _____ have very adventurous lives.
2. The woman decided to become a _____ because she had always liked biology and was curious to learn all she could about human traits and why they developed as they did.
3. The young girl's parents were _____ upset when she did not come home before midnight.
4. Canada and the United States have different _____ systems of measurement; Canadians use metric measures and Americans use imperial measures.

⑤ When children are dreaming of their futures, they have many different _____ from which to choose.

⑥ When walking in the forest, watch out for wild _____.

FOR DISCUSSION

» Do you think it has been important to explore space when there is still much to learn about the earth? Why or why not?

» People view the telephone with a variety of emotions, some positive and some negative. How do you view the telephone and why? Are there moments in life when you would prefer not to be near a telephone?

» In what ways have science and technology made our lives better and in what ways worse?

» Why do you think several important and famous Canadians have moved to the United States?

In Medicine

Dr. Charles Best and Dr. Frederick Banting, discoverers of insulin

Diabetics all over the world owe their lives to those two Canadians who discovered insulin: **Dr. Frederick Banting** and **Dr. Charles Best**. Banting was a medical researcher working at the University of Toronto and Best was one of his students when they made their remarkable discovery. For this important achievement, Banting received the Nobel Prize for Medicine in 1923.

Many people who come to Canada from China already know the name of **Dr. Norman Bethune**, called *Pai-Chui'en* (White Seeks Grace) in Chinese. He initially gained fame for revolutionizing battlefield care by organizing the world's first mobile blood transfusion service in Spain. Then, in 1938, he went to China to help the Chinese in the war with Japan and was recognized as a hero by the Chinese people. The Bethune Memorial House National Historic Site was created in memory of him in his hometown of Gravenhurst, Ontario.

Two other important figures in Canadian medicine whose names are perhaps less well-known are **Dr. William Osler** and **Dr. Wilder Penfield**. William Osler was one of the most respected doctors in the world at the turn of the twentieth century. His work focused on examining not only a patient's physical condition, but also his or her state of mind. He had an important influence on Wilder Penfield, one of Canada's greatest neurologists. Penfield did important research on epilepsy and the workings of the brain. He was one of the first Canadians to be honoured with the Order of Canada. He died in 1976.

COMPREHENSION CHECK

1. What medicine is used to treat diabetes?
2. Which Canadian doctor received the Nobel Prize for Medicine?
3. Why do many Chinese people respect Dr. Norman Bethune?
4. Who is well-known for increasing our understanding of how the brain works?

VOCABULARY

diabetics — people who have diabetes, a disease in which the body cannot break down the blood sugars, leaving diabetics without energy (can be fatal without treatment)

mobile — capable of being moved with relative ease from place to place

transfusion — the giving of one person's blood to another who needs it

neurologists — doctors who specialize in the study and treatment of diseases of the nervous system

epilepsy — a disorder of the central nervous system characterized by attacks or seizures where people may lose consciousness and have convulsions (violent muscle contractions)

USING NEW WORDS

Fill in each blank with a word from the list above.

1. People of the Jehovah's Witness religion teach their members not to get a blood _____ because they believe the Bible says they should not.
2. _____ must be very careful of what they eat and how often, to maintain steady blood sugar levels.
3. The man went to see several _____ for help with his nervous condition.
4. A car used to be called an *automobile* because it is _____ and moves by its own power (that is, without horses pulling it; it was originally called a horseless carriage).
5. Though she had _____, the woman actively enjoyed life.

FOR DISCUSSION

» Do you think it is important for doctors to consider a patient's emotional, as well as physical, condition? How do you think your state of mind affects your health?

» Terry Fox is a hero to many Canadians; Dr. Norman Bethune is a hero to many Chinese people. Who is your favourite hero or heroine? What qualities do you think heroes and heroines have?

In Politics

Nellie McClung, suffragette

Emily Murphy, suffragette

It is not easy to single out a few politicians for special recognition because many deserve credit for their contribution to democracy in Canada. Regardless of which party they support and what positions they take, politicians give up a lot of time and energy as well as personal freedom and privacy to support the practice of democracy in Canada.

Before Confederation, a well-known person who was called a traitor by some and a martyr by others was **Louis Riel**. Riel was the Métis leader hanged for treason in 1885 for his involvement in the North-West Rebellion. He was charged with leading his people in an armed rebellion against the Queen and the Canadian government. To the Métis and other Aboriginals, he was the fiery speaker who stood his ground against the Canadian government and the settlers who were taking Métis and First Nations lands without asking or consulting them. When peaceful means of protest were ineffective, Riel and his followers took up arms. Following his death,

there were strong feelings of nationalism in both Ontario and Quebec. Many French Canadians took offence at his death because most Métis were half French, and Riel had fought for the rights of the Métis to keep their French language and culture. Many people in Ontario believed Riel was a traitor to the Canadian government and deserved to be hanged.

John A. Macdonald is one name most new Canadians learn when they are studying for their citizenship test. Macdonald was the first prime minister of Canada and was instrumental in building the national railway. He served as prime minister from 1867 to 1873 and again from 1878 until his death in 1891.

Women in Canada owe a debt of gratitude to **Nellie McClung** and **Emily Murphy**, as well as the other suffragettes at the turn of the twentieth century. These women faced humiliation from some men at the time who did not want women to gain equality at the ballot box.

In 1916, Nellie McClung helped women win the right to vote in Manitoba. In that same year, Emily Murphy became the first female judge in Canada and in the British Empire. Her job was not easy. Many lawyers challenged her right to sit as a judge, arguing that she could not have that privilege because women were not legally *persons*. On October 18, 1929, women were at last declared to legally be persons. They then had the right to serve as judges and to be appointed to the Canadian Senate.

A quarter of a century later a Canadian external affairs minister, who went on to become prime minister, achieved international recognition for his work in establishing the United Nations Emergency Force in 1956. This force kept peace in the Israeli-Egyptian border region for 10 years. The man was **Lester B. Pearson**. His achievement won him the Nobel Peace Prize in 1957. We also remember Pearson as the leader who gave us our current Canadian flag.

The prime minister who immediately followed Pearson was **Pierre Elliott Trudeau**. Trudeau was well-known around the world for his vision of a global community, his support of developing nations, and his idea of a just society. Controversial in Canada for his candour and charm, Canadians seemed to either love him or hate him. It was under Trudeau that Canada finally brought home our constitution, which until 1982 had remained in Britain as the British North America Act of 1867. Trudeau's government also worked to have the Canadian Charter of Rights and Freedoms made a part of our constitution, ensuring Canadians legal protection for many cherished rights. Trudeau served as Canada's prime minister for a total of 15 years between his first election in 1968 and his resignation in 1984. Trudeau believed in a strong central government, which he was convinced would enable all Canadians to enjoy the same standard of living regardless of where they lived.

Canadians are very proud of their national medicare system, which ensures that everyone has free access to basic healthcare services. **Tommy Douglas**, a former premier of Saskatchewan, is known as the Father of Medicare. He introduced universal health care in

Pierre Trudeau, prime minister 1968–79 and 1980–84

his province, and later helped to ensure everyone in the country was covered by medicare. In 2004, Douglas was named The Greatest Canadian of all time by the CBC.

Canada's only female prime minister to date was **Kim Campbell**, a British Columbia politician who served in provincial politics before joining the federal government. She served as Minister of Justice in the federal government under Prime Minister **Brian Mulroney**. Following Brian Mulroney's resignation, she served as prime minister for five months before the disastrous election of October, 1993. In that election, Campbell's Progressive Conservative party lost all but two members in the House of Commons. Some say Canada was not ready for a female prime minister, while others say that Kim Campbell was paying for Canadians' dissatisfaction with the previous Progressive Conservative government.

Stephen Harper was elected prime minister in 2006. He is leader of the Conservative Party of Canada and makes his home in Calgary, Alberta. He led two minority governments through the difficult times of recession, and in 2011 went on to lead Canada's first majority government since 2004.

COMPREHENSION CHECK

Match each description on the left with the correct person on the right.

1 this person brought home Canada's constitution from Britain   a) Kim Campbell
2 this person was important in the completion of the national railway   b) Emily Murphy
3 fighter for women's voting rights   c) Pierre Elliott Trudeau
4 Canada's first female prime minister   d) Tommy Douglas
5 leader of the North-West Rebellion   e) Brian Mulroney
6 winner of the Nobel Peace Prize   f) John A. Macdonald
7 first female judge in Canada   g) Stephen Harper
8 Progressive Conservative prime minister in the 1980s   h) Louis Riel
9 prime minister of Canada elected in 2006   i) Nellie McClung
10 named The Greatest Canadian of all time   j) Lester B. Pearson

VOCABULARY

traitors	people who are disloyal or who betray their country, duty, or friend
martyr	a person who gives his or her life for a cause
treason	the act of betraying one's country; a betrayal of trust
instrumental	of special importance; providing the way or means to accomplish a task
suffragettes	women who fought to help women gain the right to vote
humiliation	great personal embarrassment
ballot box	the box in which people place their votes during an election; symbolizes the democratic electoral process
candour	honesty and openness
cherish	value greatly
resignation	official withdrawal from one's responsibilities (such as a job)
unanimous	completely in agreement

USING NEW WORDS

Fill in each blank with a word or term from the list above.

1 Even as a young woman, she never forgot the _____ of a teacher laughing at her in front of all her friends when she made a mistake.

2 Most Canadians _____ their country and feel terribly sad at the thought that Quebec might separate and no longer be part of the country.

3 When a political party loses an election, party members sometimes ask for the _____ of the party leader.

4 Those caught spying for the enemy during wartime are most often convicted of _____ and put in prison for a long time. They are _____ to their country.

5 It is difficult today to believe that women and First Nations peoples have only quite recently gained equal rights at the _____.

6 _____ in any country often face strong opposition as they fight for equality.

7 Although brothers, the two men were very different; one was known for his _____ while the other always said what he thought others wanted to hear.

8 The people of the town council were _____ in their decision to honour their local doctor of 40 years by naming the new school after her.

9 A _____ has the courage to die for his or her beliefs.

10 Nellie McClung was _____ in gaining women the right to vote in Canada.

FOR DISCUSSION

» Thanks to the efforts of women like Emily Murphy, women have more rights today than they did during her lifetime. Do you think women have equality in Canada now, or do they still have fewer rights than men in some situations? Do you know of other countries in which women have far fewer rights than men? Do you know of any countries in which women have more power than they do in Canada?

» Why do you think some people like to be politicians?

» Why would you like or not like to be a politician?

In Literature

Margaret Atwood, author and poet

Yann Martel, author

One of Canada's best-known authors internationally is **Lucy Maud Montgomery**, who wrote the Anne of Green Gables books in the early 1900s. The books have become classics and are still widely read today in many different languages. The series has brought many visitors to Prince Edward Island where the author lived and wrote her stories.

Another popular Canadian novelist is Saskatchewan's **W.O. Mitchell**. Through his novels we gain an understanding of life on the Canadian prairies. A good example is *Who Has Seen the Wind*, a novel which can be enjoyed by young people and adults alike.

In 2004, Canadians lost one of their favourite authors and journalists, **Pierre Berton**. For many years Canadians watched him on CBC's *Front Page Challenge*, a popular TV show which tested panelists' knowledge of current affairs in the country. Pierre Berton has contributed to Canadians' knowledge of and appreciation for their own country in more than 20 books of colourful Canadian history.

Canada also has many wonderful writers who have become recognized around the world. **Margaret Atwood** is one. She has written many novels including *The Handmaid's Tale* and *Oryx and Crake*, as well as some poetry. Other award-winning authors include **Margaret Laurence**, **Mordecai Richler**, **Robertson Davies**, **Michael Ondaatje**, **Rohinton Mistry**, **Alice Munro**, **Carol Shields**, and **Yann Martel**. Many of these authors have won the Governor General's Literary Award, which is given each year to the best book published by a Canadian author. Some have also won international awards.

A popular Québécois author is **Roch Carrier**, whose works have been translated into English. His most famous story is "The Hockey Sweater." This story was particularly significant as it was written during a time of conflict between the sovereigntists and the federalists in Quebec. In this story, a young boy's mother orders a replacement for the boy's worn-out Montreal Canadiens hockey sweater from the Eaton's catalogue. Since they are out of Canadiens sweaters, they send him a sweater from the Toronto Maple Leafs instead. He angrily refuses to wear it but his mother insists, much to his embarrassment and the amusement of his teammates.

COMPREHENSION CHECK

1. What other word or words do you know with the same root as the word *literature*?
2. Who wrote a very popular series of books for young girls in the early twentieth century?
3. Who was a journalist as well as a popular Canadian author?
4. Who wrote a French children's story which has become symbolic of the French-English issue in Canada?
5. Name two authors in Canada.
6. Name the famous Canadian author who wrote about the prairies.

FOR DISCUSSION

» Do you enjoy writing? If so, what kind of writing do you enjoy?
» Do you enjoy reading? If so, would you rather read fiction or non-fiction? If you do not enjoy reading, do you know why?
» Some books are popular for many, many years after they are written. We call such books classics. In your opinion, what makes a book able to stand the test of time?

SPEAKING ACTIVITY

» Choose any one of the authors mentioned above and research his or her life and work. Make an oral presentation to your classmates that will make them want to read some of the author's writing.

In Music

k.d. lang, musician and singer

Bryan Adams, musician and singer

Canada boasts many fine musicians, as well as some serious composers. **Gordon Lightfoot** is arguably Canada's most beloved folk singer-songwriter. He is still a popular star in the summer folk festivals across Canada.

People of all ages have enjoyed the music of **Oscar Peterson**, the internationally known jazz musician and composer who started his career in Montreal. He recorded more than 90 albums, won awards in the US and Canada, and was honoured with the Order of Canada for his dedication and excellence in music. Oscar Peterson helped to keep the jazz tradition of the 1940s alive and swinging well into the twenty-first century and is missed by all who appreciated his love of music and dedication to jazz.

Shania Twain, well-known as a country and western artist, has many awards in recognition of her achievements. Those who like country and western music will also know the name of **k.d. lang**, whose powerful voice and distinctive style have put the small town of Consort, Alberta, on the map.

Quebec has also produced many well-known musicians and singers. **Céline Dion** is known all over the world for her singing and has six diamond-certified albums, the record for Canada. Another is **Gilles Vigneault**, whose patriotic poems, songs, and stories have stirred the hearts of the Québécois people. "Mon Pays" ("My Country") is one of his best-known songs.

Leonard Cohen is a long-time international favourite. A poet, songwriter, and musician, he has recorded 11 albums and been honoured with the Order of Canada, among other awards, for his haunting lyrics.

For decades, **Bryan Adams** has been an internationally loved singer, songwriter, and musician. Although he is primarily known for his singing and guitar-playing, he also created The Bryan Adams Foundation in 2006. This charity's goal is to improve the quality of people's lives worldwide, especially children who are in need of education.

More recently, the hip hop artist **Drake** has become one of Canada's most popular entertainers. He started his professional career as an actor on *Degrassi: The Next Generation*, but he became a household name when he released his first album in 2010.

Over the years, the names of **Alanis Morrisette**, **Diana Krall**, **Neil Young**, **Nelly Furtado**, **Holly Cole**, and **Michael Bublé** have been popular with listeners in many countries in addition to our own. **Justin Bieber** is a young man from Stratford, Ontario, whose baby face and youthful lyrics have young girls swooning to hear him. And we must not forget **Avril Lavigne**, a pop-rock singer-songwriter whose songs have topped the charts in many countries.

Canada has some very successful bands, too. Among the most popular are **Broken Social Scene**, known for its sometimes large number of musicians and its innovative sound. Internationally, the Montreal band **Arcade Fire** has been very successful, winning BRIT Awards and a Grammy, in addition to numerous Juno awards.

There are also Aboriginal artists whose music is gaining appreciation from mainstream audiences. One of the best-known is **Susan Aglukark**, an Inuit recording artist. Of course, there are many more emerging Aboriginal artists across Canada. The band **CerAmony** has gained a large following among young people of the Cree Nation. **Derek Miller**, from the Six Nations of the Grand River, plays a unique style of rock music that has earned him recognition and awards. Country and western star Willie Nelson even recorded a song with Miller.

COMPREHENSION CHECK

Who am I? Identify the people from the statements below.

1. I live in the Far North and sing some of my songs in the language of my people, the Inuit.
2. I am an Albertan who has become known internationally for my unique country and western music.
3. I was an actor before I became a hip hop star.
4. I sing in celebration of my nation, the people of Quebec.
5. I lived to play jazz on the keyboard.
6. I am from the Six Nations of the Grand River.

VOCABULARY

composers	people who write music
put on the map	make a place famous or well-known when it might otherwise not be
innovative	new, creative
haunting	a quality which stays in our minds
lyrics	the words of a song
emerging	becoming known

USING NEW WORDS

Fill in each blank with a word or term from the list above.

1. The teacher believed that the two young music students would one day become great _____.
2. Often one person writes the music for a song, while another person writes the _____.

❸ The woman found the bloody and violent scenes in the movie very _____.

❹ One very creative mother found an _____ use for large, empty tomato juice cans: she sewed them into footstools with a cushion on top.

❺ Many Americans had never heard of Edmonton, Alberta, until Wayne Gretzky and the Edmonton Oilers hockey team won the NHL championship. You could say that the Oilers _____ Edmonton _____.

FOR DISCUSSION

» Have you heard the music of any of the musicians named in this chapter? If so, which ones, and how did you like it? If not, you may want to search for some clips of their music online.

» What role does music play in your life? What is your favourite kind of music and why?

» What role can music play for a people or country?

» As a successful and popular artist who is also openly homosexual, k.d. lang is in a position to make people aware of her view that homosexuals deserve equal rights and fair treatment in society. Do you know of any other artists who fight for some minority group through their art?

In the Visual Arts

The Group of Seven artists have already been introduced to you in Chapter 8. In breaking away from the traditional European style of painting popular in the 1920s, these men had a great impact on Canadian art. Their depictions of Canada's rugged landscapes are famous. Although **Tom Thomson** was not a member of the Group, his style of painting and subject matter were similar. He is often associated with the Group of Seven, though he died very mysteriously before the group was formed. Similarly, **Emily Carr**'s paintings of west coast forests and Aboriginal scenes have also sometimes been associated with the Group of Seven's work, though she was not officially a member. The Emily Carr University of Art and Design on Granville Island in Vancouver is named after this artist.

A very famous wildlife painter who lives on Saltspring Island off the west coast is **Robert Bateman**. His originals and prints are very popular and therefore often expensive. They bring life to wild animals in a way that makes you look twice to see if they are actually paintings. They are so realistic, you might think they are photographs.

Canada also has some excellent photographers. One was **Yousuf Karsh**, who came to Canada from Turkey in 1924. He made the decision to concentrate his work on people of influence. He photographed some of the most famous people of the twentieth century all over the world, including Winston Churchill in 1941. This photo was printed on the cover of *Life* magazine.

Another photographer who gained international recognition was **Roloff Beny**, originally from southern Alberta. He published numerous travel books with exquisite photographs. More recently, **Bryan Adams** has become known for his photographs in addition to his music.

Totem Walk at Sitka, by artist Emily Carr

COMPREHENSION CHECK

1. Which famous artist painted west coast scenes?
2. What is the name of a university for art studies that is located on Granville Island in Vancouver?
3. Who produces very realistic paintings of wild animals?
4. Whose photographs are often seen in travel books?
5. Whose death is still a mystery?

VOCABULARY

depictions	representations (such as drawings or paintings)
prints	artistic representations which are made in many copies from one master
impact	a strong effect or influence (on)
exquisite	extremely beautiful and displaying excellence

USING NEW WORDS

Fill in each blank with a word from the list above above.

1. Nikki Yanofsky's song "I Believe," which she sang in the 2010 Olympics, had a big _____ on me, as her emotions were similar to mine.
2. The child's _____ of his parents had big faces with stick-like arms and legs.

❸ The fashion designer was very talented and his new dress designs were _____.

❹ The _____ are limited in number and each of them is signed by the artist.

FOR DISCUSSION

» Different people have different views about what makes good art. Many artists believe their work should be provocative, while others want to create beauty for the viewer. What makes good art, in your opinion?

» Good photographs can teach us a lot about the world around us. Some photographs, however, can be exploitative or unfair to those being photographed. Can you think of examples?

ACTIVITY

» Other famous Canadian artists include **Harold Town**, **Jack Bush**, **Michael Snow**, and **Joyce Wieland**, to name a few. Some well-known Aboriginal artists include **Alex Janvier** and **Norval Morrisseau**. Choose one of these artists and research his or her life and work for presentation to your classmates. (You will find that the last artist mentioned has an especially interesting—while somewhat tragic—story.)

In Movies and Television

Canada has produced many fine actors. All too often, these men and women find that they have to move south of the border to advance their careers. **Ryan Gosling**, for example, is from London, Ontario, and **Michael J. Fox** is originally from Edmonton, Alberta. **Paul Gross**, another Albertan is well-known throughout Canada and the US for his key role in the TV series *Due South* and many other roles in plays, TV shows, and movies. **Gordon Pinsent** comes to us from Newfoundland and is well-known and loved across the country. The veteran actor **Donald Sutherland** is from New Brunswick. Two well-known comedians from TV and movies, **Dan Aykroyd** and the late **John Candy**, are from Ottawa and Toronto, respectively. **Jim Carrey** is both a comedian and an actor. His 2003 movie *Bruce Almighty* grossed 242 million dollars in the US alone. **Keanu Reeves**, the handsome star of *The Matrix*, was born in Lebanon but has called Canada home for most of his life. Many other popular actors are Canadians, including **Michael Cera**, **Elisha Cuthbert**, **Rachel McAdams**, **Ryan Reynolds**, and **Seth Rogan**. Did you know these actors were Canadians? Can you identify any other famous Canadian TV or movie personalities?

Aboriginals are also gaining more recognition in theatre, movies, and television. **Tom Jackson**, a Métis actor and musician, is perhaps one of Canada's favourites. Well-known for his role of chief in the *North of 60* TV series, he also received the Order of Canada in 2000 for both his music and his exceptional humanitarian work. Another frequently seen face in movies and television is **Tantoo Cardinal**, a Cree-speaking actress from Alberta. **Graham Greene** from the Six Nations Reserve in Ontario is familiar to us from movies such as *Dances with Wolves*, in which he co-starred with Kevin Costner, as well as television programs.

Canada has a growing number of film production companies whose films tend to do very well at the annual international Cannes Film Festival. In addition, Canadian directors have given us some great movies, such as **Sarah Polley**'s *Away from Her*, **Deepa Mehta**'s *Water*, and **James Cameron**'s films, which include classics like *The Terminator*, *Titanic*, and *Avatar*.

COMPREHENSION CHECK

1. Name two famous comedians from Ontario.
2. Which very well-known actor is originally from Edmonton?
3. Which actor speaks Cree?
4. Which popular Aboriginal actor comes from Ontario?
5. Where do Canadian films receive many awards?

FOR DISCUSSION

» Canadian films win many awards at international film festivals, but are generally less popular than American films. Have you seen any Canadian films? In what ways are they different from most American films?

» What disadvantages do you think Canadian filmmakers have in trying to make good films relevant to Canadians, which will also make enough money to cover costs?

In Sports

Rick Hansen, the Man In Motion

Perdita Felicien, world-class hurdler

Canada has many athletes of whom we are proud, but if asked who they considered to be a genuine hero, many would probably choose **Terry Fox**. In April of 1980, Terry Fox began running across Canada in what was called The Marathon of Hope to raise money for cancer research. He had lost the lower part of one leg to cancer but was determined not to die in vain. His courageous run across Canada attracted supportive viewers and generous donors who will always honour the courage and determination he displayed. By September of that same year, he fell seriously ill again and could not continue. He died in June of 1981 but not before raising 24.7 million dollars for cancer research and setting a standard of excellence to which all Canadians still look with pride. Terry Fox Runs are now an annual event in many cities and continue to raise millions for cancer research.

Others were inspired by Terry Fox's courage. **Steve Fonyo**, who had also lost a leg to cancer, retraced Fox's steps and completed his run in 14 months. His journey raised another 13 million dollars for cancer research. **Rick Hansen**, a man who is paralyzed from the waist down, set off on a world tour in his wheelchair. In 17 months, he wheeled through 34 countries and across four continents. He did not stop at that. He returned to Canada and in 1986 retraced the journey made by Fox and then Fonyo. After 26 months on the road, he arrived back in Vancouver. The Man In Motion, as he was called, had raised 26 million dollars for spinal cord injury research and set an admirable example for people with disabilities. He inspired many people not to focus on what they *cannot* do, but at what they *can* do.

One of our earliest and best-known sports heroes was **Barbara Ann Scott**. She captured the hearts of the world when she won Canada's first Olympic gold medal in figure skating in 1948. Canada has since produced many excellent figure skaters, not the least of whom is **Kurt Browning** from Alberta. Browning took the men's World Figure Skating Championship for four years. We remember him for being the first to land the difficult quad—a jump with four revolutions—in competition. **Elvis Stojko**, from Richmond Hill, Ontario, followed in Browning's footsteps and also won the men's World Figure Skating Championship. Stojko combined his skating skills with a martial arts background and gave us a new level of disciplined performance. More recently, **Patrick Chan** won the World Figure Skating Championship in 2011 and his score in the short program set a world record.

The twenty-first century has seen many successful Canadian athletes. **Steve Nash** is one of the National Basketball Association's (NBA) most successful point guards of all time, and received the Order of Canada for his charity work. Tennis player **Milos Raonic** first began playing the game when he was eight and turned professional

in 2008, at the age of 18. Within three years, he became one of the highest-ranked tennis players in the world. In the world of mixed martial arts, **Georges St-Pierre** is an important name. He won the Ultimate Fighting Championship's welterweight title many times and was named Canadian Athlete of the Year in 2008, 2009, and 2010.

A list of great Canadian athletes would not be complete without mentioning our hockey players, some of whom have become legendary. The names of **Maurice "Rocket" Richard** and **Gordie Howe** are on the lips of many young aspiring hockey players. The most famous of all, however, is **Wayne Gretzky**, who went on to break almost every hockey record possible. Gretzky first played in the National Hockey League with the Edmonton Oilers, then a relatively new team that captured four Stanley Cups in a row with him as captain. Then, to the great dismay of many Canadians, he was traded to the Los Angeles Kings and eventually to the New York Rangers. **Sidney Crosby** is one of Canada's best-known hockey players today, in part due to his gold medal–winning goal at the 2010 Olympics.

Canadian athletes have made their country proud at international competitions in many sports. **Perdita Felicien** is a successful hurdler from Pickering, Ontario. She has won medals for the 60-metre and 100-metre hurdles at numerous American and worldwide track championships. **Christine Sinclair**, captain of the Canadian women's national soccer team, is an energetic forward who has been named one of the players of the year many times throughout her career.

Canadian athletes have been noted for their pluckiness in the face of difficulty. **Silken Laumann** impressed everyone at the 1992 Olympics when she won a bronze medal in rowing in spite of just recovering from a severe broken leg. She had suffered a serious accident prior to the competition but was determined to compete. For her endurance and strength, she was named athlete of the year in both 1991 and 1992. At the 1996 Olympics, she won a silver medal for Canada. At the 2010 Olympics, while **Joannie Rochette** was practising for her short program, she found out that her mother had died. Rochette decided to skate in her mother's honour, and took home the bronze medal and the Terry Fox Award.

COMPREHENSION CHECK

1. Who first completed the run that Terry Fox was unable to finish?
2. Who went through 34 countries in a wheelchair to raise money for spinal cord injury research and to encourage people with physical disabilities?
3. Which Canadian was named Athlete of the Year for his skill in mixed martial arts?
4. Who is today acknowledged as one of the best players hockey has ever known?
5. Which Canadian figure skater took four world championships?
6. Which Canadian athlete competed internationally in spite of a severe injury shortly before the competition?

VOCABULARY

paralyzed	unable to feel or move certain parts of one's body
aspiring	hopeful, ambitious
pluckiness	bravery, courage in the face of difficulty
endurance	ability to finish something in spite of great obstacles

USING NEW WORDS

Fill in each blank with a word from the list above.

1. The young swimmer showed her _____ by swimming in the competition with a miserable head cold.
2. A distance runner requires great _____ to win, while a sprinter primarily needs speed.
3. The car accident left one man dead and another _____ from the waist down.
4. _____ athletes in any sport need to have a lot of patience, drive, and self-confidence.

FOR RESEARCH

» Canada won 26 medals at the 2010 winter Olympics, 14 of which were gold medals. List the gold medal winners and choose one male and one female. Prepare an introduction about them for your classmates. (Seven of these gold medals were awarded to teams. You can choose an individual from one of the teams to introduce, if you like.)

FOR DISCUSSION

» How do you feel about participating in sports? Which ones do you like to participate in?

» Which sports do you like to watch and why?

» What do you think about professional athletes who earn millions of dollars per year?

» How much financial support do you think our government should give to athletes who compete in international events?

CHAPTER REVIEW

Test your memory to see which of the following significant Canadians you can identify. You need to provide last names only using the following clues.

1. G_____ is one of the world's most famous hockey players.
2. F_____ is the young man who inspired Canadians by running across a large part of the country with one artificial leg.
3. B_____ is the man whose invention people love to talk on for hours.
4. S_____ is the well-known scientist who urges us to take care of our environment.
5. R_____ is the Métis leader who fought for Métis rights in Manitoba.
6. M_____ and M _____ are two of the women who worked to gain women the right to vote in Canada.
7. T_____ is the prime minister who brought Canada's constitution home from Britain.
8. M_____ is the author who made Canada's smallest province famous with her stories of a red-haired girl.
9. C_____'s movies include *The Terminator* and *Titanic*.
10. Emily C_____ brings the dark, wet forests of our west coast to life in her magnificent paintings.
11. B_____ is an artist who paints wild animals.
12. M_____ was Canada's first prime minister.

(You can find the answers on page 251 at the back of the book.)

13

Chapter Thirteen

Challenges for Canadians Today

Life is always changing and sometimes, it seems like change is happening more rapidly today than ever before. The following questions reflect some of the changes and challenges identified in this chapter.

» What does it mean to be a Canadian today?

» Is Canada made up of ten provinces and three territories, or two nations, or both?

» How does our membership in an increasingly global economy affect the average Canadian?

» What are Canadians willing to sacrifice in order to have a sustainable future?

» How can we ensure that we continue to have a quality healthcare system to meet the needs of an aging population?

» What values will we see shaping tomorrow's education?

» Are Canada's oil sands an economic boon or an ecological burden?

» How can all Canadians support Aboriginals in enjoying a lifestyle that reflects both their traditional cultural values and the opportunities modern Canadians enjoy?

» How can we control our food safety when our cold climate makes it difficult to avoid importing most of our produce?

» What role do Canadians want to play in international politics: the traditional role of peacekeeper or the recent role of combatant?

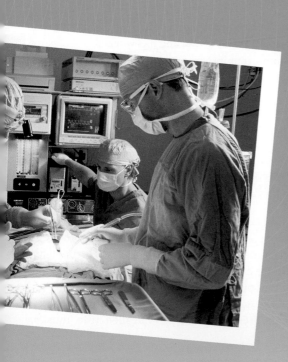

Introduction

The world has changed a lot in the past few years. Canada is increasingly part of a large global community. The balance of power is shifting as nations like China and India take a larger share of power and economic activity in the world, while the United States (US), long Canada's dominant trading partner, finds itself facing growing challenges. The demographics of Canada have changed significantly, due to large numbers of immigrants coming from all parts of the world. Our society is more diverse than ever before. This, together with a recent recession and numerous other changes, has posed new challenges for us as Canadians. This chapter is far from complete in identifying all the challenges, and, as you read, it is hoped that you will ask yourself which challenges you and your friends find to be most urgent.

Canadian Voices

Jeffrey Bullard wrote his answer to the question of what it meant to him to be a Canadian for the first edition of this book. Thirteen years later, he writes the following—a testament to the valuable work he has done in the intervening years and an inspiring way to start this chapter.

> *Canadians are privileged to live in a country blessed with such natural beauty and abundant resources, a productive economy, strong democratic traditions and a commitment to pluralism and universal human rights. At the same time, we cannot ignore the reality that not all Canadians share in the bounty this country has to offer.*
>
> *For me, being Canadian means challenging the status quo and working to improve the lives of those left behind. We need to be aware, and critically engaged in addressing the social and economic challenges faced by many in this country. As Canadians, we must also look beyond our borders, to support the advancement of democratic traditions and human rights around the world.*
>
> *Being Canadian means not being complacent.*

Jeffrey Bullard is the Director of Horizontal Policy at the federal department of Human Resources and Skills Development. He has been a federal public servant for 25 years, and has worked on a range of social policy issues in Canada, including immigrant integration, citizenship, multiculturalism, homelessness, poverty, social exclusion, and community development.

The Question of Our Identity as Canadians

Canada, as we know it, was created by two founding nations—England and France—and the country still reflects these two great solitudes. Keeping the country together has been a challenge. The Bloc Québécois, for years a major force in Quebec, had a clear agenda to defend the rights of Québécois to define their own cultural identity, and fought hard in our federal parliament to do that. There are people in Quebec who would like the province to separate from the rest of Canada. Fortunately, there are many others who appreciate the rich history that our two founding nations have given us.

Our national anthem was originally written in French by Calixa Lavallée (the music) and Adolphe-Basile Routhier (the lyrics) in 1880. While it quickly became very popular with French-Canadians, it was not heard in English Canada until the early twentieth century. Robert Weir gave us the original English translation, then changes were made in the 1980s—this most-recent version is the official wording you see below.

O Canada!

O Canada! Our home and native land!
True patriot love in all thy sons command.
With glowing hearts we see thee rise,
The True North strong and free!
From far and wide,
O Canada, we stand on guard for thee.
God keep our land glorious and free!
O Canada, we stand on guard for thee.
O Canada, we stand on guard for thee.

O Canada! Terre de nos aïeux,
Ton front est ceint de fleurons glorieux!
Car ton bras sait porter l'épée,
Il sait porter la croix!
Ton histoire est une épopée
Des plus brillants exploits.
Et ta valeur, de foi trempée,
Protégera nos foyers et nos droits.
Protégera nos foyers et nos droits.

Translation of French Lyrics
O Canada! Land of our forefathers
Thy brow is wreathed with a glorious garland of flowers.
As in thy arm ready to wield the sword,
So also is it ready to carry the cross.
Thy history is an epic of the most brilliant exploits.
Thy valour steeped in faith
Will protect our homes and our rights
Will protect our homes and our rights.

As you can see, the English and French versions are quite different from one another. This is symbolic of the great differences which have always existed between English- and French-Canadian visions of Canada. Many French-Canadians see Canada as two distinct nations. English-Canadians see Canada as ten provinces with three territories, and respect that Quebec is certainly different from the rest of Canada in many ways. In fact, both views are correct, as Quebec is considered a nation within a nation. Our federal politicians have long supported a policy of bilingualism across Canada but this policy has become a thorn in the side of many who resent paying taxes which are used to translate all federal documents into French, even in regions where French is rarely, if ever, spoken. People in the West resent the fact that federal civil servants in Western Canada have to speak French as well as English if they want to get the best jobs. We use the term *the two solitudes* to refer to English and French Canada because there is so much misunderstanding between these two perspectives.

Increasingly, we are hearing a much larger question than the challenge of English-French differences in Canada. We are hearing from Aboriginal and ethnic voices that they too want to have a place in defining our identity as a nation. In addition, the ways in which we identify ourselves in Canada are more than just ethnicity or language. We may also identify ourselves based on our nation, region, race, or religion. The popular media (Internet, TV, radio, newspapers) show us that all these voices want to be heard. Those in the West live in a different reality than those in the East. Maritimers often feel cut off from the mainland. Aboriginals may feel cheated of the lands of their ancestors and want to enjoy the same prosperity as the rest of the country. Newcomers wonder where they fit into the national mosaic. Victims of racism wonder how they can be treated as equals. Many Muslims in large cities are finding a newfound openness to their desire for prayer space during the workday and for Friday afternoons off to go to the mosque. Chinese immigrants have created Chinatowns within the larger urban areas where they can do all their business in their own language, as have other ethnicities in the metropolitan areas.

The face of Canada has changed and, with that, values we used to take for granted are being questioned. What does it mean to be a Canadian today?

Canadians express their identities in many different ways

COMPREHENSION CHECK

1. Who originally wrote our national anthem?
2. How do some western Canadians feel about the national policy of bilingualism?

VOCABULARY

demographics	the physical characteristics of a population such as age, gender, ethnicity, or marital status
ignore	pay no attention to; act as if something is not there
pluralism	a form of society in which minorities maintain their own cultural traditions
bounty	abundance
complacent	smugly self-satisfied; calmly content
integration	the intermixing of people previously segregated; bringing together groups of people who are different from one another
social exclusion	a lack of belonging, acceptance and recognition, leaving the excluded ones economically and socially vulnerable
lyrics	the words of a song
solitude	the state of being alone, or socially isolated

FOR DISCUSSION

» Many countries have a history of conflict among different cultural groups. English and French Canada are one such example. Can you think of other examples of this challenging situation? How best do you think we can work towards understanding and appreciating those who are different from ourselves?

New Economic Realities

The world slid into an economic recession in 2008. Stocks dropped in value. Jobs were lost. Real estate plummeted in value. Unemployment rates soared. Banks went out of business. Canada was not as badly hit as many other countries, in part because our regulatory system for banks was better than in some countries. The stock market recovered and real estate regained its value. But governments had to increase their deficits and social programs suffered as the governments that fund them strove to lower costs and keep taxation to a minimum. Gone were the days when a good idea would surely receive funding from the government.

Canada is rapidly integrating into the global economy. What does this mean for the average consumer in Canada? It means we are buying things like clothing and household goods from China instead of goods that have been locally produced. It means we increasingly speak to someone from the US or India on the telephone

Your Honda may have been produced here in Canada

when we dial a Canadian company that has outsourced many of its communication functions. It means that our gasoline prices go up when the world conglomerate of oil companies decides to raise its rates. It means that when we buy a so-called Japanese car, such as Honda or Toyota, it was probably produced in either Canada or the US by a Japanese company. It means that Canadian companies have to work harder and harder to supply products and services that other countries want and cannot buy more cheaply elsewhere. How can we maintain a moderately high standard of living with an economy that is increasingly integrated with the economies of other countries?

COMPREHENSION CHECK

1. In what year did the most recent recession begin?
2. Name one way governments responded to the recession.

VOCABULARY

recession	an extended decline in economic activity
plummeted	dropped rapidly
soared	climbed high
deficit	the amount by which expenses exceed income over a particular period of time
strove	tried very hard (He strove for excellence.); past tense of strive
outsource	assign responsibilities for job tasks to people outside a company or outside the country, generally to save money
standard of living	a level of material comfort as measured by the goods, services, and luxuries available to the average person in a large group of people

FOR DISCUSSION

» The average Canadian family wants to have a house, a car, a computer, a TV, and enough money for a summer holiday each year. What do you see as essential to being happy in your life? What do you expect to have in your life?

A Sustainable Future

The whole world is becoming aware that humanity has done a lot of damage to the planet. Animal species are disappearing from existence. Air and water are highly polluted in many areas. The rainforests, which have provided medicinal plants to humans for centuries, have been stripped of their trees and replaced, in some cases, with concrete and pavement. Many people no longer want to eat tuna or other fish from the sea because they have come to contain a dangerously high amount of mercury, which is toxic to human beings. Oil, a very important resource in an industrial society, is being used up at alarming rates. It is evident to most people that we cannot continue to live as we do now and survive as a species ourselves.

A nation with three long coastlines and many large lakes and rivers, Canada at one time had generous supplies of fish for its own population and for export. But in recent years, the Grand Banks off the coast of Newfoundland and Nova

Scotia have been overfished, mostly by people from other countries who failed to respect the fishing limits posted by the government. As a result, the people of this area have lost their livelihoods as fishermen, work done by generations of their families. Many Newfoundlanders and Nova Scotians have migrated to other parts of Canada, such as Alberta and the North, where employment has been growing. They miss the ocean and the communities they came from.

Alberta's oil sands

Fishing villages like this one in Newfoundland have suffered because of overfishing

The search for alternative lifestyles that will give the planet time to heal while still sustaining a modern lifestyle for people is a quest for everyone in the world today, and Canada is no exception. Being a northern (often cold) country as well as a developed country, we use more resources per person than most of the world does. We have to find ways to be more conservative in our use of resources. How can we use fewer resources?

In addition, the world's eyes are on Canada's oil sands. Alberta and Saskatchewan both have large areas filled with this valuable resource. But due to the manner in which it has been extracted up to now, there are many people in the world who think of it as dirty oil and don't want it. They call it dirty oil because the extraction process has contaminated land and water and has diminished the water supply in some areas. Scientists continue to work hard to find economical alternatives for extracting the oil from the bitumen in which it is found so that these problems can be prevented in future.

If we are all to contribute to making a sustainable future for our country and for the world, we have to be willing to sacrifice some of the material wealth that we have come to take for granted.

What would you and your family be willing to sacrifice so that the planet could be healthy once again and everyone could have enough to survive and be healthy?

COMPREHENSION CHECK

1. Name two ways in which humans have damaged the planet and its resources.
2. What happened to the fish off Canada's east coast?
3. Which two provinces in Canada have large areas of oil sands?
4. Why do some people call oil from the oil sands dirty oil?

VOCABULARY

rainforest	a dense forest with large amounts of annual rainfall, such as the tropical rainforest of Brazil
bitumen	various tarlike mixtures of hydrocarbons found naturally or extracted from coal
diminished	decreased in size or volume
sustainable	that conserves an ecological balance by avoiding depletion of natural resources; capable of being maintained

FOR DISCUSSION

» A large part of Alberta's economy is dependent on the oil sands and all the jobs connected to them. How do you think the people of Alberta feel when American politicians say that people should not buy Alberta oil?

» Why do you think fishermen from other countries continued to fish for cod in the Grand Banks when they had been warned that the fish supply was shrinking and would disappear if people continued to fish?

Health Care

If you were to ask the average Canadian what the most important issue in Canada is, many people would say "Health care!" We once had a healthcare system that was the envy of most of the world. After World War II, the Co-operative Commonwealth Federation party in Saskatchewan brought in a radically new system of universal care for people of that province. Then, under the leadership of Tommy Douglas, who is widely known as the Father of Medicare in Canada, the province's system of free and universal care came to the whole country. The system is enshrined in federal legislation and funding goes to the provinces, who decide how to administer the system to their residents. In the 1970s, Canadians felt very lucky to have a system of care like this when they often saw their American neighbours going bankrupt if they had to go into hospital. In the 1980s, it became evident that this was an expensive system to have in Canada and the demands on that system seemed unending.

Should the focus be on treating or preventing illness? Who should be deciding which services are basic and which ones are luxuries we cannot afford? What about patients with diseases which are extremely expensive to treat? And then there were the costs of pharmaceuticals, which were not covered by medicare unless the individual was in the hospital at the time. Most of the money went to staffing and doctors, especially specialists who often need to be paid a lot of money to remain in Canada. In the 1980s, many of our doctors left for the US because they could earn a lot more money there than they could here. The whole situation has been very challenging.

In the West, Albertan premier Ralph Klein decided deficit reduction was the priority and, between 1992 and 2000, Albertans saw the quality of their health care decline significantly. Wait times for surgery and treatment escalated and people suffered as a result. Suddenly, people could not find a family doctor. And if someone needed a specialist, he or she could wait up to a year or longer to see one. Hospitals in Edmonton and Calgary were closed down—and in some cases demolished—leaving the cities with a bed shortage and no capacity for emergency situations. Other provinces started to follow Alberta's example.

In 2001, the attacks on the World Trade Center injected fear into the entire world. How could human beings plan terror attacks of such size and brutality? Health authorities began to wonder what would happen if there were a terrorist attack in their jurisdiction. In 2003, SARS (Severe Acute Respiratory Syndrome) hit Toronto and the city almost shut down as conferences were cancelled and business trips postponed indefinitely. The hospitals were unprepared for an epidemic of any kind. In 2005, avian flu reached Canada from Asia and we wondered how badly this illness would affect Canadians.

There is a strong public perception that our healthcare system is broken. The doctors, nurses, and other staff working in the system have been heroic in their attempts to make it work, but even they are speaking out and saying that something has to change. People value medicare and want to see it protected at any cost. However, many people have been victims of this broken system and are beginning to ask whether people should have the option of seeking private care if they want it. (Canadians with enough money can go to the US, Mexico, or India to get the surgery they need in a timely manner, and some do.) At present, the cost of treatment is taking up so much money that there is little or none left to research preventive medicine or alternative medicine. So, the big question is, how can Canadians begin to take more accountability for their own health? And in the meantime, is some combination of private and public health care needed?

The 2003 SARS outbreak strained Toronto's hospitals and economy

COMPREHENSION CHECK

1. Who is credited with being the Father of Medicare?
2. How do most Canadians feel about the state of their healthcare system today?
3. What is the name of the epidemic that hit Toronto in 2003?

VOCABULARY

enshrined	protected as if it were sacred
pharmaceuticals	prescription drugs produced by the big drug companies
alternative medicine	healing responses that do not include the administration of drugs that suppress symptoms (for example, acupuncture, energy medicine, naturopathy, homeopathy)

Education

While no one doubts that education is a critical service to provide to the Canadian population, there is a growing perception that public education is not doing all it could be to support our children in becoming creative, ethical, and participatory members of society. Like health care, education has suffered funding losses to support lowering government deficits and keeping people employed during the recession.

For the most part, Canadians can be proud of their educational system. Public education is free from kindergarten through Grade 12, and students get a well-rounded education inclusive of the basics (math, science, social studies) as well as a variety of options in most schools.

Increasingly, however, there are fees and costs associated with education that were not present in the past. Children in many systems pay a yearly rental fee for the use of their textbooks, as well as various costs for field trips during the year. Sports and other extracurricular activities can also cost parents a great deal of money for equipment and uniforms.

Changes that worry parents include the following:

Violence and bullying in many schools. For the first time ever, a child was murdered at school by another child. This happened in Taber, Alberta, in 1999. In 2006, one student was killed and 19 others wounded—six critically—at Dawson College in Montreal. While we have read about such tragedies in the US, we were shocked to find them happening in Canadian cities.

Bullying is traumatic for many children, and some have taken their own lives in despair. Can we find better ways of creating safe atmospheres for our children in schools and in the community?

A shift away from a liberal education, inclusive of the arts and second languages, towards courses that are geared towards the workplace and research. In other words, governments have decided that schools owe their primary allegiance to the economy. This is not to say that a liberal education is not available to many students, especially in the larger cities, but when budgets get cut, the arts suffer first. The economy is important and we want our children to be employed in good jobs

Canadian students get a well-rounded education

as adults—but can we find a balance so that they can also enjoy music, art, dance, and theatre, all of which contribute to the quality of life?

An increasing trend towards valuing only that which can be readily measured with tests. From the sixties through the seventies and even eighties, there was an appreciation for healthy self-esteem, creativity, healthy pursuits, intercultural understanding, and ethical citizenship. Those things were not easily measurable and they seem to have been replaced with skill training that more directly results in readiness for the workplace. Standardized testing consumes an increasing amount of classroom time. Could some of that time be better spent teaching and learning?

Mainstreaming has become the norm for many special needs learners, including ESL learners. While teachers' aides are still provided in many cases, many wonder if the placement of special needs learners in regular classes is a less-than-optimal way to approach their learning and is also taking time away from the needs of regular students. How can society best serve the learning needs and potential of all learners?

A failure to teach values directly and openly in the school system. Teachers are cautioned against teaching values in the schools because they do not want to offend any group who may not agree. It is unrealistic to think that anyone can teach without imparting values. But when we try to hide those values or—more likely—are unaware of them, the outcomes are not always what we would hope for. In some cases, the response of the public has

been to open more private schools or to do home schooling with their children. The latter was unheard of 40 years ago, but is increasing every year as parents struggle with how to ensure that the individual learning needs of their children are met and that their values are reinforced by the school system. In South Korea, all children take a subject called Moral Education throughout their schooling. Koreans are shocked to come here and find there is nothing that instructs ethics and morals in the schools. How can we hope to maintain strong Canadian values if we do not intentionally teach these values in our schools? How can we begin to name those central values that define us a country and a culture?

These are controversial issues and good arguments can be made for all points of view. Again, it is hoped that you will consider your own views on these topics and discuss them with people you know. If we were to summarize the issue of education, we might ask,

Is the purpose of education

to enable individuals to reach their highest potential for their own good and also for the good of the community?

or

to serve the interests of the status quo, ensuring that all the jobs that need to get done to maintain those interests are done?

What do you think?

COMPREHENSION CHECK

1 Although education for kindergarten to Grade 12 is free in public schools, there are some costs associated with it. Can you give two examples?

2 In what small Alberta town did one student murder another in 1999?

3 What subjects does a liberal education often include?

4 What is one subject that all South Korean students study that Canadian students do not study?

VOCABULARY

bullying	persecuting or oppressing by force or threats
mainstreaming	placing students with special needs in regular classrooms for all or part of the school day
controversial	open to argument and dispute
status quo	the existing state of affairs; the existing balance of power

FOR DISCUSSION

» What do you think are some of the values that Canadians cherish?

» There is a zero-tolerance policy for bullying in many schools now. This means children are suspended from the school if they are found to be bullying other students. How do you think we can best understand the cause of bullying and how can we put an end to it?

» Some people believe that Canadians have lower standards of morality than those in other countries. Can you think of things you have seen or heard in Canada that make you uncomfortable? What is the primary purpose of education, in your opinion? Defend your answer.

Aboriginal Issues

Our Aboriginal citizens have faced far more than their share of problems ever since people from many lands colonized the land from coast to coast. There are many stories of Aboriginals helping the newcomers to face the harsh winters when they first came here. In addition, they taught the newcomers how to use the native herbs to cure sickness. Imagine how angry they must have felt when told they had to leave the land they had known and move to some small reserve where they could no longer follow the animals to hunt from season to season. Their whole way of life changed radically with the coming of the Europeans. In the Aboriginal tradition, no one owned the land. The land was given to everyone by the Creator. Suddenly, the Europeans arrived and start putting coloured ribbons on sticks to signify that they had bought a square of land. The Aboriginals found that no one was allowed to walk on, or take anything from, claimed land unless they had the piece of paper saying they owned it.

Now Aboriginal citizens are struggling to find a way to co-exist with the new populations who have taken over. Some have grown up on reserve

In the Aboriginal tradition the land belonged to everyone

lands that have living conditions which range from fair to appalling. Others live in poverty in the cities. And of course, others have integrated well into the lifestyle of the majority and are living well. Issues such as land claims, inadequate housing, health, education, and reconciliation for victims of residential schools continue to plague Aboriginal Canadians and to be disturbing to all Canadians who care about social justice for all. In addition, a far greater proportion of Aboriginals are caught up in our correctional system than one would expect of the general population. How can the country as a whole work together with our Aboriginal citizens to support them in creating solutions that work to resolve these problems?

COMPREHENSION CHECK

❶ When the first European immigrants came to Canada, who helped them to survive the first winters?

❷ Who owned the land before Europeans came?

VOCABULARY

appalling	shocking, unpleasant, bad
residential schools	schools run by the Christian churches for Aboriginal children who were taken forcibly from their parents, forbidden to speak their own languages, and lived in residences where they were taught how to live like white people
reconciliation	the process of recreating friendly relationships when these have been destroyed
correctional system	a euphemism for prisons and jails

FOR DISCUSSION

» The process of kidnapping children from their families and communities in order to teach them how to live like white people happened all over the world: in Australia, in the US, and in Africa. How do you imagine those who did this justified their actions to themselves? In other words—what were they thinking?

» Can you think of other situations today where one group of people think that everyone else should live and believe what they do?

» As humans, how can we work and learn together to accept others as they are and value our differences?

Food Safety

While in general the Canadian food supply is much safer than in many countries, we still have concerns about this topic because so much of our food is imported and we have had problems in the past with contaminated foods. Local and imported foods are treated with pesticides, herbicides, preservatives, and various other chemicals, and some are contaminated with salmonella, other bacteria, or parasites. We worry about GM (genetically modified) foods since little is known about the long-term effects of such foods on our health. We are concerned when we find out that potatoes, onions, or other vegetables imported from the US are irradiated to prevent deterioration before we buy them. We don't know what long-term effect such irradiation has on our health. We pasteurize our milk and cheese products and freeze the fish used in our sushi, and yet we read about people who suffer health problems unless they can drink raw milk, which is outlawed in most provinces.

The 100-mile diet has been proposed by some as the best way to ensure that we eat healthy, safe foods. This means that, as much as possible, we should buy food that has been grown and prepared within 100 miles (160 kilometres) of where we live. Then, chances are good that we know what is in it, how old it is, and how it has been handled before it reaches our tables. That is a challenge in a country in which we can only garden outdoors for four to six months a year.

Canada's food supply is one of the safest in the world, and yet people still worry about threats to their health from food. What are we willing to do to ensure that our food supply is safe?

The Canadian Food Inspection Agency exists so the government can make sure that food produced in Canada and abroad is safe and healthy. Even so, many people go to health food stores and read alternative literature on good health so they can be informed and make up their own minds about what is safe and what is not. And wherever possible, many people buy produce, meat, and poultry from local farmers' markets.

COMPREHENSION CHECK

1. Name three things that can contaminate the food we buy in the stores.
2. What must be done to fish before it is used to make sushi (a Japanese food) sold in restaurants?
3. What is the 100-mile diet?

VOCABULARY

pasteurize	to heat milk to kill any bacteria in it before packaging for sale to the public
genetically modified (GM)	modified in character by the manipulation of genetic material (for example, adding the genes of a fish to a tomato plant so it will repel insects)
sushi	a Japanese snack prepared with rice, vinegar, salt, and sugar and garnished with raw fish, egg, seaweed, or vegetables

FOR DISCUSSION

» In many countries, people eat only local foods. In Canada, most of us would find this difficult. Why?

» What experiences have you had of getting sick when you ate something? Could that have been prevented? If so, how?

» Find a farmers' market in your city and go on a "field trip" with your classmates. How is the experience different from going to a grocery store?

Our Changing Role in World Conflicts

Canadians have long been proud of their role as peacemakers in situations of world conflict. While other countries have chosen to send soldiers to join the fight in other countries, until recently, we have chosen to send our soldiers to keep the peace and rebuild the countries when a war finishes. Our priority has been on human rights, regardless of whether the Liberals or the Conservatives were in power. Under Brian Mulroney, Canada showed leadership in fighting South Africa's apartheid policies and in promoting the Convention on the Rights of the Child in 1989. Under Jean Chrétien, Canada urged nations to adopt the concept of the Responsibility to Protect, meaning that government's first responsibility should be to protect its citizens from exploitation and abuse. As a result, we fought against the use of landmines.

The Stephen Harper government changed our priority on human rights and on peacemaking. Diplomats in many countries first noticed the change in terminology used by the Canadians under Harper. *Child soldiers* became *children in armed conflict. International humanitarian law* became *international law.* Some felt that watering down the language of world diplomacy like this signalled a change in Canadian foreign policy, and they were right. For the first time since the Korean War, Canadian soldiers were involved in intense combat (fighting alongside the Americans in Afghanistan). While some supported this, others are saddened that our tradition of peacekeeping, which we have long valued as Canadians, seems to have been taken from us. How can we best support our global neighbours in creating a peaceful world for us all?

COMPREHENSION CHECK

1. Who was the prime minister of Canada when we were fighting South Africa's apartheid policy?
2. What did Prime Minister Chrétien and his government believe was their first priority in governing the people of Canada?
3. Under which prime minister did our soldiers change from peacekeepers into armed soldiers in active combat?

VOCABULARY

exploitation	taking advantage of people for selfish reasons
abuse	poor treatment of a person with no thought to their best interest
landmines	explosive devices buried under just under the surface of the land which are triggered when stepped on or run over by a vehicle
foreign policy	the decisions made by a government to determine our relationships with other countries
watering down	softening the language so that people have trouble seeing what is really being said; making the language less clear so as to hide the meaning

FOR DISCUSSION

» Why do you think Prime Minister Harper changed our foreign policy away from peacekeeping and towards active combat?

» What role would you like to see Canada play in international politics? Explain your answer.

CHAPTER REVIEW

» Choose the issue from this chapter that you think is the most important and present two different perspectives on this issue, either in writing or verbally. Ask others what they think the solutions are to the problem or problems presented.

Answer Key

Page 15

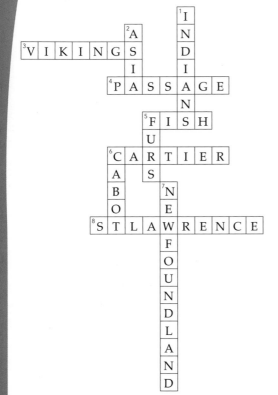

Page 43

Page 58

ESL	English as a second language
LINC	Language Instruction for Newcomers to Canada
CEC	Canada Employment Centre
EAL	English as an additional language
EI	Employment Insurance

Page 21

VERB	NOUN	ADJECTIVE	ADVERB
reinforce	reinforcements	reinforced	- - - - - -
threaten	threat	threatening	threateningly
embitter	bitterness	bitter	bitterly

Page 99

Rosemary Brown: first Black woman elected to a provincial legislature (BC, 1972)

Oscar Peterson: famous jazz musician

Lincoln Alexander: first Black cabinet minister in the government of Canada; first Black Lieutenant-Governor (Ontario, 1985–91)

Mary Ann Shadd: first female editor of a North American newspaper (Chatham, Ontario, *Provincial Freeman*, 1853)

Michaëlle Jean: a journalist and the 27th Governor General of Canada

Page 101

```
F M E Z P C E B O N T C V Z X R
I J A P A N H O P Q K O R E A B
U S A C U Y T I N D I A V R F S
X R L E B A N O N Q G E L U T N
N B E P Y T I E B A E S D S C C
M R T P O L A N D N R M X S C A
G R E E C E P G V Y M A I N R R
D Z E B H O R L O V E K I A K G
R A T Y U P B A N M N C H I L E
E M V V I E T N A M Y G M N X N
T B Y Z Q A S D P L R E G Y P T
A I D O B M A C H T A R E S D I
D A C I A M A J N M G H P X F N
E B C S T H A I L A N D L R S A
F P L K Q V E N E Z U E L A B G
P A K I S T A N O P H E I C S Y
```

Page 104–5

1. Christianity
2. Shamanism
3. Judaism
4. Sikhism
5. Islam
6. Hinduism
7. Buddhism
8. Islam
9. Judaism
10. Shamanism

Page 129

1. charm
2. hub
3. ecologists
4. mind
5. cedar
6. ancient
7. domestic
8. harsh
9. balmy
10. port
11. warn
12. hippies

Page 145

1. A L B E R T A
2. D I N O S A U R S
3. L E T H B R I D G E
4. P O T A S H
5. S A S K A T O O N
6. R I E L
7. B A N F F
8. J A S P E R
9. C H U R C H I L L
10. B E A R S
11. E D M O N T O N
12. C A M P I N G

Page 160

1. straddles
2. innovative
3. gracious
4. distinctive
5. adventure

Page 172

1. pilgrim
2. prestige
3. trend
4. voyage
5. rough

Page 186

Toronto: Torontonians

Calgary: Calgarians

Alberta: Albertans

Edmonton: Edmontonians

Quebec: Quebecers (sometimes spelled Quebeckers)

Montreal: Montrealers

Winnipeg: Winnipeggers

Newfoundland: Newfoundlanders

Vancouver: Vancouverites

Prince Edward Island: Prince Edward Islanders

Page 207

Verbs	Adjectives	Nouns
sustain	sustainable	sustenance
collide	colliding	collision
extinguish	extinguishable	extinction
distinguish	1. distinct 2. distinctive	distinction

Page 233

1. Gretzky
2. Fox
3. Bell
4. Suzuki
5. Riel
6. McClung and Murphy
7. Trudeau
8. Montgomery
9. Cameron
10. Carr
11. Bateman
12. Macdonald

Glossary of Words and Expressions

The following is a list of the words and expressions found in the vocabulary lists throughout the book, along with the pages on which they are defined.

Index

Photo Credits

Text Credits